Children's Rights: A Comparative Perspective

Issues in Law and Society
General Editor: Michael Freeman

Children's Rights: A Comparative Perspective

Edited by
MICHAEL FREEMAN
University College London

Dartmouth

Aldershot • Brookfield USA • Singapore • Sydney

Published by
Dartmouth Publishing Company Limited
Gower House
Croft Road
Aldershot
Hants GU11 3HR
England

Dartmouth Publishing Company
Old Post Road
Brookfield
Vermont 05036
USA

British Library Cataloguing in Publication Data
Children's Rights: Comparative Perspective
I. Freeman, M.D.A.
341.481

Library of Congress Cataloging-in-Publication Data
Children's rights : a comparative perspective / edited by Michael
Freeman.
    p.   cm. — (Issues in law and society)
    Includes index.
    ISBN 1-85521-678-7 (hb). — ISBN 1-85521-683-3 (pb)
    1. Children's rights.   2. Children — Legal status, laws, etc.
3. Convention on the Rights of the Child (1989)   I. Freeman,
Michael D. A.   II. Series.
K639.Z9C455   1996
323.3'52—dc20   95-34903
                                                                 CIP

ISBN 1 85521 678 7 (Hbk)
ISBN 1 85521 683 3 (Pbk)

Typeset in Great Britain by Manton Typesetters,
5–7 Eastfield Road, Louth, Lincolnshire.
Printed and bound in Great Britain by
Biddles Limited, Guildford and King's Lynn.

Contents

List of Contributors

Coby de Graaf is a Lecturer in Juvenile Law and Justice at the University of Amsterdam.

Michael Freeman is Professor of English Law, Faculty of Laws, University College London. He is co-editor of the *International Journal of Children's Rights* and General Editor of this series.

Lis Frost is Associate Professor of Family Law and Medical Law at the University of Aarhus. Secretary of a Law Reform Commission regarding adoption. Author and editor of a number of books and articles relating to the family and children.

Cecilia P. Grosman is Professor of Family Law, Law Faculty, University of Buenos Aires, and Principal Researcher of the National Council of Scientific and Technical Research. Author of a number of books and articles relating to the family and children, including *Divorce Process: Law and Reality, Family Violence* and *Child Maltreatment*.

Olivier Guillod is Professor of Private Law and Director of the Institute of Health Law, University of Neuchâtel, Switzerland.

Mark Henaghan is Senior Lecturer in Law, University of Otago, Dunedin, New Zealand, specializing in Family Law. Co-author of *Family Law in New Zealand* (6th edn 1993, Butterworths) and *Family Law Policy in New Zealand* (1992, Oxford University Press, Auckland). Deputy Chair of the New Zealand Committee for Children 1985–87; Consultant for the New Zealand Commissioner for Children 1994–95.

Elżbieta Holewińska-Łapińska is Dr Juris in Civil Law at Warsaw University; member of the Judicial Decisions Bureau of the Supreme Court in Warsaw; member of the Family Law Group within the Committee for Civil Law Reforms.

Olga Khazova is Senior Research Fellow, Institute of State and Law, Russian Academy of Sciences. She is a specialist in comparative family law and a member of the Working Group for the new Family Court in Russia.

Yukiko Matsushima is Professor of Law at Dokkyo University; attorney-at-law and mediator of the Tokyo Family Court; executive member of the All Japan Family Law Association; Vice-President of the International Society of Family Law.

Linda Nielsen is Dr Iuris, Associate Professor of Family Law and Contract Law at the University of Copenhagen. Member of the Danish Council of Ethics and of a number of law reform commissions including the Children's Law Reform Commission. Member of the Executive Council of the International Society of Family Law. Author of a number of books and articles relating to the family and children.

Ana Maria Pessoa works in the Ministry of Justice in Maputo, Mozambique.

Luis Filipe Sacramento is a Justice of the Supreme Court in Maputo, Mozambique.

Wanda Stojanowska is Associate Professor in Family Law at the Maria Grzegorzewska College for Special Education in Warsaw and in the Institute of Justice in Warsaw; judge of the Provincial Court; member of the International Society of Family Law; member of the International Society for Prevention of Child Abuse and Neglect; author of a number of books, articles and investigations relating to the family, children and family law.

Stephen J. Toope is Dean of the Faculty of Law of McGill University. Previously served as a law clerk for the Right Honourable Brian Dickson, P.C., C.C., Chief Justice of Canada. Educated at Harvard (A.B., 1979), McGill (B.C.L., LL.B., 1983) and Cambridge (Ph.D., 1987), Professor Toope teaches and conducts research in the areas of International Law, Human Rights and Family Law. His book, *Mixed International Arbitration – Studies in Arbitration Between States and Private Persons* is published by Cambridge University Press.

1   Introduction: Children as Persons

Michael Freeman

The United Nations Convention on the Rights of The Child, finalized in 1989, is a landmark in the history of childhood. And, no matter from what perspective one examines it, its gestation period was lengthy. On one level, the Convention can be traced to the United Nations Declaration of 1959;[1] on another to the Geneva Declaration of 1924.[2] That there is a Convention at all is due to the initiative of Poland which in 1979 – the International Year of the Child – pressed for the 1959 Declaration to be turned into a Convention (it is therefore appropriate that Poland should feature in this survey). Yet, even then, there was a protracted debate on whether or not there should be a convention and what it should contain.

The children's rights movement can be traced back way before these international stirrings. An early awareness is found in Jean Vallès's novel *L'Enfant*, written in 1879 in the aftermath of the Paris Commune. But Vallès, concerns, like those of the child-saving movement[3] which spawned the juvenile court, the orphanage and the modern school, was with children's welfare and protection rather than with the child as an individual. Clearly, the orientation towards nurture precedes any emphasis on self-determination. Nevertheless, by the end of the nineteenth century such writers as Kate Douglas Wiggin[4] in the USA and Janusz Korczak[5] in Poland were already forcibly expressing ideas which later come to be associated with the identification of children's rights accompanied by a recognition of the child as an autonomous individual.

These ideas were not central to those who drew up the 1924 Geneva Declaration, which betrays its origins as a document emerging from the First World War. The Declaration views children very much as an investment for the future, with a dividend of peace and harmony between nations (note the emphasis on socialization to serve others). It is a statement of mankind's obligations towards children: mankind, we are told, 'owes to the child the best it has to give'.

It was 35 years before children's rights received international recognition again. We can gain considerable insight into attitudes towards children's rights in the late 1950s – when civil rights issues were only just beginning to make an impact – from the discussions which took place at this time. The French delegate to the Commission on Human Rights in 1959 believed that

> ... the child was not in a position to exercise his own rights. Adults exercised them for the child and in doing so were subject to certain obligations. Thus it could be said that a child had special legal status resulting from his inability to exercise his rights.[6]

But despite ideological conflicts and religious divisions and the concerns of Third World countries that they did not have the means to implement rights such as compulsory education, only Cambodia and South Africa, then in its darkest period, were unable to agree the United Nations Declaration of the Rights of the Child of November 1959.

The ten principles adopted were:

1   non-discrimination;
2   special protection and opportunities and facilities by law and other means to develop physically, mentally, morally, spiritually and socially in a healthy and normal manner and in conditions of freedom and dignity;
3   the right to a name and nationality;
4   the right to the benefits of social security, adequate nutrition, housing, recreation and medical services;
5   the right of a special-needs child to the treatment, education and care required by his or her particular condition;
6   the need for love and understanding so that the child, wherever possible, grows in the care and responsibility of his parents, and in an atmosphere of affection and moral and material security;
7   entitlement to education, which should be free and compulsory, at least in the elementary stages;
8   to be among the first to receive protection and relief;
9   protection against all forms of neglect, cruelty and exploitation, including that associated with employment (there was a Soviet proposal to extend this to embrace corporal punishment, but it met with considerable opposition);
10 protection from practices which may foster racial, religious and other forms of discrimination.

The scope of this Declaration is undoubtedly wider than that of the Geneva Declaration, but its emphasis is still firmly on protection and welfare. There is no recognition of a child's autonomy, no understanding of the importance of a child's wishes and feelings, and no appreciation of the value of empowerment. The child remains an object of concern, rather than a person with self-determination.

It was only after 1959 that these ideas were rediscovered. In 1972 Robert Ollendorf argued for the adolescent's rights to self-determination and to participation in decisions.[7] And it was self-determination that Richard Farson saw as being at the root of all other rights that children were entitled to claim.[8] He argued that whether such a right was good for children was beside the point; children should be granted rights for the same reason that adults were. His case was ideological – a belief in the value of freedom. And it was accompanied by an acknowledgment that freedom is a 'difficult burden for adults as well as for children'.[9]

Although the so-called children's liberation movement of the 1970s is now history, it has left its impact on the United Nations Convention[10] – and nowhere more clearly than in Article 12 which, in many respects, is its linchpin. This requires State Parties to assure to the child, capable of forming his or her own views, the right to express those views freely in all matters affecting the child. In particular, the child is to be provided the opportunity to be heard in any judicial and administrative proceedings which affect him or her, either directly or through a representative or an appropriate body. This right is significant not only for what it says, but because it recognizes the child as a full human being, with integrity and personality, and with the ability to participate fully in society.

The Convention contains:

1 *General rights.* These encompass the right to life, the prohibition against torture, freedom of expression, thought and religion, the right to information and to privacy.
2 *Rights requiring protective measures.* These include measures to protect children from economic and sexual exploitation, prevent drug abuse and other forms of neglect and abuse.
3 *Rights concerning the civil status of children.* These include the right to acquire nationality, the right to preserve one's identity, the right to remain with parents (unless their best interests dictate otherwise) and the right to be reunited with their family.
4 *Rights concerned with development and welfare.* These include the child's right to a reasonable standard of living, to health and basic services, the right to social security, to education and to leisure.
5 *Rights concerning children in special circumstances or 'in specially*

difficult circumstances'. These extend to such children as children with special needs, refugee children and orphans. There are special regulations on adoption, the cultural concerns of minority and indigenous children and rehabilative care for children suffering from deprivation, as well as a prohibition on the recruitment of soldiers under 15 years of age.

Article 4 of the Convention – on a practical level the most important – pledges states to translate all the rights set out in the Convention into reality. Most of the world – even belatedly the USA[11] – has agreed to do so. But what is the status of the children in the nations of the world? This book, containing essays by leading experts in a representative sample of countries, should give an insight into the progress that is being made to bring the status of children into line with the norms of the Convention. It is a survey and it is by no means exhaustive. But, unlike the reports prepared for the UN Committee on the Rights of the Child, which monitors progress in the different States Parties, it has the value of candour and independence. In all the countries surveyed there is divergence between the new international norms and the law and practice of the countries themselves.

Of course, it would be wrong to assume that the Convention is itself the last word on children's rights. Stephen Toope, in particular, acknowledges, in Chapter 3, the many faults in the Convention, and others have done so elsewhere. Writing in the context of Canada, Toope acknowledges that one major problem with the Convention is its resources implications. However, if this is the case in the wealthy nations of the world, how much more of a problem must it be in the developing world or in those countries such as Russia whose infrastructure has failed to survive the collapse of communism? Olga Khazova's essay on Russia (Chapter 11) exudes pessimism. That the rights of children in different countries are a global responsibility is emphasized by Toope and also by Luis Filipe Sacramento and Ana Maria Pessoa in their essay on Mozambique (Chapter 8). Mozambique was selected for this sample because, though one of the world's poorest nations, it sets an example to the world in the way in which it sees its future as lying in better prospects for its children.

Each of the countries surveyed has its own problems in dealing with the Convention. It is a common phenomenon to think that one is complying with the Convention when clearly there is a considerable shortfall. This emerges in several of the essays in this collection. Too many states ratified the Convention – no other international instrument has been responded to so rapidly by so many – without giving serious thought to their own laws and practices and to what would be entailed in ratifying the Convention. Part of the explanation for this may lie in the ways childhood has been socially constructed. Thus, even where substantive provisions have been changed to promote the interests of children, the procedures and processes in operation may still fall well short of the Convention ideals. Several contributors, Cecilia Grosman writing on Argentina, Stephen Toope on Canada, Linda Nielsen and Lis Frost on Denmark and Mark Henaghan on New Zealand, all indicate obstacles impeding the presentation of a child's viewpoint, thereby demonstrating failures to address the ideals of Article 12.

Each country has its own history and culture, and the problems it confronts in complying with an international convention of this nature reflect this. In two of the countries surveyed, Canada and New Zealand, there is a greater awareness of multiculturalism and the problems this creates for norm-setting authorities. Two of the countries in this study – Argentina and Poland – are predominantly Catholic, and the impact of this on the definition of child, particularly in relation to abortion, stands out. Japan's history and its cultural heritage, in particular its concepts of the family, not surprisingly provide a constraint on its ability to implement the Convention: discrimination against illegitimate children, now removed by most countries, still remains in Japan, despite, or perhaps because of, the fact that the illegitimacy rate is very low there. Because of different histories and cultural traditions as well as divergent ideologies, concepts, such as what constitutes abuse, are not constant, and this is reflected in what is deemed to be abuse in different parts of the world, including the countries surveyed in this collection. For example, five countries[12] – but not Denmark, though it is frequently included within the list – have made it unlawful for parents to hit children; the Danish law is explained by Nielsen and Frost in Chapter 4. England stands in contrast: one of the legal controversies of 1993–94 centred upon whether a childminder was allowed corporally to punish a pre-school child in her care;[13] another issue which aroused much public debate centred upon the right and propriety of a Singaporean court to inflict a sentence of caning upon a US teenager.[14]

The essays in this volume must be allowed to speak for themselves. Drawn from both the prosperous 'North', the developing 'South' and from former Communist countries, from all five continents, from the common law world as well as from civil law systems, from countries which have ratified the Convention as well as from one, Switzerland, which, as Guillod explains in Chapter 12, has not yet done so, they will give the reader an insight into the status of children today and into the progress that is being made to recognize children's interests and uphold their rights. The picture that emerges is not entirely gloomy. Children's rights are being taken more seriously than was the case only a generation ago.[15] But this book, as an audit conducted in the years immediately following the formulation of the United Nations Convention, shows the enormous work that still needs to be done and highlights the responsibilities of the world community to create a better future for the citizens of the next century.

NOTES

1   For the text of this Declaration, see Philip Veerman (1992), *The Rights of the Child and the Changing Image of Childhood*, Dordrecht: Martinus Nijhoff, p. 465.
2   The text may be found at *ibid.*, p. 444.
3   On which see A. Platt (1969), *The Child Savers: The Invention of Delinquency*, Chicago: University of Chicago Press.
4   K.D. Wiggin (1892), *Children's Rights: A Book of Nursery Logic*, Boston: Houghton.
5   On Korczak see Betty Jay Lifton (1987), *The King of Children*, London: Hodder and Stoughton.
6   M. Juvigny, quoted in Veerman, *op. cit.*, note 1 above, p. 164.
7   In P. Adams, *et al.* (eds) (1972), *Children's Rights*, London: Granada, p. 97.
8   Richard Farson (1978), *Birthrights*, Harmondsworth: Penguin.
9   *Ibid.*, p. 31. See also Howard Cohen (1980), *Equal Rights for Children*, Totowa, NJ: Littlefield Adams.
10 On the movement see Beatrice Gross and Ronald Gross (eds) (1977), *The Children's Rights Movement – Overcoming the Oppression of Young People*, Garden City, NY: Anchor Press; also Patricia Vardin and Ilene Brody (eds) (1979), *Children's Rights: Contemporary Perspectives*, New York: Teachers College Press.
11 It signed the Convention on 16 February 1995.
12 Sweden, Norway, Finland, Austria and Cyprus.
13 Eventually resolved in favour of allowing a childminder to hit a child if the parent gave permission to do so.
14 The precedent so attracted Americans that several states are considering introducing caning for juvenile offenders. A British MP, Elizabeth Peacock, has argued for televised whippings at peak viewing hours (*The Independent*, 21 March 1995). On its roots see Philip Greven (1992), *Spare The Child*, New York: Vintage Books.
15 The subject now has its own journal: *The International Journal of Children's Rights*, 1993.

2 Argentina – Children's Rights in Family Relationships: The Gulf Between Law and Social Reality

*Cecilia P. Grosman**

INTRODUCTION

On 27 September 1990 (by Law 23.849) Argentina ratified the UN Convention on the Rights of the Child. We propose, in this chapter to examine, four years later, how far Argentine legislation and judicial decisions meet the standards required by the Convention, and what reforms would be required to give full effect to the rights it enshrines. Our information and comments will concentrate on certain of the child's rights in family relationships, and the divergences which frequently appear between statutory rights and social reality.

THE IMPORTANCE OF THE CONVENTION FOR ARGENTINA

In Argentina, 37.7 per cent of the population is under 18; in a number of provinces this rises to over 45 per cent. The satisfying of children's rights, in conjunction with meeting their basic needs, is a national priority. According to official statistics, 20 per cent of the population lives in extreme poverty[2] and that percentage increases dramatically in some regions of the country. In Northern Argentina, between 40–50 per cent of the people live in wretched conditions and infant mortality exceeds 33 per thousand.[3] In the city of

*Professor of Family Law in the Law Faculty of the University of Buenos Aires and Principal Researcher, the National Council of Scientific and Technical Research. Translated by Peter Schofield.

Buenos Aires itself, there are quarters where more than one in four of the people are without means, inadequately housed and have defective sanitary conditions. In some cities in Buenos Aires Province approximately one in three children under 12 have no provision for their most fundamental needs.[4] Consequently, a significant proportion of Argentinian children are malnourished, inadequately housed, have health problems and leave school because they have to contribute to the family budget. This situation worsens daily due to the effects of economic policy, unemployment and cuts in social benefits. In short, the situation of poor families places children at risk – unprotected and abandoned.

However, there is also a need to press for recognition of the child as a 'subject of protection' – as a human being whose rights and freedoms must be respected as much by parents as by society as a whole. Children are still perceived socially as 'objects of protection', forgetting their role as thinking and feeling persons. Considered to be 'under incapacity', fragile, vulnerable and dependent on adults, they often fail to be perceived as persons with their own individuality and rights. Thus, although improving the quality of children's lives is an overriding priority, this is not restricted to supplying their basic needs, but also includes respect for what they say and feel and for their dignity.

Legislative improvements in the situation of children in their families have been a notable result of the establishment of democracy in Argentina since 1983. Concern for children's rights is part of the process of democratization as seen in the field of family relations within the philosophy of the protection of human rights, which may not only be violated by governments but may also be endangered within the privacy of the family and in other aspects of daily life. Several provincial constitutions enshrine the various rights of children (to life, sufficient food, health, identity, education and recreation) explicitly;[5] likewise, in 1985 a reform of the law of filiation and paternal authority[6] raised the status of the child, although there is still a long way to go. It is, nonetheless, necessary to remember that to ensure the efficacy of such reforms, they have to be accompanied by action to ensure the social, economic and cultural rights of children as enshrined in the Convention.

IMPLEMENTATION OF THE CONVENTION[7]

The principles of the Convention on the Rights of the Child are part of Argentine law, as international treaties are incorporated into national law.[8] The Argentine Constitution incorporated the UN Convention on the Rights of the Child in June 1994. Since then, the Convention as well as other treaties on human rights have become part of the Constitution and, in due course, of the Supreme Law (Art. 75, inc. 22 Constitución Nacional). Argentina has to take the measures necessary to fulfil the obligations she undertakes. On the one hand, the country must pass the required laws to apply the rights these principles enshrine; on the other hand, pending the passage of such laws, ratification of a treaty obliges the country to ensure that its administrative and judicial organs apply those rights in any actual cases which arise.[9] Under Article 27 of the Vienna Convention, ratified by Law 19.685, placing international treaties above internal laws, it is not open to Argentina to plead the lack of legislation, or the existence of a contrary rule, to negate the force of the rights enshrined in the Convention. In a recent decision, the Supreme Court of Justice held that any international treaty takes precedence over laws, regulations and other internal rules of a legislative nature which contradict it.[10] Since the 1994 constitutional reform, there is no doubt that the rights enshrined in the UN Convention on the Rights of the Child constitute an operative instrument.

DEFINITION OF THE 'CHILD' IN THE CONVENTION (ARTICLE 1)

Majority is attained at age 21 in Argentina.[11] Two kinds of minors exist in law - minors below puberty up to age 14 and minor-adults aged between 14 and 21[12] who have a wider civil capacity than children in the younger category (to recognize their children, to work with parental consent, to give evidence in court and so on). A reform which would lower the age of majority to 18 is currently under discussion.

Argentina's ratification of the Convention was subject to a reservation relating to Article 1. This declares that the said article must be interpreted in the sense that the term 'child' includes any human being from the moment of conception.

In Argentinian legislation, the existence of a person begins at conception in the mother's body,[13] giving rise to rights which become irrevocable at live birth.[14] Property can be acquired through a legal representative by a child *en ventre de sa mère* (that is, in the mother's womb), by gift or inheritance.[15] Labour law protects the unborn child through the protection of the pregnant employee, which ranks as a constitutional provision in some provinces; social security law provides antenatal benefits to cover the major expenses of pregnancy.[16] Also, paternal authority takes effect from the child's conception.[17]

Consistently, doctrine permits recognition of an unborn child. Typically, the father's impending death leads to an admission of paternity ahead of time. Conversely, a husband or his heirs can challenge paternity of a child before birth.[18]

THE CHILD'S PARAMOUNT INTERESTS (CONVENTION, ARTICLE 3)

'The paramountcy of the child's interests' is expressly recognized as a principle in Argentinian laws and is constantly applied in the courts in the various aspects relating to the child's person and property. Judges likewise use this principle to resolve conflict between adult carers and the child. It is invoked also as a basis for state intervention in the family when it is judged that the father or mother may harm the child by their actions.

The 'paramount interest of the child' principle is a step forward respecting the personality of the child and his needs, and implies an undertaking to defend the rights of those unable to exercise them themselves. But we must not overlook the fact that it is ill-defined and depends not only on the understanding and construction of each society and historical period, but also to interpretation by judges who define, case-by-case, the content of that interest in accordance with its particular history and with their own beliefs and world-view. This may just as easily lead to acting to the child's advantage as to acts of an arbitrary nature.[19] To escape the trap of personal subjectivity, one must have recourse to other knowledge and to other disciplines which enable one to identify in any given situation the true interest of the child. Because of this risk of personal value judgements, it would seem useful, as has already been pointed out by other authors, to link the 'interest of the child' with his or her fundamental rights, since failure by parents or others to respect any of these rights damages the 'paramount interest of the child'. Of course, there is, however, no escaping the fact that, even if this test adds greater precision to the concept, this does not overcome its ill-defined nature.

It must be noted that, both Argentina's laws and its courts, demonstrate a systemic focus since, to resolve the practical situation, not only is the interest of the child taken into consideration, but also the interests of the whole family.[20] Concern to protect the family as a whole through the notion of the 'family interest' is found in various provisions of the law. Efforts are made to combine the 'us', representing the family unit, with the 'me' that symbolizes the autonomy and individual development of its members.

NON-DISCRIMINATION. THE CHILD'S RIGHT TO LIVE IN A FAMILY AND TO KNOW HIS PARENTS (CONVENTION, ARTICLES 2, 7, 8, 9, 10 AND 11)

Children who have no family life

From the moment of birth a child has a right to identity as a unique and un-repeatable being, though one integrated at the same time into a family group, a society and a culture. That is what is expressed in the right to a name, a nationality and, within the limits of what is possible, to know and be cared for by his parents (Article 7, Convention on the Rights of the Child). Many of the Convention's provisions (among others, Articles 8, 9, 10 and 11) affirm this essential right of the child to live in a family, and hence not to be separated from parents, except when this is necessary in the child's interests (Article 9).

Despite this, in Argentina many children have no family life; these are the abandoned street children, runaways from home, abused and violated by their parents, or sold and thus denied their history and links with their origins. Street children, deprived of all family support, are a fact of life in both Argentina and in Latin America as a whole. These children and adolescents enjoy none of the constitutional rights, contrary to the principle of non-discrimination established in Article 2 of the Convention. Their physical and mental health are at risk, they inhale toxic substances, fall into child prostitution and become victims of sexual abuse and economic exploitation.

Nor do the numerous children and adolescents, described as 'minors in an irregular situation', kept in public institutions, live in a family environment. They are stigmatized and cut off from the mainstream of society which, claiming to save them from danger, only succeeds in labelling them as 'dangerous'.

Certainly, to give effect to the child's right to live in a family, the state has to adopt preventive policies to improve the living conditions of families so that they can raise and educate their children. The Constitution (art. 14 bis) guarantees the full protection of the family and efforts have been made to realize this, both by legal provisions and action programmes. Recently, the Consejo Nacional del Menor y la Familia has been set up to promote a better system of helping families, or their members, at risk; public and private programmes have been developed to reinforce the bonds between parents and children and, in the case of irreversible breakdown, to offer the child a substitute family. Likewise family centres have been set up to give direction and support to families (presidential decree 1606/90). There is no lack of laws, but it is necessary to give concrete reality to these legislative good intentions.

Children born out of wedlock

Argentina has abolished one form of discrimination which gave greater rights to children of a marriage than to those born out of wedlock. Regadless of the status of their parents, all children have equal rights of filiation to both parents. Likewise, marital, extramarital and adoptive filiation have the same effects.[21]

Filiation on the mother's side

Maternity, in or out of wedlock, is fixed by birth, with no requirement of an act of recognition. The mother's rights and duties attach by operation of law.

Filiation on the father's side

Argentina has abolished one form of discrimination which gave greater rights to children of a marriage than to those born out of wedlock. Nowadays all children, whatever the status of their parents, have equal rights and all can claim filiation on the paternal side without restrictions. But the real practical obstacles to achieving a paternal filiation are not overcome by formal equality.

Considerable progress has been made. The reforms of 1985 brought in changes to facilitate paternity actions. Treating the child as one's own, by caring, feeding, bringing up as a 'child of the family' (*posesión de estado*) are equivalent to express recognition, in the absence of proof that there is no biological relationship;[22] analogous to the presumption raised by marriage, the fact of cohabitation with the mother in the conception period establishes paternity unless, of course, it is proved that there is no biological relationship.[23]

The governing principle, supported by doctrine and by judicial decisions, is that all forms of evidence including biological evidence are admissible and relevant.[24] The progress of science now allows genetic links to be established with a probability approaching certainty. In Argentina, biological evidence is supported by the setting up of the Banco Nacional de Datos Geneticos (Law 23.511), with the objective of obtaining and storing genetic information to help resolve conflicts over filiation. The law provides for genetic tests in cases involving a person's filiation, indicating particular aspects to be investigated (art. 6).

All the same, we are now faced by what the law says and by the realities of experience. And what do these realities tell us? That the country lacks the laboratory facilities in many places and that, in addition, the defendants in filiation claims are often unwilling to provide samples. Doctrine and judicial decisions have tended to maintain that, on a refusal, compulsion to undergo a blood test is inadmissible on the principle of individual autonomy and inviolability. Nevertheless, such resistance is taken to create a strong presumption against the person refusing, and this may be corroborated by other evidence. A problem arises where, as often happens, the mother has no other evidence and relies only on biological tests, to prove paternity. Here, if the man refuses a test and there is no other evidence, the child cannot achieve paternal filiation. In such a case, although judges tend to regard the mere refusal of a test as insufficient evidence on which to base a judgement,[25] a recent decision has taken a more drastic position, affirming that refusal to undergo biological tests can raise a presumption of paternity which may only be rebutted if the defendant proves he is *not* the child's father.[26] Thus, refusal of a test is of itself a ground for a paternity judgement. The doctrinal argument is that the putative father cannot, by his own decision, obstruct justice and prevent the determination of paternity. Cooperation by both parties is required to reach the truth, and the procedural act of the party seeking to deny the claim is construed accordingly.[27]

One superior court, the Corte Suprema of Santa Fé Province, has held that a person cannot refuse biological tests on grounds of privacy, physical inviolability, control of one's own body or personal freedom, since the child's right to have his paternity determined and know his origins overrides those other rights.[28]

Many fathers do not recognize their children. Reasons of a psychological, social or economic nature, outside the scope of this chapter,[29] prevent the bringing of an action by the mother on behalf of the child. Thus many children, usually of single and poor mothers, are registered as of unknown paternity. As a recent investigation has shown,[30] about one extramarital child in three is in this position. Such children have no rights vis à vis the man who fathered them. This is a serious problem in a country such as Argentina, since the lack of a father's support and the mother's poverty result in abandonment of the child. The state does not have sufficient resources adequately to fulfil its duty to feed and provide for the health and education of such children.

Furthermore, psychosocial research indicating that non-recognition by a father imposes a real social stigma on a child, affecting his development of a sense of identity and giving rise to psychological complications, has been judicially recognized. Consequently, judges have ordered men against whom paternity is proved to compensate the child for lack of prompt recognition.[31]

At the same time, the father's ability to evade liability demonstrates an inequality between men and women, for the mother alone has to raise the child and the father can evade his responsibility, in contravention of Article 18 of the Convention. Thus, the right to separate sexuality from parenthood benefits only the man; the woman is in no position to choose and must accept responsibility for the child. To overcome this, the law[32] provides for the Ministerio Público de Menores to claim against the putative father for recognition and, on refusal, to bring filiation proceedings with the mother's consent. However, this legal power is, at present, rarely effective, as mothers often refuse to name the father and do not want the action to be brought. In this way, the actions of the adult parties victimize the child who remains of indeterminate paternity.

We believe that, since from the private law viewpoint it is necessary to develop responsible parenthood, this direction should be accompanied on the public law side by measures which give women, as well as men, in conditions of equality, the right to choose freely their maternity and paternity and provide, to this end, adequate guidance and support services.

It must be emphasized, as this is an argument often put forward to criticize the rule, that state action by the Ministerio Público de Menores in no way contravenes the mother's or the putative father's right to privacy. This right, which merits serious protection, cannot be allowed to undermine the child's right to have his paternity established. Once born, the child's new life in being is not the property of the parents. It is his, and cannot be concealed at the whim of his progenitors.

The right of the child born in marriage to determination of his true filiation and the principle of biological truth

The principle of equality in determining filiation, which affirms implicitly that of non-discrimination, is linked to the principle of biological truth, and to the child's rights to know his parents and to be cared for by them.

The child's right to obtain his true parentage is shown also in the action to challenge the husband's paternity. The current legal approach is an open one (Civil Code, art. 258) allowing the true relationship to be determined, unlike the former situation which restricted displacement of the presumption of paternity to exceptional cases set out in the law. The reform gives an action to deny paternity not only to the husband, but also to the child. In the previous system only the husband during his lifetime could bring it. Now, the child's right to his true filiation is fully realized (art. 259 CC).

The child resulting from medically assisted procreation: the need for legal regulation

The techniques of assisted procreation have revolutionized filiation procedures, yet despite the extensive use of such methods, there is still no legal provision for the diversity of situations which can affect the family status of the resulting children. These procedures need legal regulation, protecting children's rights, and preventing abuse and dangerous concealment. The National Congress is currently studying a proposed legal text which would restrict the use of such practices to cases of sterility or infertility, approved by an interdisciplinary team of the medical centre which would specify the treatment to be given (art. 1.). Preselection of sex would be banned save for the purposes of preventing hereditary diseases (art. 10).

The desire for transcendence through children, to create a living being and to give it affection, is a human need worthy of respect. But, since there are no absolute rights, it will be necessary to consider what may be the solutions when this wish is at odds with the children's rights or social interests. Examples could be attempts to choose the child's sex or other characteristics, or merely to find an alternative to natural fertilization. The quest for a child must not be reduced to shopping for a consumer commodity.

Children carrying the HIV virus

We should refer briefly to AIDS in relation to children's rights, particularly that of non-discrimination, bearing in mind that this is a disease that grows ever more widespread and which has especially adverse consequences for children and women. Argentina has promulgated Law 23.789 and regulatory decree 1244/91 to deal with this problem. Many provisions in these concern children's rights enshrined in the Convention, such as those guaranteeing the dignity of the person, privacy, equal treatment, and prohibition of any treatment leading to marginalization, stigma or humiliation of the patient. Among these provisions, is the duty of the professional who detects the virus to inform the patient of the infectious/contagious nature of the disease, of the manner and form of its transmission, and of his or her duty to obtain adequate help (art. 8). In the case of a minor, his or her legal representative is entitled to be informed (art. 2). We believe that this latter should be reformed, since a child of sufficient maturity has the right to be told. There is also provision for covering the subject in educational programmes at all school grades. Infected children are not excluded from school, this being seen as unnecessary as mere physical contact does not transmit the disease, and exclusion would contravene constitutional rights of access to education.

THE CHILD'S RIGHT TO MAINTAIN HIS IDENTITY (CONVENTION, ARTICLE 8)

The case of children whose parents have disappeared

In relation to this right of the child to live in a family, we cannot ignore the children of parents who disappeared as a result of the state repression operating in Argentina between 1976 and 1983. The disappearances that then took place, and the fate of the children, are facts of Argentine history which cannot be suppressed in any discussion of children's rights. These children, snatched when their parents were arrested or born in captivity, were taken away from their families of origin and deprived of their name and family contacts. Their filiation was falsified, others claiming them as their own or adopting them.[33] In short, they were robbed of their individuality as persons and of the right to know their personal history – indeed, robbed of their rightful identity. This right of every person to know his origins is a road to the truth which may not be obstructed.[34] At present, after the constitutional reform, the child's right of identity is expressly enshrined in the National Constitution as well as in some Provincial Constitutions.[35]

The case of adoption

Currently, no legal provision allows the child to know his origins. In the case of full adoption, which breaks the child's links with biological family, birth certificates which do not even disclose that the child is adopted are issued (Civil Code, art. 241).

A bill is under consideration, giving the adopted person a right to know his origins from the age of 18. The child's right to know his origins raises many questions which future legislation must resolve, such as the age at which the child may demand information, the manner of applying the right and authority responsible for supplying it.

The case of assisted procreation

As previously noted, assisted procreation is unregulated in Argentina. A bill aimed at providing a legal framework for this would require the medical centre to maintain a register of the gamete donors which could be consulted by the child, his legal representative or the person authorized by a judge if the latter considered there was justification for this, or to avoid prohibited marriages.

THE CHILD'S RIGHT NOT TO BE PARTED FROM HIS PARENTS AGAINST THEIR WISHES (CONVENTION, ARTICLE 9, PARA. 1). STATE AID FOR CHILDREN TEMPORARILY OR PERMANENTLY OUT OF THEIR FAMILIES (ARTICLE 20)

Under Argentine law various circumstances justify the removal of children from their families: first, all the causes which result in ending the progenitors' parental authority (crimes against the child, abandonment, endangering the safety, physical or mental health or the morality of the child, by maltreatment, evil example, notorious misconduct or delinquency);[36] second, any situation involving moral or material danger to the child.[37] In such cases the child is in an 'irregular situation' and the judge decides his fate, either entrusting him or her to a relative or other person or placing him or her for adoption or in a public or private sector residential placement.[38] Nationally, there are 24 institutions, and an average of 200 children a month enter them. There is temporary accommodation in the system called *amas externas* and the *régimen de sequeños hogares* where children and adolescents up to the age of 21 live, pending long-term placement.[39]

The separation of the child from his or her family has no fixed term, and his or her return home rests on the decision of the judge. Should the judge find the conditions which led to removal still to exist, the minor may stay placed until his or her majority – that is, until age 21. For the child this amounts to a sentence of indeterminate placement, infringing, as such, the right to due process. This detention in institutions is a real deprivation of liberty for the children, who are thereby punished for the acts of the adults who victimized them. The majority (90 per cent) of detained children are from the poorer social groups, with unsatisfied basic needs in the case of over 90 per cent.

This produces a vicious circle. For want of preventive state assistance for families, parents cannot function properly, so, faced with this inadequacy, the state intervenes, removing the children considered 'at risk' from these families. Thus, in order to fulfil the Convention's norms, the essential problem is to attend to the needs of the families, enabling them to care adequately for their children and fulfil the responsibility of parenthood. This means improving the economic situation of families, developing programmes against domestic violence and helping families in crisis or in case of drug or alcohol abuse.

It remains to note that one of the aims proposed by the Consejo Federal de Protección del Menor y la Familia (1992) is to cut progressively the number of children institutionalized for want of care, by means of supporting families and of developing alternatives to institutionalization.

CHILDREN OF SEPARATED PARENTS (CONVENTION, ARTICLE 9 SS. 3)

Custody of children

Argentine law, regardless of the way child custody is organized, makes an attribution in favour of only one person, preference being given to the mother where children are under five years old. Above this age, failing agreement by the spouses, they are entrusted to the parent whom the judge considers most suitable for this purpose (art. 206, Civil Code). However, in judicial practice the custody of children, by agreement or by judicial order, usually goes to the mother.

Communication with the non-custodial parent: so-called visitation rights

Argentine law is consonant with to the terms of the Convention in that it gives the parent not living with the child rights of contact. In case of *de facto* separation, separation order, divorce or nullity, it is for the parent with custody to exercise the parental rights, the other parent retaining the right to have sufficient contact with the child and oversee his upbringing.[40] However, to harmonize the system with the Convention, it should be set out expressly that the right to contact is not merely a parental right, but also belongs to the child, as is already recognized in doctrine and judicial decisions.[41]

Although the child has this right to contact with both his parents on a regular basis, social and judicial practice shows it to be ineffectual in many cases. A clear example of the child being regarded as an object of parental property occurs when the parents divorce. Here he or she becomes a bargaining counter, or is fought over, without regard to his or her need, wishes or feelings. This disregard for the person of the child emerges in conflicts over custody, over the management of contact with the non-custodial parent and over maintenance – conflicts which ultimately harm the child. These disputes originate, beyond any doubt, in the inability of many parents to distinguish between their conjugal relationship and their parent–child relationship. In these cases, the father quite often stops seeing his children and cuts himself off altogether from their upbringing and education. By the same token, the mother often resists contact by the father. Judicial reaction is severe, through sanctions against a mother who obstructs such contact.[42] Access is only stopped if the behaviour of the non-custodial parent could harm the minor or threaten his physical or mental health.[43] Similarly, in awarding custody, the parent who is best able to facilitate contact with the other has been considered the more suitable.[44] Indeed, in one particular decision, custody was taken away from the parent resisting the children's contact with the other parent and granted to that other parent.[45]

A recently passed law punishes by imprisonment the parent or third party who illegally impedes or obstructs contact between minors and parents not living with them. It also imposes a penalty on the parent or third party who, to impede contact of minors with the parent not living with them, changes his address without judicial authorization. These increase if the parent takes the child abroad without judicial authorization (Law 24.270/930).

One reason given by mothers to their opposition to fathers seeing their children is the non-fulfilment of a maintenance obligation. Previously, judges would, on the mother's request, suspend the father's visitation rights on this ground, but the tendency now is to maintain contact with the father, as this is an essential right of the child and to deny it imposes a double punishment, since the child benefits neither from support nor from contact with his father. However, it is often the child or adolescent who opposes contact with the absent parent. Where he or she takes this position, the court investigates whether his or her stance is spontaneous or induced, or justified.[46] In one case it was ruled that the mother must make her children comply with the visiting arrangements on pain of modification of her custody order.[47]

Argentine judges – increasingly the senior ones – understand that these conflicts cannot be settled by penalties which benefit neither child nor the family unit and therefore seek, with behavioural science experts, to diagnose and apply therapy to this dysfunction, and to have recourse to mediation techniques. Recently, some decisions have attempted to overcome resistance and conflicts by ordering the parents to accept therapy, under threat of sanctions for non-compliance. It is said that, for the child's sake, the court cannot stand idly and indifferently by, and must seek an adequate solution to the family conflict.[48]

To ensure the principle of joint parenthood after divorce, so that the child really maintains regular contact with both parents, as required by the Convention, I believe that Argentine law must now accept shared custody, which would have a positive psychological effect on both parents. The mother would benefit by knowing that all important decisions were taken jointly and the father would likewise benefit by no longer feeling cut off and excluded. This latter point is important, as it would encourage the father's compliance with his support obligations. Many studies have confirmed that the more contact the father has with the child, the more committed he is to paying maintenance and fulfilling his parental responsibilities. Reluctance to pay maintenance increases precisely in line with the passage of time and the cessation of the father's contact with his children. Argentine courts have usually rejected joint custody agreements with alternate care because they consider it affects the child's upbringing.[49] But ultimately, and increasingly, judges see it as the right of parents to make such agreements for shared custody.[50]

One current problem for jurists is to work out how the law should operate to maintain the child's contact with both parents when one of these is infected with AIDS. Doctrinal opinion is that suffering this disease is not in itself a ground justifying a change in custody arrangements or cutting off the infected non-custodial parent's contact with the child. If, however, the patient falls into chronic depression, neglects the child or suffers a personality change, these factors, not the illness itself, justify action.[51]

ILLICIT REMOVAL OF CHILDREN FROM THE COUNTRY, TRAFFIC IN CHILDREN. WAYS OF STOPPING ABDUCTION, SALE AND TRADE IN CHILDREN (CONVENTION, ARTICLES 11 AND 35)

Argentina has a widespread problem of purchase and trade in children, usually caused by the practice of impoverished and mainly adolescent mothers giving up their child due to lack of family support. There are also cases where divorced or separated parents illegally take the child abroad, or withhold him or her.

Argentina is a signatory of the Hague Convention, which is ratified by Law 23.867, of 26 October 1990. At a regional level, the country signed a bilateral treaty with Uruguay in 1980 (ratified by Law 22.546 of March 1982), and has also taken part in specialized Interamerican Convention on Private International Law, signing the Interamerican Convention on the International Restitution of Minors, ratified on 24 November 1992 by a law not yet in force. The object of this Convention is to ensure the prompt return of minors whose habitual residence is in one participating state and illicitly removed to another, or who after being taken there legally are unlawfully kept there. Another object is to ensure respect for the exercise of visitation rights, custody and care on the part of those entitled thereto.

Argentina also participated in a conference of Latin American experts on traffic in children held in Mexico, on 13–16 October 1993, preparing for the

Fifth Special Congress on Private International Law (CIDIP V), accepted a project for an Interamerican Convention on the international traffic in minors including civil and penal aspects. Its objectives are to identify, prevent and punish illegal retention and international traffic in children, and the abduction abroad of a child without the consent of the person entitled to give it or the order of the competent authorities of the state of habitual residence.

THE CHILD'S RIGHT IN RELATION TO THE EXERCISE OF PARENTAL AUTHORITY (CONVENTION, ARTICLES 12, 13, 14, 16)

In Argentina, *patria potestas* is 'a bundle of rights and duties which the parents have over their children, for their protection and total development'.[52] The concept of 'domination' has been replaced by that of 'protection' and the power attributed to parents or their substitutes has as its exclusive goal the child's or the adolescent's welfare.[53] However, this is insufficient to implement one of the central ideas of the Convention: to consider the child a 'subject of protection' rather than as an 'object of protection'. Perceiving the child as 'a subject of protection' means seeing him or her as a human being in relationships with adults, with the possibility of expressing his or her wishes and needs, taking part in his or her own development and enjoying a growing autonomy as each new stage is reached. Consequently, to guarantee that his or her upbringing is the result of interaction between adult and child, Argentine law needs the three following reforms:

1   establishing that, in exercising parental authority, the particular needs, requirements, aptitudes and aspirations of the child in question must be considered at each stage of life. This would ensure that the child is not seen as an abstract 'object' whose expectations and wishes are identical with those of the parents; such a view, despite the best intentions, frequently hinders the development of his individuality and character.
2   establishing the child's or adolescent's participation in the educational process. This idea, which implies letting the child speak for him or herself, promotes the democratic principle of the search for consensus within the family, rejecting imposed decisions. The child's duty to obey, which Argentine law affirms,[54] is not one of carrying out orders in a subordinate relationship, but of accepting a decision as the result of interchange, the child or adolescent being allowed to express an opinion even if the adult has the last word.
3   setting out in law the levels of autonomy and freedom of the child in the

family sphere, and establishing mechanisms at the same time to resolve conflicts which may arise.

Argentine law considers the minor aged 14 to have reached the age of discretion (Civil Code, art. 921) and particular provisions give the right to perform a series of personal acts in social life before reaching legal majority. However, the law has made limited progress in developing the child's rights to impose parental authority. If in practice many parents and parent substitutes ignore the wishes of the child, the will of the child or adolescent signifies little in law. Considering the minor as a subject of rights in his relation to his parents means allowing him or her space to complete his apprenticeship in autonomy in his or her progression to adulthood, preparing him or her for an independent and responsible life in society (Convention, Preamble and Article 29, ss. d). Thus, once he or she has reached a certain stage of development, the participation and the will of the minor must be considered, in relation to: choice of religion; right to the care of his or her own body (for example, in relation to medical consultations and treatments, hospitalization); right to privacy of correspondence and papers, choice of friends and so on. Also, even if the education and training of a child or adolescent remain subject to the direction of parents or parent substitutes, it is appropriate to give the child access to the courts when the action of the parents is an abuse of right and the child's fundamental rights are infringed (in terms of religious freedom, choice of work or of studies, personal, physical or psychological inviolability, right to identity and so on).

In Argentina, if parents refuse to authorize blood transfusions for a sick child on religious grounds, court decisions have ruled that health is a most personal right which parents cannot override, and that refusing to let a minor receive blood transfusions implies an abuse of parental authority justifying state intervention to protect the child's interests.[55] There is a proposal currently before the National Congress to provide that, in case of unjustified refusal by parents of medical treatment necessary because of the child's state of health, a judge may authorize it.

IS THERE A CONFLICT BETWEEN RECOGNIZING THE CHILD'S RIGHTS AND THE ADULT'S POWER TO GUIDE AND DIRECT? (CONVENTION, ARTICLE 5)

Many contend that emphasis on the child's rights will create more conflicts, since having rights implies the means of vindicating them in court, and children or adolescents may challenge parental authority thereby depriving parents of the ability to raise and train their children. Such fears lose their force when one sees that – as is enshrined in the Convention, Article 5 – asserting the rights of the child is not a defence of the prerogatives of the child in derogation of the authority of parents and of the family unit. Parents or their substitutes remain responsible for the training and education of the child, but it is necessary to find a balance between the parents' freedom to educate, their right to train the child and the respect due to the child as a person. Respecting the child does not imply leaving him or her to his own devices and abstaining from all guidance and persuasion. Parents and teachers must provide children with coherent models of right behaviour, while simultaneously giving them the opportunity to participate in their own growing up. As is enshrined in Article 29 of the Convention, affirming the child's right to take the initiative means, at the same time, teaching him or her respect for human rights and calling for responsible and collaborative behaviour, in accordance with his or her age, towards parents, the family and society as a whole.

THE CHILD'S RIGHT TO BE HEARD IN JUDICIAL PROCEEDINGS (CONVENTION, ARTICLE 12)

Many of the conflicts involving children are resolved in court. Hitherto, on the assumption that the court looked after the interest of the minor, child or adolescent, the latter remained a silent figure whose feelings, wishes and needs were unknown. Now, the minor is sometimes allowed to speak in a proceeding affecting his person. For instance, where the mother and father disagree as to the exercise of parental authority, the judge, to decide what best serves the interest of the child, may also hear evidence from the minor, if he or she has sufficient understanding and it seems advisable in the circumstances.[56] Likewise, in adoption cases the judge may hear the adopted person if he thinks it necessary, and provided he or she is over the age of ten. Where the adopter already has biological children, they may also be heard by the tribunal, if the judge considers it necessary and they are over the age of eight.

Provincial rules of procedure expressly establish the need to hear the minor in proceedings affecting his person. In the Province of Mendoza, the Procedure Code[57] provides that, in cases involving *patria potestas*, tutorship or adoption, the judge must see and hear personally the minors involved, so far as is reasonable. In the Province of Buenos Aires, in proceedings before the Court of Minors, the judge must likewise hear the minor.[58]

In addition to the particular instances above, nowadays, in cases concerning problems of custody or access, the judge listens to the minor, particularly if he or she is an adolescent, and determines the best solution for him or her, taking the minor's views into account with the other elements of the case.[59]

We believe that it is now necessary for a general rule that, in all proceedings in which the judge hears a minor (in relation to divorce, rights or access by grandparents or others, tutorship, adoption, or in any case where the child or adolescent is in physical or moral danger), Argentine law should conform with the Convention.

The debate as to whether the views of the child or adolescent should be heard raises many questions for jurists and specialists in other disciplines to answer. For instance, should there be a specific age from which it is obligatory to hear the child, or should this be left to the discretion of the judge in each individual case? Who should hear the child? How? And what weight is attributed to his views?

The defence of the child's rights in civil matters

In civil matters, the Argentine state body charged with defending and representing the interests of children is the Ministerio Público de Menores. However, its function, in practice, is somewhat limited. It rules and gives opinions in cases in which children's interests are at stake, and supervises the acts of parents or others who represent them in the lawsuit. Where there is conflict between the interests of children and of parents a *tutor special* (equivalent to a *guardian ad litem*) is appointed.[60]

Our view is that current procedures in Argentina fail to satisfy the requirements of due process. The Ministerio Público de Menores should actively represent the child's interests, taking the initiative itself where necessary to defend them. To this end it should act with the help of experts in the various specialized disciplines concerned with children's problems in order to accumulate all the information needed by a judge to decide the most appropriate solution for the child or adolescent. Some authors believe that the mere presence of the *Ministerio Público de Menores* does not assure the child's right to natural justice, and that a child should have his own advocate or representative, including in actions undertaken for his own protection whenever he is in a situation of risk.[61]

CHILD ABUSE (CONVENTION, ARTICLE 19)

Society delegates the function of raising and educating the child to parents or their substitutes. These, according to their experience and social and moral values, guide the actions of the child in daily life. To fulfil their task, society gives parents a right to discipline their children, but this right is expressly limited: '… the power of correction must be exercised *moderately*, to the exclusion of maltreatment, punishments or acts which harm or humiliate minors physically or mentally'.[62]

However this right of 'moderate' correction is, in the understanding of society, often taken to mean a right to use corporal punishment 'moderately'. Often actions which public discussion define as unlawful acts to be condemned are felt by the actors themselves to be normal behaviour and a natural consequence of the duty to educate. We therefore consider a reform of the law is called for, to ban once and for all every form of physical or mental punishment of children.

What sanctions are established in Argentina for abusive acts against children? First, *patria potestas* can be withdrawn from parents who maltreat their children.[63] Furthermore, when the use of force has damaged the body or the health of the child, this amounts to the serious offence of *lesiones* (bodily harm) and the offender is dealt with under the ordinary law. If the maltreatments of minors by parents, tutors or guardians do not amount to a serious offence, the law gives the judge power to impose lesser penalties, which may be suspended if the offenders give assurances as to their future conduct.[64] The penalties for sexual abuse are identical to those for these offences under the Penal Code – *violación* (rape), *estupro* (seduction by deception or breach of confidence) *corrupción* (corruption of a minor) and *abuso deshonesto* (indecent assault).

The purpose of a recently sanctioned law (24.470, December 1994) are: to make it possible for accusations of family violence to come before the family courts in order to increase public awareness of the problem (bearing in mind the proportion of cases that go undetected) and to adopt measures to protect the victims and to impose therapeutic and educative treatment on the offenders. Recent research shows that criminal proceedings are ineffective; few prosecutions are brought and, when cases come to court, convictions result from only the very serious.[65]

ADOPTION (CONVENTION, ARTICLE 21)

Forms of adoption[66]

National norms on adoption[67] meet the standards set out in Article 21 ss. a) of the Convention. In Argentine legislation two forms of adoption are established – so-called full adoption and simple adoption. Adoptive filiation under the first form takes the place of the adopted person's original filiation, extinguishing all relationship to his birth family save for impediments to marriage. This is the form of adoption ordered where there is a irreversible breach between the minor and his biological parents. In the second form, simple adoption, the adopted person receives the status of a child of his adopters' marriage, but still belongs to his blood family, save for the exercise of *patria potestas*.

Procedure

The application of the adopters necessitates a judicial process in which the judge investigates the applicants' social conditions, taking into account their means and moral qualities, and whether adoption is appropriate for the child or adolescent. Application must be made to the judge of the adopters' domicile; and the adopters must be Argentine residents, whether of Argentine or foreign nationality. The public and private sector agencies keep registers of would-be adopters, Argentines or foreigners, who are qualified by two years' residence in the country or by being employed there.

Social practice

As we have already noted, children are frequently given away by single, adolescent mothers, abandoned by male partners, without family support, lacking resources and in no position to raise the child. It is estimated that each year 85,000 young, mainly poor, women given birth in Argentina,[68] and this has been increasing since 1985. More than 30 per cent of births in Buenos Aires Province are to young adolescents. While middle-class women have recourse to abortion, even though abortion is prohibited in Argentina, in the poorer classes most young women carry the baby to term, regarding it as 'one more misfortune'. Pregnancy is not a matter of choice and, after the birth, the mother, unable to maintain or care for it, gets rid of the child.

The clandestine handing over of children is a frequent practice; the children are then registered as their own by those who want to raise and educate them. There is reluctance to undertake formal adoption proceedings which is thought to be a long and complicated process. Also, 'adopters' want to conceal the transaction so that the biological parents are unable to reclaim the child in the future. At a guess, only one in five adopted children are legally adopted, the rest being registered with a false filiation. In Argentina, social paternity is still undervalued, and adoption is a matter of fear and shame.

International adoption

Argentinian law lacks norms for 'international adoption', covered in Article 21 ss. (b), (c), (d) and e) of the Convention. In ratifying the Convention, Argentina placed an express reservation excluding these provisions within its jurisdiction, on the ground that a rigorous regime of legal protection would be a prerequisite to control trafficking and sale. Argentina thus rejected the concept of 'open adoption' contained in the Convention, and pronounced in favour of 'closed adoption'.

Contradictory positions are taken in Argentina over this problem. Some totally reject international adoption on the grounds that it uproots the child from his society of origin, and denies his or her rights to live in the land of his birth and to his or her own identity. They maintain that it increases illegal trafficking in children and encourages agencies acting with commercial objectives.

Other authors, while opposing the involvement of profit-motivated institutions or individuals, accept the possibility that those domiciled abroad may adopt children living in Argentina, provided they meet the conditions required by Argentine law and the adoption is advantageous for the child - that is, in cases of abandoned children in institutions, and where there are no potential nationals to adopt them.

In the proposed Convention on International Adoption which the meeting of Latin American experts approved in Quito in 1983, it was ruled that international adoption should only be used if all possibilities of keeping the child in his birth family, or in an adoptive family of his birth nationality, were exhausted. Likewise, it decided that the law of habitual residence governs capacity, consent, procedure and formalities of creating the bond of adoption, while that or the adopters' domicile governs their capacity and the other requirements of adoption. This restrictive approach is in line with current Latin American and international thinking.[69]

We believe that Argentina should regulate international adoption as follows:

1 A foreign domiciled person should be allowed to adopt if adoption and care cannot be given in the birth country (Convention, Article 21 ss. b);
2 Any adoption based on crime (such as kidnapping or abduction or minors) should be invalidated;
3 Intervention by private agencies, institutions or other bodies in the process of adoption should be banned;
4 International judicial cooperation in adoption proceedings, even preliminary or subsequent to the order, should be established;

5   Disclosure to the child of his or her origins in support of his right to an identity should be facilitated;
6   The jurisdiction of the courts of habitual residence and of domicile of the child or adolescent should be determined;
7   It should be made possible for the child to be heard in court;
8   The law of the adopted person's domicile, save as to the adopters' capacity, should be applied;
9   Measures both before and after the order should be a matter of international judicial cooperation.[70]

HANDICAPPED CHILDREN (CONVENTION, ARTICLE 23)[71]

In Argentina several laws provide overall protection for the handicapped, including handicapped children,[72] containing a series of state obligations in line with the requirements of the Convention. We may cite as examples: the organization of rehabilitative services; trade and professional training for the handicapped; special regimes of social security and educational provision in ordinary schools or, if the degree of handicap makes it impossible for the person to attend ordinary schools, in a special establishment; creating protected workshops with both therapy and the production of goods and services as their objectives; creation of assessment and guidance centres; training specialized teachers and professionals; free transport and architectural adaptation to facilitate the mobility of disabled persons; social benefits for their integration, such as the provision of cars,[73] telephone service,[74] free entry to shows and special parking permits.

The protection of the handicapped is completed by a law banning any arbitrary discrimination against the disabled, ensuring their equal exercise of constitutional rights and guarantees, providing for the ending of such practices and compensation for any physical or mental harm they have caused. Taking part in organizations or producing propaganda based on theories of superiority of a particular group with discriminatory intent is also punishable.[75]

Other preventive rules take account of possible future disability, requiring newborn children to be tested for early diagnosis of conditions leading to mental retardation (such as phenylketonuria, hypothyroidism).

THE STATE AND THE RIGHTS OF THE CHILD

Finally, I would like to make a few brief reflections on a much debated problem closely linked to children's rights. I refer to the autonomy of the family and state intervention.

We must distinguish two levels: state action to protect the family expressed in acts of a social nature, and intervention by the state in the functioning of the family.

At the first level, the child's rights established in the Convention put responsibilities on parents and on the state. Parents have a duty to nurture and educate their children, but the state must appropriately help them to discharge this duty (Convention, Articles 18, 24, 27, 28). Educating and training the child is both a private function and a social responsibility. Parents are often criticized for the inadequate care of a child, forgetting that the cause is their poverty, alienation through poor living conditions and lack of education. Therefore, it is necessary to consider what the state and the community must do so that social rights should become effective policies for living, employment, education and culture rooted in family life. In Argentina the Consejo Nacional del Menor y la Familia has proposed various programmes, such as preventing abandonment, subsidized care, emergency subventions for household expenses and preventive measures to support families in situations of deficiency or crisis. It is now a question of realizing these intentions so families are not left to their own devices.

At the second level, relating to the exercise of *patria potestas*, the basis of Argentine law is that the state only has a subsidiary role in family life, the parents' will being sovereign in caring for the moral and material interest of the child or adolescent. State control is therefore restricted to cases where there are clearly elements of danger for the children or their care and education are abandoned or neglected.[76]

However, it must be borne in mind that, despite increasing autonomy and privatization of the family, there is at the same time a greater intervention by the public interest, precisely as a consequence of recognition of children's rights. Society increasingly requires parents to act in particular ways in relation to the care and education of their children, such as compulsory schooling and vaccination, medical checks, showing clearly demonstrating the interest of society as a whole in the life and development of children. Equally, the courts act with ever increasing frequency in defence of the child against abusive acts of his parents or their substitutes which could harm his physical or mental well-being or frustrate his opportunities. Yet, at the same time, in the attempt to achieve consensus, personal freedom and family autonomy are being encouraged, using such resources as mediation, so that the parties can resolve their conflicts themselves by agreement and bargaining.

NOTES

1   Formosa, Jujuy, Chaco – Indec, Synthesis no. 2, 1993.
2   *Clarin* (daily), 16 April 1994, and *Pagina 12* (daily), 17 April 1994.
3   Argentine UNICEF data, based on the *Encuesta Permanente de Hogares, Niños en cifras* (Permanent Statistical Review of Households and Children), Indec, Synthesis no. 2, 1993.
4   Argentinian UNICEF data based on the *Encuesta Permanente de Hogares, Niños en cifras* (Permanent Statistical Review of Households and Children), 1993.
5   Among these are Catamarca, Salta, Rio Negro, Tierra del Fuego.
6   Law 23.264.
7   Grosman (1993), Cecilia P., 'Significado de la Convención de los Derechos del niño y en las relaciones de familia', *La Ley*, 26 May 1993.
8   *Martin y Cia Ltda. S.A. c. Administraciôn General de Puertos s. repetición de page* (C.S. 6-11-63, Fallos de la Corte Suprema, V. 257).
9   This doctrinal rule, which grows stronger all the time, does have its opponents who maintain that a law ratifying a treaty only implies a promise to adjust internal laws to meet the norms of the international instrument.
10 Corte Suprema de Justicia de la Nación, 7 July 1992, *Ekmekdjian c. Sofovich, La Ley* review, t. 1992-C, p. 563.
11 Civil Code, art. 126.
12 *Ibid.*, art. 128.
13 Some provincial constitutions expressly provide for protection of the child from conception, for example, San Luis, art. 49; Catamarca, art. 65 and Santiago del Estero, art. 78.
14 Civil Code, art. 70.
15 *Ibid.*, art. 64.
16 Law 20590.
17 Civil Code, art. 264.
18 Civil Code, art. 258.
19 Cecilia P. Grosman (1994), *Los derechos del niño en la familia. La ley, creencias y realidades*, work undertaken for UNICEF, Losada, Buenos Aires, p. 73.
20 Cámara Nacional Civil, Sala E, 14 September 1989, *ED* 137, p. 400; Cámera Nacional Civil, Sala A, 5/6/92, *La Ley* review, t. 1992-E-236.
21 Civil Code, art. 240.
22 Civil Code, art. 256.
23 Civil Code, art. 257.
24 Civil Code, art. 253.
25 Cámara de Apelaciones Civil y Comercial, Mar del Plata, Sala I, 30 August 1988, *ED*, 137–747; Cánara Nacional Civil, Sala E, 2 October 1987, *ED*, 130–331.
26 Cámara Nacional Civil de la Capital, Sala M, 8/6/93, *La Ley* review, 14 January 1994.
27 C. Grosman and C. Ariana (1992), 'Los efectos de la negativa a someterse a los exámenes biológicos en los juicios de filiación paterna extramatrimonial', *La Ley* review, 20 May 1992.
28 Corte Suprema Pcia. de Santa Fé, 19/9/92, *La Ley* review, 8 October 1992.
29 For more information see data in: Cecilia P. Grosman (1981), 'El hijo extramatrimonial no reconocido por el padre', *Revista de Ciencias Jurídicas*, University of Costa Rica, Law Faculty, May–August, p. 105; C. Grosman and C. Ariana (1992), 'Hacia una mayor efectividad del art. 255 del C. Civil', *Jurisprudencia Argentina* review, 15 April.
30 Work referred to in note 29 above.

31   Decision of Instancia Juzgado Civil Comercial San Isidro, no. 9 29/3/88, *El Derecho* review, t. 128–331. In the judgement it is held that 'a feeling of repudiation' gives rise in the child to 'a sense of inferiority, of lack of psychological protection and of insecurity felt by one who cannot rely on a certain, visible and responsible person', referring also to the 'social humiliation' suffered by one registered as of father unknown.

32   Civil Code, art. 255.

33   Until now, 50 children of disappeared parents have been found; 25 have been restored to their families and 13 bear their true names, know their origins, even while still living with the families that were bringing them up, by agreement between the two families. The legal problem that has occurred is that, in most cases, the persons claiming to be parents of the child, already now adolescent, refused immunogenetic HLA or DNA tests. Some cases, since a crime, abduction, had been committed, were resolved by compulsory restoration, imposed on the children as much as on their carers. (Elena Mendoza: 'El derecho del nino a preservar su identidad. *El caso* de los ninos desaparecidos', unpublished.)

34   Opinion of Drs Petracchi and Fayt in the decision of the Corte Suprema de Justicia de la Nación, 13 November 1990, *La Ley* review 1991-B-470.

35   Río Negro, Tierra del Fuego, Atlántida and South Atlantic Islands.

36   Civil Code, art. 307.

37   Civil Code, art. 21; Law 10.903.

38   Law 10.903, Law 19.134 and art. 234 Civil Procedure Code.

39   Silvia S. Chavanneau, Maria Teresa Maggio and Elbio Raul Ramos (1993), 'El derecho del nino a permanecer junto a sus padres', paper presented to a Seminar on the Convention on the Rights of the Child, unpublished.

40   Civil Code, art. 264 inc, 2.

41   Lidia Makianich de Basset (1993), *Derecho de visitas*, Ed. Hammurabi: Buenos Aires, p. 293.

42   Cámara Nacional Civil, Sala C, 1 November 1990, ED 141, p. 795 and Cámara Nacional Civil, Sala A, 23 February 1989, *LL*, 1989-C, p. 401. Courts have ordered measures such as arrest for disobeying the court order (five days per visit prevented), exclusion of the mother from the house by public authority to let father visit, fines, and placing the minor in a college in order to allow unobstructed visits.

43   Bossert, G. and Zannoni, E.A. (1989), *Regimen legal de la filiación y patria potestad*, Ed. Astrea: Buenos Aires, p. 278; Cámara Nacional Civil, Capital, Sala C, 1/11/90, *LL*, 1992-B-1.

44   Cámara Nacional Civil, Sala L, 12/9/91, *La Ley* review, t. 1991-E-503; remarks of the assessor of minors in decisions; Cámara Nacional Civil, Sala B, 22/11/89, *LL*, 1990-E-170.

45   Remarks of Asesor de Menores de Cámara, Cámara Nacional Civil, Sala I, 12 Sept. 1991, *LL* 1991-E p. 503; Cámara Nacional Civil, Sala C, 1 November 1990, *ED*, 141, p. 795.

46   Cámara Nacional Civil, Sala B, 3 August 1989, *ED*, 137, p. 563.

47   Cámara Nacional Civil, Sala C, 1/11/90, *La Ley* review, t. 1992–B–1.

48   Cámara Nacional Civil, Sala E, 20 February 1989, ED, 136, p. 685; Cámara Nacional Civil, Sala E, 31/5/88, *La Ley* review, 14/12/89; Cámara Nacional Civil, Sala E, 26/5/86, *La Ley* review t. 1989–E–437.

49   Cámara Nacional Civil, Sala E, 9 December 1983, LL, 1984–D, p. 679; Cámara Nacional Civil, Sala D, 31/8/83, *La Ley* review, t. 1983–C–225.

50   Cámara Nacional Civil, Sala F, 23 October 1987; Cámara Nacional Civil, Sala B, *La Ley* review, t. 1990–B–171.
51   Nelly Minyersky (1994), 'El derecho de familia frente al Sida', *Revista Derecho de Familia*, No. 8, ed. Perrot.
52   Civil Code, art. 164.
53   Augusto C. Belluscio (1987), *Manual de Derecho de Familia*, Ed. Depalma, Buenos Aires, p. 289.
54   Civil Code, art. 266.
55   Decision of la Instancia, 24/4/85, *El Derecho* review t. 114-115-945.
56   Civil Code, art. 264 ter.
57   Procedure Code, art. 309.
58   Law 10067/83, art. 40.
59   Cámara Nacional Civil, Sala F, 27/2/91, *La Ley* review 8/9/91; Cámara Nacional Civil, Sala F, 29/6/79, *ED*, t. 84-546; Cámara Nacional Civil, Sala C, 1/11/90, *La Ley* review, t. 1992-B-1.
60   Civil Code art. 397 ss. 1.
61   Aída Kemelmajer de Carlucci (1993), 'Principios procesales y tribunales de familia', *Jurisprudencia Argentina* review, 20 October.
62   Civil Code, art. 278.
63   Civil Code, art. 307.
64   Law 10.903, art. 18.
65   C.P. Grosman and S. Mesterman (1992): *Maltrato al menor. El lado oculto de la escena familiar*, Editorial Universidad: Buenos Aires.
66   Cecilia P. Grosman and Delia Iñigo (1994): 'Adoption of Children in Argentina by Local Citizens and Foreign Nationals', in Eliezer David Jaffe (ed.) *Intercountry Adoptions: Law and Perspectives of 'Sending' Countries*, Martinus Nijhoff: Dordrecht.
67   Law 19.134 of 1971.
68   Anahí Viladrich (1991), *Madres solteras adolescentes*, Cedes: Buenos Aires, 1991.
69   Youth Judges' International Congress, Rio de Janeiro, 1986; XIIIth World Congress of the International Association of Youth and Family Judges, Turin, 1990.
70   Nelly Minyersky, 'La adopción internacional', unpublished.
71   The data is taken from an exhaustive study of Argentine legislation by Drs Monica E. Vicchio and Patricia A. Levaggi in the Seminar of 'Rights of the child in the family. Bringing legislation into line with the Convention on the Rights of the Child', 1993, Law Faculty of the University of Buenos Aires.
72   Law 22.431, Law 23.876, and regulations.
73   Laws 19.279, 22.499 and 24.183.
74   Law 24.204.
75   Law 23.292.
76   Cámara Nacional Civil, Sala D, August 1987, *La Ley* review, 1988-A, p. 270; Cámara Nacional Civil, Sala D, 12/12/88, *La Ley* review, 1989-C, p. 217; Cámara Nacional Civil, Sala F, 11/4/88, *La Ley* review, t. 1989-C, p. 385; Cámara Nacional Civil, Sala A, 6/6/90, *La Ley* review, 1991-A, 198.

3   The Convention on the Rights of the Child: Implications for Canada

*Stephen J. Toope**

INTRODUCTION

During the negotiations which culminated in the final text of the United Nations Convention on the Rights of the Child,[1] many commentators argued that the Convention was little more than a 'make-work' project for foreign ministry officials and NGO activists worldwide. It was suggested that humanity was blessed with a plethora of human rights standards and that the proposed new Convention would add little to the concrete protection of the millions of children who suffer from abuse, poverty, sickness and deprivation throughout the world.[2]

Since the conclusion of the Convention, the focus of critics' attention has shifted to arguments concerning the domestic implementation of the Convention. It is now argued that the Convention will have no impact on those countries where the abuse of children's human dignity is greatest, because there will be no political will[3] or, if there is a will, no money, to improve the situation. A corollary to this argument is the view offered by other commentators who argue that in the countries of the North which promoted the Convention, nothing much will change because the standards set out in it are so general and so anodyne that while no government will challenge them, no government will feel the necessity to act upon them either.[4]

*Of the Faculty of Law and Institute of Comparative Law, McGill University. An earlier version of this paper was prepared for the Child, Youth and Family Policy Research Centre, Toronto. I would like to thank colleagues Rod Macdonald, Suzanne Peters, Elobaid A. Elobaid and graduate David Farrell for their helpful comments. Roger Stuart (1995) provided able research assistance, funded by a research grant from the Office of the Dean, Faculty of Law, McGill University.

The purpose of this chapter is to offer a perspective which challenges both the idea that the Convention adds very little to the long list of human rights contained in other international treaties and the idea that, even if the Convention is taken seriously, nothing much will have to change substantively in countries such as Canada. I want to suggest that the Convention is, in one crucial respect, a breakthrough in international human rights standard-setting. Because of the important new step taken in the Convention – a significant movement towards the explicit interlinking of civil and political, and economic, social and cultural rights – it must be viewed as a challenge to Canada and like-minded states which identify themselves as upholders of human rights and, more particularly, of the rights and interests of children. Unfortunately, a third element of the critique which has been offered by sceptics is probably accurate: the Convention will not mean very much in concrete terms to the children of the developing world, partly because of a lack of political will or governmental legitimacy within developing countries which would allow an honest reassessment of priorities, and partly because of a lack of political will in the North to allow any substantial transfer of resources to the South.

The focus of this chapter will be upon the implications of the Children's Convention for Canadian legal and social policies.[5] Before engaging in that discussion, however, I will review briefly the content of the Convention, highlighting relevant substantive elements and problems. Apart from helping to identify the Convention's challenges to Canada domestically, this discussion will highlight difficult ethical questions which relate to Canada's role in the implementation of the Convention internationally. In the second section of the chapter, I will analyse certain assumptions which underlie the Convention and which hold important implications for its implementation in Canada. I conclude with an inventory of the broad areas of social and legal policy which will have to be studied and analysed in new ways now that Canada has ratified the Convention on the Rights of the Child.[6] Although the Canadian government has produced an 'action plan for children' which purports to map out a children's strategy in response to the Declaration of the Summit on Children,[7] the plan is notably short on action. Furthermore, it does not address the Convention directly, consisting largely of a general review of the socioeconomic position of children in Canada, an enumeration of both 'challenges' facing Canadians and of certain actions already taken by the government. New initiatives are restricted in scope. The 'action plan' will nonetheless be referred to where appropriate.

RIGHTS IN THE CONVENTION: INNOVATIONS AND PROBLEMS

The Convention on the Rights of the Child is the latest in a series of major international agreements which resulted from the impulse to enunciate 'universal' standards of human rights promotion and protection. Building upon the breathtaking scope of the Universal Declaration of Human Rights,[8] these international treaties have been designed to articulate both rights applicable to all human beings and rights which are more narrowly tailored to address the challenges facing particular groups within human society.

The major innovation of the Convention on the Rights of the Child – and it is a signal achievement – is that its provisions are the first of any globally applicable human rights convention to integrate explicitly the two broad classifications of rights: civil and political, and economic, social and cultural.[9] The importance of this integration cannot be overstated. The world community spent almost 20 years attempting to codify in the form of one binding treaty the provisions of the Universal Declaration of Human Rights. Largely because of the failure to agree upon the interrelationship between civil and political, and economic, social and cultural rights, it never succeeded, and it became necessary to conclude two separate treaties.[10] Yet, in a few short years, the drafters of the Children's Convention were able to agree upon a text which treats the broad classifications of rights as interdependent and at least morally equivalent. This equivalency will open up more forceful arguments than ever before that both categories of rights should be treated as binding, although certain escape clauses continue to undercut the force of the enumerated economic, social and cultural rights.

Before the Children's Convention, states could divorce the two classes of rights because they were physically divorced in the key international Conventions. Economic, social and cultural rights could be measured against the lowest common denominator whereas civil and political rights could be assessed against higher 'objective' standards. An important psychological barrier has been breached with the integration of both categories of rights in the Children's Convention, for it has become harder to identify those rights which are meant to have practical force immediately and those that need not even be addressed until a 'higher' stage of development is achieved. Within the Convention, many provisions are framed clearly as 'oughts', whether they relate to civil or to economic and social rights.

For example, in Article 3, the Convention states that in all actions 'undertaken by public or private social welfare institutions ...' the 'best interests of the child *shall* be a primary consideration'. In Article 6, states are instructed to 'ensure *to the maximum extent possible* the survival and development of the child'. Article 24 contains a recognition by states of the 'right of the child to the enjoyment of the *highest attainable* standard of health'. Finally, states agree in Article 28(a) that they '*shall*, in particular, make primary education compulsory and available free to all' (my emphasis). Lest these rights seem breathtakingly novel, even radical in their implications, it must be noted that each of them is subject to important caveats. In every case, the social and economic rights are made at least partly conditional upon national circumstances. States remain under relatively loose obligations to implement basic rights; they must 'strive to ensure' basic health care (Article 24(2)), to provide social security 'in accordance with their national law' (Article 26(1)), and to achieve the right to education 'progressively' (Article 28(1)). The right to an adequate standard of living is subject to 'national conditions' and a state's 'means' (Article 27(3)).

All the economic, social and cultural rights enumerated in the Convention are further made conditional upon a rather broad escape clause: 'State Parties shall undertake such measures to the maximum extent of their available resources and, where needed, within the framework of international cooperation' (Article 4). Although this general qualifier could be read to undercut the economic, social and cultural rights of the Convention to a large degree, I would argue that the qualifier contains one element which could actually be of assistance to children's advocates, especially when read with other provisions of the Convention.

The commitment of states to promote economic, social and cultural rights 'to the maximum extent of their available resources' should be read with Article 6(1) of the Convention whereunder 'States Parties shall ensure to the maximum extent possible the survival and development of the child'. If these commitments are to be taken at face value they will require states to reassess their spending priorities. For example, in developing states which spend a large proportion of their income upon military hardware, advocates are now presented with a legal argument justifying a substantial shift in budgetary allocations. Even in Canada, priorities for spending will have to be re-examined. In 1990 nearly one Canadian child in five lived in a low-income family.[11] The figure was much higher for aboriginal children. Children of aboriginal families are also significantly less likely to gain a secondary education; their health status is inferior to other Canadian children; and their life expectancy is markedly lower than that of children in the general population.[12] Governments will not necessarily undertake the required reassessment of priorities seriously, but those who support the goals of the Convention have been provided with significant legal ammunition to press governments to act. More importantly from a theoretical perspective, the recurring emphasis upon the need to attain the highest possible standards in economic and social rights reverses the 'lowest common denominator' approach which has marked interpretations of earlier attempts to reach international agreement upon economic and social rights. It is primarily for this reason that the Children's Convention should be viewed as a milestone in the elaboration of economic and social rights, in tone if not in its substantive norms.

The implications of this attempt to link and make more commensurate the categories of rights could be enormous precisely because advocates may now invoke a text from which they can justifiably advance claims relating to the reallocation of resources. It has long been argued, rather simplistically, that the implementation of civil rights does not cost money, but that the promotion of economic and social rights is expensive.[13] It was therefore possible to favour the wide promotion of civil rights, but to treat economic and social rights as mere *desiderata* which could be postponed to the day when resources were no longer so scarce.[14] After all, economic and social rights were not really 'rights' in the same sense as rights to be free from arbitrary arrest or torture.[15] The Children's Convention advances the argument that economic and social rights are *fully* rights and that they deserve a degree of commitment to promotion and protection commensurate with that accorded to civil and political rights.[16] One is not obliged to argue for an unattainable 'equality' in the distribution of economic goods, merely for serious attention to allocation decisions and some reordering of priorities.

For children's advocates in Canada and elsewhere, the Convention contains a broad range of provisions which may ground claims for various types of government action. Hammarberg has suggested that the range of human rights protections dealt with in the Convention may usefully be divided into three categories:

1 the provision of basic needs;
2 the protection of children from harmful acts and practices; and
3 the participation of children in decisions affecting their lives.[17]

I agree that this categorization is helpful. It is especially effective in revealing the areas in which Canada is likely to experience challenges in fully implementing the terms of the Convention. Although it could be argued that Canada has already gone a long way in offering protection to its children from harmful acts and practices, the provision of basic needs is not uniformly adequate. The participation of children in decisions affecting their own lives is a very difficult and controversial area where the present state of Canadian social and legal policy may not mesh with the requirements of the Convention.

In the next section, I will review some key provisions of the Children's Convention using Hammarberg's categorization. It will not be possible to discuss each of these provisions in detail. Rather, I will focus upon provisions which are innovative, or which give rise to concerns about Canada's ability to abide by its Convention commitments.

Canada's implementation of the Convention has recently been assessed by the Committee on the Rights of the Child. Under the terms of Article 44, states agree to submit a report to the Committee 'on the measures they have adopted which give effect to the rights recognized herein' within two years of the entry into force of the Convention for the state concerned, and thereafter every five years.[18] Although commending Canada for its 'commitment … to adopt measures in order to face the increasing poverty and to reduce existing disparities', the Committee nonetheless expressed concern about 'the emerging problem of child poverty, especially among vulnerable groups' such as aboriginal children. Canada was asked to take 'immediate steps to tackle the problem of child poverty' and to allocate resources 'to their maximum extent to ensure the implementation of economic, social and cultural rights'.

Provisions relating to the basic needs

The Convention recognizes 'the right of the child to the enjoyment of the highest attainable standard of health and to facilities for the treatment of illness and rehabilitation of health' (Article 24 (1)). This right is made more precise, albeit still uncertain in scope, in a series of provisions concerning the diminution of infant mortality (Article 24 (2)(a)), the provision of primary health care and safe drinking water (Articles 24 (2)(b) and (c)), pre- and postnatal health care (Article 24 (2)(d)), health education (Article 24 (2)(e)), and preventative health care and family planning (Article 24 (2)(f)).

Education is also treated as a basic need. Every child has a 'right to education' (Article 28(1)) which includes free and compulsory primary education (Article 28 (1)(a)) and 'available and accessible' secondary education, both 'general and vocational' (Article 28 (1)(b)). Higher education is to be made 'accessible to all on the basis of capacity' (Article 28(1) (c)).

Like the Universal Declaration of Human Rights, the Convention guarantees the right to social security, but makes that right specifically applicable to children (Article 26(1)). Although parents bear the primary responsibility to maintain and support children (Article 27(2)), the state must assist parents and their children in need. In other words, the Convention treats income support programmes and state provision of basic needs as rights.

All of these provisions may be seen as subcategories of the basic 'right of every child to a standard of living adequate for the child's physical, mental, spiritual, moral and social development' (Article 27(1)). Poverty alleviation is also a right which may be demanded by the children of the world.

These provisions would not seem to be substantively problematic for a country as wealthy as Canada. However, the health and education standards remain unsatisfied as far as poor children and many aboriginal children are concerned. Moreover, to the extent that Article 4 requires resource transfers from the North to the South to ensure the attainment of basic needs,[19] Canada's Official Development Assistance policies, and World Bank policies to which Canada subscribes, should come under intense scrutiny. This issue will be explored in more detail below.

Provisions relating to the protection of children

From a Canadian perspective, most of the Convention's protection provisions are uncontroversial. The dominating ideology is that all legal and administrative acts and decisions are to be accomplished with 'the best interests of the child' as 'a primary consideration' (Article 3(1)). In terms of Canadian social and legal policy, the only likely objection to this formulation is that it is not sufficiently strong; for a number of years now, Canadian legislatures and courts have been insisting that, in many contexts, the 'best interests of the child' should be *the*, not *a*, primary consideration in decision-making.[20]

The fundamental right to protection contained in the Convention is found in Article 2(6)(1) which recognizes the child's inherent right to life.[21] The second broad protection for children is a general anti-discrimination provision, contained in Article 2.[22] From a Canadian viewpoint, most of this Article seems uncontroversial, given the existence of the broad equality guarantee in s.15 of the Canadian Charter of Rights and Freedoms,[23] as well as in provincial and federal anti-discrimination legislation.[24] However, the inclusion of language, social origin and property as prohibited grounds of discrimination could open up creative new anti-discrimination debates in Canadian courts.[25] Although the Convention will not apply automatically in Canada unless 'incorporated' into national law,[26] Canadian courts have been inclined to interpret Canadian legislative and administrative actions in the light of Canada's international obligations.[27]

Another congeries of provisions relates to the protection of children by public authorities in cases where parents cannot, will not, or are incapable of providing a healthy environment for their offspring. Legislative, administrative, social and educational measures are to be undertaken to protect children from 'all forms of physical or mental violence, injury or abuse, neglect or negligent treatment, maltreatment or exploitation including sexual abuse' (Article 19(1)). Separation from parents is only to be accomplished through decisions of competent authorities subject to judicial review (Article 9(1)). Provision should be made by the state for protection through foster case, adoption, Kafala of Islamic Law[28] or institutional care. In the case of adoption, only public adoption should be recognized (Article 21(a)). For international adoption, states should ensure that no 'improper financial gain' is involved (Article 21(d)).

The Canadian government, at the behest of national aboriginal organizations, entered a reservation to Article 21 precluding the application of its provisions 'to the extent that they may be inconsistent with customary forms of care among aboriginal people'. This reservation evidences a concern of the Canadian government that the Convention is not drafted in a manner which is particularly sensitive to aboriginal cultures. The cultural bases of the Convention will be discussed more fully below.

Juvenile justice standards and protection for children within the legal system are not extensively dealt with in the Convention. However, one potentially important provision requires that 'the child shall ... be provided the opportunity to be heard in any judicial and administrative proceedings affecting the child, either directly, or through a representative' (Article 12(2)). This statement is open-ended, and could affect all criminal and civil proceedings relating to children, including prosecutions involving the Criminal Code and the Young Offenders Act,[29] divorce and child custody cases, and youth protection proceedings.

One legal protection for children contained in the Convention has already proved to be problematic for Canada. In its instrument of ratification, Canada entered a reservation concerning Article 37(c) which relates to the provision of separate detention facilities for adult and juvenile offenders. Canada has accepted the 'general principles' of the Article, 'but reserves the right not to detain children separately from adults where this is not appropriate or feasible'. This reservation probably reflects three problems with the Canadian implementation of the Convention. The first is the need to coordinate federal and provincial action. Although criminal law is a federal head of jurisdiction under the Constitution Act 1867, the administration of justice falls within the legislative authority of the provinces.[30] Not all provinces were willing to abide by Article 37(c), largely for reasons relating to cost. Second, it is arguable that an unmodified commitment to the provision of separate detention facilities could interfere with a parallel development in Canada: the creation of local detention centres designed to allow contact between detainees and their families. This is especially important in the north and in aboriginal communities. Finally, recent federal initiatives in the treatment of young offenders have been based upon a assumption that flexibility is required, that some violent young offenders may be more appropriately incarcerated with adults than with other youths for whom they might constitute a threat. This issue is particularly applicable to people accused while under age 18, but convicted and jailed after the age of majority. The Canadian government apparently believed that the Convention was not sufficiently clear whether or not such people should be treated as 'youths'.

The Convention's most innovative provision concerning the protection of children relates to privacy. Article 16 contains the bold proposition that '[n]o child shall be subjected to arbitrary or unlawful interference with his or her privacy, family, home or correspondence'. The state is to provide 'the protection of law against such interference or attacks'. Clearly this provision raises difficult questions concerning the relationship between the child, his or her parents and the state. For example, certain US lobby groups have worked hard to encourage states to pass laws requiring doctors to divulge to parents any request by a minor for birth control devices or drugs. Any such law would seem to run directly counter to even a limited conception of children's privacy, but one must ask whether there is any distinction to be drawn between an 11 year-old asking for such information and a 17 year-old.[31] In the new Civil Code of Quebec, which entered into force on 1 January 1994, a minor over the age of 14 may give her or his consent to medical 'care' if such care is elective. Presumably, reproductive health 'care' could fall within the ambit of this provision.[32] Implicit in this provision is a reconception of the traditional relationship between parent and child. Such a reconception is also one of the grand themes of the Convention, and it will be explored in some detail in a later section of this chapter.

Provisions concerning the participation of children in decision-making

Hammarberg suggests that the provisions which seek to enhance the autonomy of the child are the weakest of the Convention.[33] This should come as no surprise as they were also likely to be the most controversial. Children's rights are a relatively new concept and they upset the 'traditional' concept of the parent (usually the father) who 'knows best'. In the words of Martha Minow:

> Children's rights make adults uncomfortable because they represent new ideas, or old ideas in new forms, and signal that adults and existing practices have to change.[34]

Bennett notes that the European child did not even 'attain a juridical personality until the nineteenth century'.[35] In the USA, children were not expressly recognized as full legal persons until 1969.[36] In many cultures children have historically been treated as property vested in their parents.[37] Conceiving of children's 'rights' separate from those of the parent requires significant changes in social attitudes in almost all nations of the world, including Canada.

Apart from prompting a conservative resistance to children's rights generally, the adoption of autonomy as an underlying conceptual theme in the Convention should also raise concerns for progressive scholars and activists who question the descriptive and normative power of any pure doctrine of individualism, at least in the context of children and their families. As Colleen Sheppard has noted:

> Children's rights may take the form of claims for autonomy and non-interference; they may, however, entail claims for care and protection, or claims for relationships with others.[38]

Martha Minow has also questioned the utility of any discourse which gives undue emphasis to 'autonomy, rather than need, especially the central need for relationships with adults who are themselves enabled to create settings where children can thrive'.[39]

Yet the Convention does seem to focus upon autonomy as the moral basis for children's rights to participate in decision-making. In addition to the right to privacy already noted, the Convention states in its Preamble that 'the child should be fully prepared to live an individual life in society'. Although this statement is obviously intended to focus upon the developmental aspect of childhood, it reveals an underlying assumption that society is constructed principally by autonomous individuals, not by people grouped in families, clans or tribes. This assumption is given some practical import in Article 12(2) which, as we have already seen, provides for the right of a child to be heard in any judicial or administrative proceeding affecting him or her. The first paragraph of the Article goes further, insisting that a 'child who is capable of forming his or her own views' be accorded the right to 'express those views freely in all matters affecting the child'. Under Article 13(1), children are stated to have a more general right to 'freedom of expression' and to 'impart and receive information'. This right is not specifically conditioned by a parent's right to filter expression or information.

It is arguable that all children's rights in the Convention are affected by the 'responsibilities, rights, and duties' of parents referred to in Article 5. But this provision raises far more questions than it answers. The Convention provides little guidance on questions such as:

1   Is a parent entitled to censor the reading material or television viewing of a child in the home?;
2   Does a parent have a right to 'supervise' the lessons a child receives at a public or private school?;

3   Can a parent legitimately speak for his or her child in establishing what materials a child should be allowed to borrow from a public library?

The following two concrete situations, which are far from extraordinary in contemporary Western society highlight the issues more clearly. First, should a parent be able to prevent a 16 year-old boy from exercising his 'freedoms of information' by viewing pornography? Is the answer different if the pornography is violent? Second, if that same boy wishes to wear Nazi paraphernalia to school should his parents, or the school authorities independently of the parents, have authority to stop him? At a purely practical level, the answer to these questions may be simple: unless they exercise force and possibly destroy the relationship, how can the parent's will possibly prevail? But the more interesting question is whether the Convention should lead us to the conclusion that these forms of expression are rights vested in the child as an aspect of autonomy. The appropriate scope of parental 'responsibilities, rights, and duties' is entirely unclear in the moral universe of the Convention and will probably be the subject of heated debate. This is an area which requires extensive research, both as to legal rights and social practices.

Problems with the Convention

Commentators have already noted many weaknesses in the Convention – weaknesses that have a direct bearing upon the extent of the Convention's potential impact upon Canadian social and legal policy. The most obvious weakness is in Article 1, the very definition of 'child'. For the purposes of the Convention, a 'child' is defined as a 'human being below the age of 18 years, unless, under the law applicable to the child, majority is attained earlier'. The practical effect of this provision is to allow any state to evade the requirements of the Convention simply by lowering the age of majority. Arguably this could be done either generally or for specific purposes. Although it is unlikely that Canadian authorities will engage in such pernicious behaviour, there could be some hypothetical circumstances where, for particular purposes, a lowering of the age of majority might be proposed. For example, the age of majority for criminal prosecution as an adult could be lowered in response to public outcry about 'gang violence'.

The Convention has also been widely criticized for being rather loosely, if not sloppily, drafted. Many provisions have been described as 'vague' or 'mushy'.[40] This criticism is entirely valid and holds some important implications for Canada and for advocates of children's rights in Canada. First, the Canadian government, like all governments, will be able to rely upon vague obligations to avoid substantive commitments. The government's action plan for children, *Brighter Futures*, already manifests this tendency. Although generally applauded by children's rights activists for its tone and rhetoric, the plan has been criticized for its lack of 'measurable goals, objectives and time frames'.[41] Second, the Canadian government may confront difficult situations in which other states will enact self-serving, but empty, legislative provisions purporting to implement the vaguely phrased rights of children. These same states could then criticize countries such as Canada, for example in the UN Human Rights Commission, for taking too long to implement the terms of the Convention, when in reality the government is seeking to enact realistic and meaningful legislation, which usually takes longer than mere showpieces.[42] Third, the vagueness of the formulation of many Convention provisions will open up the possibility of endless debate as to the scope of those provisions, and will provide opportunities for less-than-honest interpretations of the Convention. This latter concern has already manifested itself in Australian debates, where opponents of the Convention offered bizarre interpretations in order to discourage ratification.[43] It was suggested, for example, that the Convention, having been promoted by Poland, was a socialist plot to destroy Christian families and to centre all power in the state. Parents would no longer have any say in the lives of their children, who would now live an Orwellian existence of state thought control![44]

An issue of even greater concern is the seeming inability of the drafters of the Convention to come to terms with the issue of cultural pluralism. This failing seems to be endemic in texts designed to promote universal human rights. Barsh has noted that the 'family' as conceived of in the Convention appears to be the late nineteenth-century European ideal of the nuclear family.[45] Gomien complains that the Convention fails to 'ensure that extended family relationships are respected throughout its substantive provisions'.[46] It is certainly true that the 'family' usually makes its appearance in the Convention in the guise of 'parents'.[47] Only Article 5 makes reference to the role of parents 'or, where applicable, the members of the extended family or community as provided for by the local customs'. The lack of involvement of the extended family in the life of the child, as reflected in the terms of the Convention, is often treated as a North–South issue. The emphasis upon autonomy as the model of human relationships noted above has been said to reflect a deep misperception of traditional African and Asian cultures.[48] But it must be emphasized that the orientation towards the individual and the nuclear family could prove to be problematic within Canada both from the perspective or aboriginal communities and more recent immigrant communities whose understanding of 'family' may not mesh neatly with that of the drafters of the Convention. An escape clause is provided in

Article 30 which seeks to provide cultural protections for children of minority groups, particularly of aboriginal communities.[49]

Apparently, the Canadian government did not believe this protective clause to be adequate and therefore felt obliged to enter a reservation and a 'statement of understanding' concerning the Convention's impact upon aboriginal communities. The reservation to Article 21, which has been criticized by the Committee on the Rights of the Child, protects from the Convention's adoption provisions the 'customary forms of care among aboriginal peoples in Canada'. Given the historical abuse of adoption laws in Canada to remove aboriginal children from their families and communities, this reservation would appear to be in good faith.

The 'statement of understanding' is an interpretive guideline making it plain that Canada will give great weight to Article 30 of the Convention in interpreting the government's duties towards aboriginal children. The protection of a child's right to participate in his or her community, and the community's right to protect its language, religion and culture, will be accorded a high priority. One implication of the statement is that these 'community' rights may at times conflict with individual rights, particularly civil and political rights. In such cases of conflict, the Canadian government wants to reserve its position to support the aboriginal community, rather than a particular individual. It seems obvious that this interpretive statement was designed to please the principal aboriginal organizations during a particularly fraught phase of Canada's seemingly interminable process of constitutional renegotiation. It must be noted, however, that some aboriginal groups, particularly those representing aboriginal women, have called into question this strategy of preferring community rights for aboriginal people over individual rights.

The greatest 'problem' with the Convention has nothing to do with drafting lacunae, with cultural or sociological issues, or with 'mushy' language. The greatest problem is that, if the Convention is taken seriously, it will cost a great deal of money to implement. Macdonald concluded his brief review of the implications of the Convention for Canada by noting that if Canadians truly want implementation, the governments of Canada 'must be pressured into reallocating their expenditures towards providing the necessary services, or higher taxes must be imposed'.[50] There is as yet no evidence that Canadians are really interested in seeing a shift in the allocation of resources away from present social spending programmes. Nor is there evidence of a willingness to bear a higher tax burden; indeed, quite the opposite mood appears to be dominant in public opinion. The economic reality implies that, strategically, advocates of children's rights should devote a great deal of attention to public education to build up their constituency. Direct pressure upon governments is not likely to result in greater resources devoted to children unless the governments themselves are convinced that any reallocation is politically sustainable. In the interim, lower cost initiatives should be advanced, which are likely to capture public imagination and to build interest in children's issues.

The question of resource allocation also gives rise to an important moral and ethical issue. The provisions of the Convention are to apply to all the children in ratifying states throughout the world. In a number of Articles, it has been recognized specifically that only international action and cooperation can bring about the changes necessary to provide better lives for the world's children.[51] Even if Canadians, and their governments, were willing to reallocate resources or to increase tax levels to support the economic, social and cultural rights of children within Canada, would it be morally acceptable to do so without providing substantially greater resources for the international campaign to upgrade the living standards of children in the developing world? Are children's advocates in Canada ethically obliged to become global children's advocates? I believe that they are. Even though the Canadian bureaucracy is subdivided into domestic and international components, and even though the budgetary allocations for work in Canada and abroad are distinct, all public resources are ultimately derived from the same source – the Canadian taxpayer. It is not ethically sound to advocate that ever-increasing resources be devoted to children in Canada without demanding a commensurate reallocation of resources to children outside Canada's borders.

In a brief but provocative article, Fran Olsen has bemoaned the common tendency to dichotomize issues of rights, and issues of children's rights in particular. She refers to the 'our children/their children' syndrome.[52] It is easy to see that syndrome domestically. For the middle and upper classes nothing is too good for 'our children': hence the child safety industry, the baby formula industry, the child clothing industry and the toy industry. But 'their children', those of the dispossessed, the single-parent family, the aboriginal family, the unemployed, continue to suffer hunger and other forms of deprivation on the periphery of Canadian society without causing any great public outcry. Economically deprived inner-city children are subjected to substandard education while middle-class suburban parents demand 'community control' of schools to establish a proportionately higher tax base to support the education of their children alone. Funding for 'head-start' programmes and vocational training is cut because the constituency for such initiatives is politically weak. Young professional couples devote enormous resources to employ full-time home care workers, often under exploitative conditions, while access to subsidized day care for the working poor is increasingly restricted.

The syndrome exists even more starkly in the international context. Children of the North are blessed with resources and lavished with services undreamed of by the vast majority of children in the South. Yet the Convention seems to point to the moral conclusion that 'their children' are 'our children' as well. The Convention posits an ethical universe in which all children are entitled to respect as human persons,[53] and in which they may claim a fair share of the world's resources. The ethical implications of that conclusion are enormously challenging for Canadian economic, social and foreign policy.

ASSUMPTIONS UNDERLYING THE CONVENTION

The Children's Convention is an attempt to work through the complex, and shifting, relationship between the child, his or her family and the state. For generations, a powerful myth shaped attitudes in many cultures; the myth contained a vision of the family as a purely 'private' sphere which was, and should be, shielded from public scrutiny.[54] Then the doctrine of the 'best interests' of the child gained ascendancy, and it was no longer possible to argue that parents necessarily knew best or that state intervention in the family was wrong. For many children, the home was the site of their deepest oppression, and it became necessary to use state power to protect the child from that oppression. But once state power was seen as an appropriate vehicle to 'protect' children, often from their own families, the family and the life of the child had clearly become public commodities. Once openly public, it was a short logical leap to assert that a 'best interests' doctrine was inadequate to protect children fully.

When measured by courts, 'best interests' becomes an external viewpoint. Even though judges may try to place themselves in the position of the child whose parents are fighting over custody, for example, that position is largely fictitious, for the judge will inevitably bring his or her socially constructed and experiential appreciations of what is best for a child into the particular case before the court. Best interests is potentially paternalistic; it is arguably stronger, therefore, to treat the goal of protecting the child not as a social interest, but as a *right* inherent in the child herself.

These ideological transitions are all apparent in the Convention, but they exist simultaneously, leading to what may be an inevitable theoretical incoherence. It is best to accept that there is no single manner in which to describe the appropriate relationship between the child, parents and the state. Children's lives within families are private in some senses and public in others. Children may need protection in a paternalistic manner, but they may also wish to claim rights on their own behalf. Because these conflicting stances are all present within the Convention, they will lead to radical disagreement concerning the appropriate interpretation of the Convention's provisions. Commentators have already identified various assumptions within the Convention which give rise to significant dissent. Due to limitations of space here, I will simply highlight these assumptions and suggest the controversies they are likely to generate.

Socially defined 'best interests' override parental rights

In a short comment upon the Convention, Chen argued that he could identify within it a 'preferred policy':

> ... to secure family integrity and provide a stable family environment for a child's healthy growth, psychologically as well as physically. Thus, under normal conditions, it is in the best interests of the child to respect the rights of the parents to raise children as they see fit, free of governmental intrusion.[55]

I do not share this reading of the policy imperatives in the Convention. Although it does make reference on a number of occasions to the 'rights' of parents,[56] the overall thrust of the Convention is to declare that 'best interests' of children may not be what parents think they are. I have already noted the provisions concerning privacy (Article 16), freedom of expression (Article 13), and freedom of thought, conscience and religion (Article 14), all of which undercut any notion that the parent may dictate what is 'best' for a child. Instead, in cases of conflict, public actors – typically courts – will increasingly be called upon to evaluate a child's best interests and order the parents to abide by the court's interpretation or face state-enforced sanctions, including the ultimate enforcement of the removal of the child from parental custody.

The state may properly define the obligations of private actors towards children

The Convention assumes that states will enact legislation and engage in regulatory behaviour designed to promote in private actors appropriate behaviour towards children – that is, behaviour in the 'best interests' of the child. A large number of provisions is designed to influence the behaviour of parents, legal guardians and families, by imposing obligations upon states which can only be fulfilled by shaping the actions of private actors. For example, state parties are told to 'assure' that a child who is capable of forming views is listened to concerning decisions which will affect him or her (Article 12). In most cases, such decisions will be made by parents, and the state will have to ensure that whenever contact is made between children and the state legal system, the child's right to be heard is validated. The point will be largely educative: to send the signal to parents that they must listen to their children. Similarly, private welfare agencies must be instructed by the state how to behave in the 'best interests' of the child (Article 3(1)). This vision of adult–child relationships continues to be largely paternalistic because the appreciation of a child's best interests will be made by public authorities who will tend to use socially constructed notions of what is best for a child in rendering these decisions. Of course, the public authorities may be instructed to give heavy weight to the voices of the children affected by the decision before the decision is rendered. A requirement to listen to children would go some way towards lessening the paternalistic element of public decision-making concerning children.

The language of rights is more powerful than the language of interests or of welfare

Despite the references in the Convention to the best interests of the child, the dominant language is that of rights. This development seems to be inevitable as soon as one moves the discussion of children, their protection and fulfilment, into the 'public' realm. If states are to ensure the best interests of children, the fear soon arises that states will not adequately do the job unless compelled by a language stronger than 'interests'. Hence the emergence of children's 'rights'. These rights extend both to protection and to the provision of services. In the words of Eekelaar:

> [T]he language of rights performs an important function. It acknowledges that there are certain things which we should provide for children, not just because adults think it would be nice if they had them, but because we are prepared to recognise that children want them, or can reasonably be assumed to want them.[57]

If children are independent rights-bearers, as the Convention clearly posits, then those rights must be opposable to the state, but also, it seems, to parents. Children are no longer 'objects of social concern', but are claimants who have an 'ethical right to be heard'.[58] Although some observers have attempted to argue that there is no dichotomy of rights between parent and child,[59] this view is belied by the Convention's many provisions which recognize that the rights of parents will be subject to social appreciations of children's best interests – but now expressed in claims of rights by children themselves, or by their advocates.

Many family lawyers, sociologists and legal theorists have questioned the appositeness of rights-based discourse to family relations.[60] Given the reality of dependency and interconnectedness within many families, the idea of individual right-holders asserting claims one against the other seems not only counter-intuitive, but potentially destructive.[61] Part of the problem is definitional. A narrow definition of 'rights' would describe them as claims which arise from authoritatively and formally pronounced legal rules which, once subject to official interpretation, are enforceable through the coercive power of the state. Alternatively, rights could be viewed more broadly as:

> ... articulations – public or private, formal or informal – of claims that people use to persuade others (and themselves) about how they should be treated and about how they should be granted.[62]

On this view, all rights would be aspirational and would serve primarily as powerful mobilizers of imagination and commitment.

I am inclined to doubt both of these explanations of rights and their role. Instead, I argue for a definition of 'rights' which maintains some legal distinctiveness, distinguishing the concept from social norms generally, but which denies that rights are *created* only through state-sanctioned enforcement (or violence). In other words, rights are 'articulations ... of claims' but they are articulations in a specialized vocabulary through particular processes shaped by distinctive values such as fairness, requirements of proof, limitations on what 'counts' as argument, and the duty to hear (at least some, but not necessarily all) opposing points of view. Rights are articulated in a variety of legal and quasi-legal institutions, not solely in courts,[63] but rights are not simply political demands. Claims of rights must be tested against standards which seek to validate underlying ethical principles and not merely to respond to transient political power.[64]

With this working definition of rights in mind, the rights listed in the Children's Convention can be seen as ethical claims which have been articulated anew in a specialized legal discourse. But it is the underlying ethical commitment which needs to be upheld while the precise legal consequences of the new discourse are worked through:

> ... we need to recognize that statements about human rights, including when enshrined in law, are declarative not constitutive of the respect for persons that they require – they also articulate profound principles of *human ethics*.[65]

In this sense, the discourse of legal rights should remain only one of a number of discourses seeking to articulate our respect for children. As one commentator has recently pointed out, there may still be 'something dignified in saying we are interested in someone's welfare as well as someone's rights'.[66] Concern and empathy are qualities which are not much associated with assertions of rights. While using rights as a specialized tool of legal advocacy, advocates for children should not forget alternative discourses which may generate significant public interest and support, and hence political action. To put the point bluntly, children's advocates can work with lawyers, but they needn't become lawyers, any more than they need become doctors, social workers or professional politicians.

At a purely instrumental level it has also been suggested that cataloguing lists of abstract legal rights may be fundamentally deceptive: 'rights without services are meaningless: services without a commitment of resources cannot be provided'.[67]

One danger with the use of rights language is that, once it is invoked, the perception may arise that the battle has been won – that the right is secure. In fact, the articulation of the right is only the beginning of a social conflict in which vested interests and traditional imbalances of power are challenged through various legal, para-legal and non-legal processes. This subsequent advocacy may prove to be particularly difficult in societies which are not culturally attuned to rights discourse. Non-legal discourses such as those based upon social cohesion, tribal loyalty or familial pride may be more effective than recourse to the exigencies of legal rules. Children's advocates within Canada must remain sensitive to such alternative discourses, especially as they engage with certain immigrant and aboriginal communities.

INVENTORY OF CHALLENGES CANADA WILL FACE IN IMPLEMENTING THE CONVENTION

The following inventory focuses upon the issues and challenges facing Canada now that it has ratified the Children's Convention. Some are intensely practical; others seem to operate at the level of theory, but I have attempted to show how they, too, possess important practical ramifications.

Making children a priority in government resource allocation

The single most significant challenge facing Canadian decision-makers will be how to make children a priority in government resource allocation. The Convention requires that states maximize their efforts in the provision of social services to children; minimum standards are not acceptable. In order to act in any serious way upon this commitment, it will be necessary to assess the contemporary position of children in Canada. A number of commentators have suggested the need for a legislative audit and an administrative audit to determine Canada's current level of compliance with the terms of the Convention.[68] Whilst agreeing with this, I also suggest that an even more onerous task must be undertaken. Given the heavy emphasis upon economic, social and cultural rights in the Convention, assessing compliance will require a base standard of measurement. To achieve such a standard will probably require a wide-ranging series of studies, the aim of which would be to provide a socioeconomic audit of the status of children in Canada.[69] It is beyond the powers even of the federal government to undertake such a job. Rather, a coordinated effort of government, academia, research centres and interest groups will be required.

When specific programmes are envisioned or targets set, it will also be necessary to engage in some rather sophisticated social analysis of the potential impact of these programmes or targets upon children. In other words, if children really are to be a priority, we may need to design 'children's impact assessment' schemes. The Canadian government's 'action plan for children' refers generally to the need to assess the socio-economic situation of Canadian children, and while it notes a special need for a 'better information base' concerning aboriginal children living on reserves, it provides no detailed scheme to accomplish that task.[70] Nor does it appear that any substantial resources have been dedicated to further that goal. Indeed, the discussion of 'monitoring, evaluation and follow-up' in the action plan consists of three short paragraphs. The Committee on the Rights of the Child has noted the paucity of monitoring strategies. The government acknowledges that '[i]t will be particularly important to monitor the impact of prevention and promotion programs on the problems they are intended to address', but no monitoring strategy is suggested. Moreover, little attention appears to have been paid to the need to evaluate the situation of children in detail *before* 'prevention and promotion programs' are designed.

A number of more specific resource allocation issues will also arise:

1   The Convention requires states to promote the 'highest standard of health' for all children equally, and without discrimination. Available medical statistics indicate that children who live below the poverty line are far more likely to suffer from medical problems than children in middle-class families. The causes of this situation are complex, relating to access to medical care, nutrition, information deficits, proximity to localized environmental contaminants and so on. Any remedy would require a substantial financial commitment by governments. The health status of aboriginal children is even more compromised in Canada today. The aboriginal infant mortality rate is more than double the average rate for other Canadians.[71]

2 The right to education enumerated in the Convention includes 'available and accessible' secondary education. Drop-out rates and illiteracy rates in Canada suggest that this right is not being universally satisfied. For example, the national high school drop-out rate is now roughly 30 per cent.[72] Moreover, the Convention categorizes secondary education as 'general' or 'vocational'. Budget cuts have restricted access to vocational programmes tremendously over the last few years. This restriction may be causally related to increasing drop-out rates, supporting the proposition that the educational system is failing to meet the needs of its clientele. If the needs remain unsatisfied, the 'right' to an education is arguably denied.

3 The right to social security is a right of children, not merely of parents. Given the increasing number of children living below the poverty line, one may ask whether basic income support programmes adequately consider the rights of children. Although one may agree with the Canadian federal government that '[t]he principal means of economic security for Canadian children are jobs for their parents,'[73] in an era of high unemployment a social security system which pays due attention to the situation of children is now required by the Convention. Similarly, the income tax provisions which treat alimentary support payments to children as taxable in the hands of the receiving spouse may contribute to inadequate standards of living for children.[74] Indeed, the very system of child support which has been developed as a corollary to divorce is increasingly under strain.[75] A related problem is how to treat the 'independent' teenager who does not live at home. Should he or she be eligible for social security at the same level as an adult claimant?

Children's rights advocates in Canada must work to create a political constituency strong enough to influence personal and governmental spending priorities. Coordination of efforts is a key to mobilizing the goodwill which sees Canadians annually devoting a large percentage of their charitable contributions to children's charities, especially those operating in the developing world. A constituency for children's rights and welfare exists, but it must be politically engaged. Meanwhile, as an interim measure, activists must suggest realistic initiatives which are sensitive to budgetary constraints. For example, pressing the provinces to create enhanced labour standards for part-time workers, many of whom are young people, could prove more fruitful in the short term than advocating the immediate creation of a fully funded national day care system when even existing social welfare programmes are under threat.

Increasing overseas development assistance for children

If Canadians and their governments are collectively to decide to increase social spending on children, I have argued that there is a commensurate legal and moral obligation to increase overseas development assistance budgets directed towards the children of the developing world. In 1991–92, the Canadian Official Development Assistance budget was roughly $3 billion. Although this sounds like a great deal of money, it amounts to less than 0.5 per cent of Canada's GNP, and the budget has been decreasing as a proportion of GNP for a number of years despite an oft-repeated commitment of the Canadian government, now temporarily abandoned, to raise the percentage to 0.7 per cent.[76] The federal government's own estimates suggest that, of the $3 billion, only $350 million 'went to activities directly benefitting children'.[77] Even though some of the remaining amount no doubt created indirect benefits for children, one must ask whether this level of commitment matches the rhetoric of both the government, and the Canadian people of 'putting children first'.

Indeed, recent initiatives call into question the stated governmental priority to help the poorest of the poor, many of whom are children. In 1993 Canadian aid programmes were 'refocused' away from many of the world's poorest countries in order to benefit middle-income countries with which Canada is seeking to promote enhanced commercial ties. Although various non-governmental aid agencies have sought to arouse the Canadian public's indignation on this issue, the refocusing of aid has been accomplished with little public outcry. Yet the Children's Convention calls upon states to address children's rights as a key element of 'international cooperation'. Children's advocates must target Official Development Assistance budgets, since they are crucial to the effective international promotion of children's rights.

Removing discrimination

In the Convention, discrimination in terms of language, social origin and property is prohibited. These grounds could be invoked in Canadian political, and to a certain extent legal, processes to challenge the laws governing language of education laws, to claim entitlements to support for the 'unpropertied', or to call into question custody decisions in divorce cases which are often based upon considerations of 'stability', where 'social origins' are often deemed by judges to be relevant.

Reviewing adoption and child care arrangements

Provincial adoption laws should be reviewed to ensure that they discourage any form of privately arranged adoption. International adoptions will have to be monitored to ensure that the people who arrange them are prohibited from any 'improper financial gain'. The position of aboriginal customary care has been protected through the Canadian government's reservation to Article 21 of the Convention, but the broader issue of cultural diversity in child care arrangements remains. The implications of the vague wording of the Convention will have to be traced out in detail.

Ensuring the rights of children to be heard

Attention must be paid to the rights of children to be heard, or represented, in all criminal and civil proceedings where their interests may be affected. Issues to consider include whether a child can choose to represent him- or herself, whether a child is free to choose a representative who is not his parent or legal guardian, and whether a child can forcibly intervene in legal proceedings which may affect his or her interests. The implications of this challenge are most broad in the family law context. In Canada, it is currently assumed that in most cases of divorce, for example, a child's interest in custody questions can be protected by the court, having heard the arguments of both parents. Children *may* be asked their opinion, but it is not required in all Canadian jurisdictions. Only rarely will children be represented by separate counsel. Similarly, in the context of deportation cases, children of refugee claimants who are denied that status find themselves deported as appendages of the parent. Should such children be entitled to an independent hearing in refugee determination hearings?

Ensuring children's rights to privacy

Privacy rights for children will prompt enormous debate. Will the state be authorized to intervene in families where the right is not adequately respected? How *can* the state, practically speaking, abide by an obligation to legally 'protect' the privacy of children?

Redefining the child–parent–state relationship

The very language of children's rights should cause Canadians to rethink quite radically the relationship between the child, the parent (or family) and the state. This will involve, at the very least, finding satisfactory answers to the following questions:

1   Does the state have an obligation to educate citizens concerning a socially dominant understanding of the 'proper' relationship between parent and child?
2   Must parents forego traditional notions of power and control over children in favour of notions of nurturing and respect?
3   Should the state intervene to foster 'healthy' parent–child relationships, based on the rights of the child?
4   What *are* the 'responsibilities, rights, and duties' of the parent?

Furthermore, will it be possible for Canadian legislatures, courts and administrative actors to deal sensitively, and in a principled manner, with issues of cultural rights, especially in the context of extended family roles and parental rights and responsibilities? This issue will be of particular importance for aboriginal peoples, but also for members of some religious groups and of new immigrant communities who may not share all of the values underlying the Convention.

CONCLUSION

The Canadian government's 'action plan for children', which might have been expected to address in some detail the types of issues set out above, does not. The document's title belies its modest aspirations. Apart from a rather sanguine description of the current socioeconomic status of Canadian children, the 'action plan' is largely a catalogue of existing programmes.[78] The section devoted to 'Directions for Federal Action' is thin. Although the general statement of aims is laudable, it is so general as to be anodyne. Many of the specific commitments are to programmes which were previously announced, such as Canada's Drug Strategy, and the Canadian Panel on Violence Against Women. The 'New Initiatives' discussion focuses upon the 'reform' of the family allowance system, the creation of a child tax credit to benefit low-income families, and a 'Child Development Initiative' which is 'aimed at preventing and reducing conditions of risk among children'.[79] The principal focus of this initiative would appear to be health promotion amongst women and children, and certain inexpensive protective mechanisms which will bolster the legal system's ability to aid children in distress. The bulk of spending commitments relate to programmes of skills development and family protection in aboriginal communities, and to a 'partnership' with Canadian community groups seeking 'to address priority health and developmental needs of high-risk children'.[80]

Although the commitment to fund aboriginal and community-based initiatives is welcome, the 'action plan' is devoid of vision. It does not attempt to put forward any comprehensive strategy to enhance the position of children in Canadian society. Rather, it presents a series of ad hoc initiatives addressed primarily to high-risk groups. That approach was no doubt deliberately adopted, for one of the three 'basic principles' expressed in the action plan is to 'respect our limits' – that is, financial limits. There is no indication of any significant shifting of priorities within the federal budget. One could criticize the government for timidity but the overall approach may, sadly, be an accurate reflection of Canadian political reality. New spending for children will not be popular if it means, as it must, cutting existing expenditures or imposing higher taxes.

I have attempted to demonstrate that if Canada is to take the Convention seriously, Canada will have to do much more than piously assert the need to 'put children first' or create legal 'rights' for children divorced from real social change; the federal government must honestly reassess priorities and consciously plan new strategies, including economic strategies. If the status quo is maintained, Canada will not be in full compliance with many of the provisions of the Children's Convention.

In a brief but telling commentary upon the importance of the Children's Convention, the distinguished writer and statesman, Vaclav Havel, warned the world community:

> As with any law, even this law can only acquire its real meaning and significance if it is accompanied by real moral self-awareness. In this case I am talking about the self-awareness of parents. That cannot be put into law. However, if it were possible, I would add another paragraph to the agreement I signed this morning. That paragraph would say that it is forbidden for parents and adults in general to lie, serve dictatorships, inform on others, bend one's back, be scared of dictators, and betray one's friends and ideals in the name of and for the alleged interest of [one's own] children, and that it is forbidden for all murderers and dictators to pat children on the head.[81]

Although Canadians may not face the immediate and frightening challenges of remaining true to ideals in the face of dictatorship, they do confront the daily challenge to seek out 'moral self-awareness'. Such awareness would require of all adults a conscious rethinking of their attitudes towards children, a reassessment of their physical, economic and social power over children, and an honest commitment to redefining social spending priorities. The Convention on the Rights of the Child calls for nothing less.

NOTES

1   UNGA Resolution of 20 November 1989, UN Doc. A/RES/44/25. Entered into force on 2 September 1990.

2   See, for example, the discussion of attitudes in W. Bennett (1987), 'A critique of the emerging convention on the rights of the child', *Cornell International Law Journal*, **20**, p. 10.

3   A former Prime Minister of Canada, who served as co-chair of the Children's Summit in 1990, has suggested that money is not the decisive factor in the 'war on child suffering. Political will is': Mulroney (1990), 'Opening statement at the Children's Summit', 30 September (mimeograph copy on file with author). It is, of course, debatable that money and political will are closely related. What may be required is a political will to spend more money, or to reallocate resources.

4   R. Macdonald (1991), 'A Canadian perspective' in P. Alston and G. Brennan (eds), *The UN Children's Convention and Australia*, 75, at p. 77.

5   When I refer to 'Canadian' legal and social policies, I include the policies of provincial authorities as well. Although the power to conclude treaties is federal, being a prerogative power of the Queen in right of Canada, the implementation of treaties requires the legislative action of the federal Parliament and of provincial legislative assemblies within their respective areas of competence. This reality is particularly striking in the case of the Children's Convention. Many of the issues dealt with in the Convention will require provincial action, because the provinces retain power over 'property and civil rights' under s. 92(13) of the Constitution Act 1867. On the other hand, certain provisions will require the action of the federal parliament under heads of jurisdiction such as 'marriage and divorce' (s. 91(26)), and 'Indians and lands reserved for Indians' (s. 91(24)). Immigration is a shared responsibility under Article 95. The requirement for significant provincial action, if the Convention is to be fully implemented in Canada, may cause political difficulties during the recurring periods in which Canadian provinces, especially Quebec, seek to assert their autonomy.

6   Canada entered its ratification of the Convention on 11 December 1991, having engaged in extensive consultations with the provinces between the opening for signature of the Convention in January 1990, and the ultimate ratification. As of 1993, some 131 states had ratified the Convention. See UNESCO (1993), *Human Rights: Major International Instruments (Status as of 31 March 1993)*, Paris.

Canada's instrument of ratification contained two reservations and a 'statement of understanding' which will be discussed below, text accompanying notes 30 to 31 and following note 50.

It should be noted that the Convention itself requires additional analysis and study authorized by the General Assembly under the terms of Article 45.

7   Canadian Ministry of National Health and Welfare (1992), *Brighter Futures: Canada's Action Plan for Children* (hereinafter *Brighter Futures*). The government had previously designated the Minister of National Health and Welfare as the minister responsible for following up the public commitments made by Canada at the Summit for Children. Within the Canadian federal bureaucracy, a 'Children's Bureau' has been created in the Department of Health and Welfare (recently renamed the Department of Health).

8　UNGA Res. 217 A (III) of 10 December 1948, UN Doc. A/811.

9　The Convention on the Elimination of All Forms of Discrimination against Women (1979) 1249 UNTS 13 (entered into force on 3 September 1981) also contains significant elements of integration between the two categories of rights. However, the linkages are more cautiously stated. In addition, the large number of reservations entered against the Convention's provisions unfortunately undercuts the moral authority of the Convention, particularly on the question of the interrelationship between civil and political, and economic, social and cultural rights.

10　The Universal Declaration was passed by the General Assembly of the United Nations on 10 December 1948. Almost immediately negotiations began to put the provisions of the Declaration into binding treaty form. It was not until 1966 that the two fundamental conventions were concluded, and only after it had been decided to create separate treaties relating to civil and political, and economic, social and cultural rights. See *Universal Declaration of Human Rights, op. cit.*, note 8 above; *International Covenant on Civil and Political Rights*, UNGA Res. 2200, 21 UN GAOR, Supp. (No. 16) 52, UN Doc. A/6316 (1966), 993 UNTS 171; and *International Covenant on Economic, Social and Cultural Rights*, UNGA Res. 2200, 21 UN GAOR, Supp. (No. 16) 49, UN Doc. A/6316 (1966), 993 UNTS 3. It should also be noted that, over the years, the Universal Declaration has become laden with normative value, so that many of its provisions are now seen to be evidence of customary international law, independently binding upon all states. See, for example, P. Sieghart (1988), 'An introduction to the international covenants on human rights', Commonwealth Secretariat, Human Rights Unit Occasional Paper, mimeograph.

11　*Brighter Futures, op. cit.*, note 7 above, at p. 27. Of these low-income families, almost 40 per cent were headed by single parents, typically mothers: *ibid.*, at p. 29. A recent UNICEF study estimated that 10 per cent of Canadian children live in poverty, 'poverty' being defined as family income below 40 per cent of the total population's median disposable income. See 'Too many Canadian kids live in poverty: UNICEF' in *The Montreal Gazette*, 22 September 1993, p. A1. For even more disturbing statistics from the USA, see E. Calciano (1992), 'United Nations Convention on the Rights of the Child: Will it help children in the United States?', *Hastings International and Comparative Law Review*, **15**, pp. 515–517.

12　Canadian Department of Health and Welfare (1990), *Children of Canada, Children of the World*, National Paper for the World Summit for Children, mimeograph.

13　This distinction was rooted in the debate concerning so-called 'negative' rights (freedom from) versus 'positive' rights (rights to). For example, the US government has long adopted the official position, at least in international fora, that only 'freedoms from' are rights. Anything requiring the active intervention of social forces, particularly the state, is better treated as an 'entitlement' which would be the subject not of rights discourse, but of political and economic trade-offs.

This position is open to challenge on a number of grounds. Most obvious is the rebuttal that even 'negative' rights have economic costs associated with their promotion and protection, for example, in the highly elaborated judicial systems which have been created to shield individuals from 'unconstitutional' state action. All rights have costs; the question is which costs society is collectively willing to sustain.

Children's advocates in the USA fear that even if the USA ratifies the Children's Convention, it will do so on the basis of a reservation stating that economic rights are merely aspirational. This would undercut even the political value of the US ratification, aside from its tendency to weaken emerging norms. See Calciano, *op. cit.*, note 11 above.

14　See C.P. Cohen (1990), 'United Nations Convention on the Rights of the Child [:]

Introductory Note' , *International Commission of Jurists Review*, **44**, at p. 37. Former Canadian Prime Minister Mulroney cautiously suggested that '[r]esources always seem to be scarce'. Mulroney, *op. cit.*, note 3 above.

15   See Bennett, *op. cit.*, note 2 above, at p. 40: 'Equating important, universally accepted rights with other less accepted rights will call into question the integrity of the Convention'. In the dominant US view, 'universally accepted rights' are almost always and exclusively civil and political rights.

16   In a useful article, Price Cohen, Hart and Kosloske suggest that: 'The Convention provides the basic framework to support efforts of those who work toward the establishment of all of the conditions of child treatment which can now justifiably be called rights?: C. Price Cohen, S. Hart and S. Kosloske (1992), 'The UN Convention on the Rights of the Child: developing an *information model*, to computerize the monitoring of treaty compliance', *Human Rights Quarterly*, **14**, p. 216, at p. 220. I agree, but question the assumption that these 'rights' only emerged with the conclusion of the Convention. Rights may exist even when they are not expressly stated in texts agreed to by states. The problem then is an essentially practical one of 'recognition' or 'enforceability' of rights within a legal system admittedly dominated by states. See, for example, M. Walzer (1983), *Spheres of Justice: A Defence of Pluralism and Equality*; and M. Minow (1987), 'Interpreting rights: an Essay for Robert Cover', *Yale Law Journal*, **96**, (1987), p. 1860. See also the discussion below, text accompanying notes 57 to 67.

17   T. Hammarberg (1990), 'The UN Convention on the Rights of the Child – and how to make it work' *Human Rights Quarterly*, **12**, p. 97, at p. 100.

18   The Committee is set up under Article 43 of the Convention and consists of 10 experts elected for four-year terms by the state parties. The principal activity of the Committee is to receive and comment upon state reports. Unlike the Human Rights Committee sitting under the First *Optional Protocol to the International Covenant on Civil and Political Rights*, UNGA Res. 2200 A (XXI) of 16 December 1966, 999 UNTS 171 (entered into force on 23 March 1976), the Committee on the Rights of the Child has no jurisdiction to hear individual complaints. See M. Santos Pais (1991), 'The Committee on the Rights of the Child', *International Commission of Jurists Review*, **47**, p. 36 (Ms Santos Pais is a member of the Committee). Canada's Report to the Committee can be found at UN Doc. CRC/C/11/Add. 3. The concluding observations of the Committee were adopted at the 233rd meeting of its ninth session (UN Doc. CRC/C/SR. 233).

19   Article 4: '... State Parties shall undertake such measures to the maximum extent of their available resources and, where needed, *within the framework of international co-operation*' (emphasis added).

20   See, for example, Divorce Act, RSC 1985, 2nd Supp., c. 3, as am., s. 16(8); *Civil Code of Lower Canada*, art. 30; and *King* v. *Low* [1985] 1 SCR 87. It should be noted, however, that some dissenting voices have suggested that the doctrine of 'best interests' is not very helpful in concrete cases and that it may serve simply as a mask for personal, and socially constructed, bias in decision-makers. 'Best interests' purports to be an 'objective' legal test, but it is not. See, for example, R. Mnookin (1985), *In the Interest of Children: Advocacy, Law Reform and Public Policy*, New York: W.H. Freeman; and M. Fineman (1989), 'The politics of custody and gender' in C. Smart (ed.), *Child Custody and the Politics of Gender*.

It has also been argued that another right enunciated in the Convention may alter fundamentally the 'best interests' calculus as it has evolved in domestic legal systems. The right to a 'family identity' (Article 8(1)) could require states to modify the evaluation of best interests by giving significant weight to existing familial biological and cultural connections 'rather than leaving best interests to a judge's discretion'. See G. Stewart (1992), 'Interpreting the child's right to identity in the U.N. Convention on the Rights of the Child', *Family Law Quarterly*, **26**, p. 221. Any such change in interpretive emphasis would be especially important in adoption cases, custody cases, and disputes involving parental mobility.

21   This provision has been controversial, for some advocates and commentators have sought to treat it as a statement concerning the question of abortion. When linked with the preambular paragraph mentioning the need for legal protections for the child 'before as well as after birth', Article 2(6)(1) could be read as a 'pro-life' tractus. It is clear from the negotiating history of the Convention, however, that this reading would be inaccurate. Abortion was not an explicit subject of discussion; all possible positions were simply 'reserved' by states whose views differed markedly on this question. P. Alston (1990), 'The unborn child and abortion under the Draft Convention on the Rights of the Child', *Human Rights Quarterly*, **12**, p. 156.

22   States commit themselves to ensure that the rights set out in the Convention will be available to each child 'without discrimination of any kind, irrespective of the child's or his or her parent's or legal guardian's race, colour, sex, language, religion, political or other opinion, national, ethnic of social origin, property, disability, birth or other status'.

23   *Canada Act, 1982* (UK), 1982, c. 11, Part 1 of Schedule B.

24   See, for example, Canadian *Human Rights Act*, SC 1976–77, c. 33; Ontario *Human Rights Code*, RSO 1980, c. 340; and Quebec *Charter of Human Rights and Freedoms*, RSQ, c. C-12.

25   For an analysis of Canadian equality theory and its relevance to children, see C. Sheppard (1992), 'Children's Rights to Equality: Protection Versus Paternalism', Paper presented to the 2nd Annual Comparative Health Law and Policy Conference, McGill and Loyola Universities, Montreal, 25–28 June, (mimeograph copy on file with the author).

26   See *R.* v. *Canada Labour Relations Board* (1964), 44 DLR (2d) 440 (Man. QB).

27   See *Re Arrow River and Tributaries Slide and Boom Co. Ltd* (1931), 66 OLR 577 (CA), rev'd [1932] 2 DLR 250 (SCC); and in the human rights context *Re Drummond Wren* [1945] OR 778, 4 DLR 674 (Ont. HC); *Reference Re Public Service Employee Relations Act (Alta.)* [1987] 1 SCR 313 (*per* Dickson CJC, dissenting on the merits); and *R.* v. *Keegstra* [1990] 3 SCR 697.

28   A system whereby children are to be protected by members of the extended family, with protections offered to the integrity of the patrimony of a receiving family.

29   RSC 1985, c. Y-1.

30   See ss. 91 (27) and 92 (14). In its Concluding Observations in response to Canada's First Report to the Committee on the Rights of the Child, the Committee asked Canada to reconsider this resolution. See *op. cit.*, note 18 above.

31   A national consultation of non-governmental organizations concerned with children's rights in Canada suggested that access to information about reproductive health should be treated as an aspect of a child's right to be heard and freedom of expression. Canadian Coalition for the Rights of Children (1993), 'NGO input into Canada's draft report to the UN Committee on the Rights of the Child', submitted to the Children's Bureau of the Department of Health, (mimeograph copy on file with the author).

32   See art. 17 CCQ 1991.

33   Hammarberg, *op.cit.*, note 14 above.

34   Minow, *op. cit.*, note 16 above, at p. 1868–9. See also M. Minow (1987), 'Are rights right for children?', *American Bar Foundation Research Journal*, p. 203.

35   Bennett, *op. cit.*, note 2 above, at p. 15. See also N. Bala and K. Clarke (1981), *The Child and the Law*, Toronto: McGraw Hill Ryerson; and Mary Ann Glendon (1977), *State, Law and Family: Family Law in Transition in the United States and Western Europe*, Amsterdam: North Holland.

36   *Tinker* v. *Des Moines Independent School District* (1969) 393, US 503 (Sup. Ct). See also Price Cohen *et al.*, *op. cit.*, note 16 above, pp. 218–20.

37   S. Hart (1985), 'From property to person status: historical perspectives on children's rights', *American Psychologist*, **46**, p. 53; and V. Zelizer (1985), *Pricing the Priceless Child: The Changing Social Value of Children*, New York: Basic Books.

38   Sheppard, *op. cit.*, note 25 above, at p. 1.

39   Minow, *op. cit.*, note 16 above, at p. 1910.

40   See, for example, D. Gomien (1989), 'Whose right (and whose duty) is it? An analysis of the substance and implementation of the Convention on the Rights of the Child', *New York Law School Journal of Human Rights*, **7**, p. 161, at 162; T. Carney (1991), 'Social security: dialogue or closure?' in Alston and Brennan, *op. cit.*, note 4 above, at pp. 54–5; and Macdonald, *op. cit.*, note 4 above, at pp. 78–9.

41   Canadian Coalition for the Rights of Children (nd), 'Will it be a brighter future?', Response to *Brighter Futures: Canada's Action Plan for Children*, (mimeograph copy on file with the author).

42   Macdonald, *op. cit.*, note 4 above at pp. 78–9. Many prominent advocates for children have suggested that the mushy language of the Convention could have been avoided if states (at the behest of certain lobbying groups) had not set a rather artificial deadline for the conclusion of the Convention – the anniversary of a previous international declaration on the rights of the child. See, for example, R. Barsh (1989), 'The Convention on the Rights of the Child: a re-assessment of the final text', *New York Law School Journal of Human Rights*, **7**, p. 142, *passim*. This comment supports the proposition that it is worth taking time in legislative initiatives, time enough to think through provisions that are likely to be influential in shaping behaviour, rather than in salving consciences.

43   See, for example, B. Burdekin (1991), 'Transforming the Convention into Australian Law and Practice' in Alston and Brennan, *op. cit.*, note 4 above, p. 6, at p. 8. (In Australia 'ratification of the Convention was achieved in the face of a much publicized, misleading, and in my view most mischievous campaign of misinformation'.)

44   One is reminded of some of the excesses of the 'debate' surrounding the proposed Equal Rights Amendment in the USA. One of the most common arguments of less sophisticated opponents was that the ERA would mean that it would not be possible to have separate men's and women's toilets.

45   Barsh, *op. cit.*, note 42 above, p. 146.

46   Gomien, *op. cit.*, note 40 above, at p. 163.

47   See, for example, Article 3(2), 10, 17 and 27 of the Convention.

48   For a discussion of conflicts between traditional African family values and contemporary articulations of universal human rights, especially individual rights, see B. Thompson (1992), 'Africa's Charter on Children's Rights: a normative break with cultural traditionalism', *International and Comparative Law Quarterly*, **41**, p. 432 (adopting a universalist stance, while recognizing the resulting cultural conflicts). For more critical discussions of universalist approaches to human rights generally, see A. An-Na'im (ed.), (1992), *Human Rights in Cross-Cultural Perspectives: A Quest for Consensus*, Philadelphia: University of Pennsylvania Press.

49   Article 30: 'In those states in which ethnic, religious or linguistic minorities or persons of indigenous origin exist, a child belonging to such a minority or who is indigenous

shall not be denied the right, in community with other members of his or her group, to enjoy his or her own culture, to profess and practise his or her own culture, to profess and practise his or her own religion, or to use his or her own language'.

50 Macdonald, *op. cit.*, note 4 above, at p. 80. A similar position was adopted by the Committee on The Rights of the Child in calling for Canadian implementation of economic, social and cultural rights 'to their maximum extent'. See *op. cit.*, note 18 above.

51 See Articles 4, 21, 22, 24, 27 and 28 of the Convention.

52 F. Olsen (1991), 'A United States perspective' in Alson and Brennan, *op. cit.*, note 4 above, at p. 73.

53 The concept of 'respect for persons' provides the ethical foundation for the legal doctrine of human rights. It is the person him- or herself who is worthy of respect, and not any interposed concept such as 'dignity', which is amenable to subjective evaluations of worth. I am indebted to my colleague Dr Margaret Somerville for this insight. See M. Somerville (1993), 'The right to health care: a human rights perspective' in J. Mann and C. Dupuy (eds), *CIDA, Santé Droit de l'Homme/AIDS, Health and Human Rights*, Annecy, France.

54 This viewpoint was ideologically based and has probably never been descriptively accurate in Western societies. Numerous commentators have demonstrated that state, social and legal policies have actually buttressed a particular perception of family life which was both hierarchical and male-dominated. See, for example, M. Freeman, 'Legal ideologies, patriarchal precedents, and domestic violence' in M. Freeman (ed.) (1984), *State, the Law, and the Family*; and J. Elshtain (1981), *Public Man, Private Woman*, Princeton: Princeton University Press. See also the discussion in S. Toope (1991), 'Riding the fences: courts, charter rights and family law', *Canadian Journal of Family Law*, 9, p. 55, at pp. 57–8. In many African and Asian traditional societies families could never have been conceived of in terms of privacy; they were quintessentially communal and linked to broader social groupings of clan or tribe.

55 L. Chen (1989), 'The United Nations Convention on the Rights of the Child: A Policy-Oriented Overview' (1989), *New York Law School Journal of Human Rights*, 7, p. 16, at p. 19.

56 See, for example, Articles 3 (2), 5 and 14.

57 J. Eekelaar (1991), 'Why children? Why rights?' in Alston and Brennan, *op. cit.*, note 4 above, at p. 21.

58 M. Rayner (1991), 'Taking seriously the child's right to be heard' in Alston and Brennan, *op. cit.*, note 4 above, at p. 34.

59 *Ibid.*, at p. 35.

60 See, for example, the discussion and references in Toope, *op. cit.*, note 54 above, at p. 56 *et seq.*

61 See Parker (1991), 'How can 'rights-talk' help children? An academic perspective' in Alston and Brennan, *op. cit.*, note 4 above, pp. 16, 18.

62 Minow, *op. cit.*, note 16 above, at p. 1867.

63 For example, 'ombudsman' processes. See G. Melton (1991), 'Lessons from Norway: the children's ombudsman as a voice for children', *Case Western Reserve Journal of International Law*, 23, p. 197.

64 See, for example, C. Perelman (1976), *Logique juridique: nouvelle rhetorique*, Paris: Dalloz; and F. Kratochwil (1989), *Rules, Norms, and Decisions: On the conditions of practical and legal reasoning in international relations and domestic affairs*, Cambridge: Cambridge University Press.

65 Somerville, *op. cit.*, note 53 above, at p. 4 (emphasis in original).

66   Parker, *op. cit.*, note 61 above, at p. 19.
67   Freeman (1991), 'A United Kingdom perspective' in Alston and Brennan, *op. cit.*, note 4 above, p. 81, at pp. 82–3.
68   See, for example, Macdonald, *op. cit.*, note 4 above, who gave greater priority to the administrative audit, believing that most of the key changes required for implementation will be administrative (or executive) in nature, not legislative; and E. Fishwick and M. Hogan (1991), 'Looking ahead: strategies for monitoring compliance' in Alston and Brennan, *op. cit.*, note 4 above, p. 86.
69   For a similar argument in the Australian context, see M. Harrison (1991), 'Does Australia Really Need the Convention' in Alston and Brennan, *op. cit.*, note 4 above, p. 29.
70   See, *Brighter Futures*, *op. cit.*, note 7 above, at pp. 33 and 47. The action plan does state, however, that CIDA has created a 'Task Force on Child Survival and Development' to oversee the implementation of initiatives relating to children. Perhaps this group will take on an evaluative function as well as a planning function vis-à-vis Canada's international commitments.
71   *Ibid.*, at p. 33. It should also be noted that the suicide rate for adolescent Indians is more than seven times the national rate.
72   *Ibid.*, at p. 34. One might respond by arguing that all that is required is the provision of an opportunity for secondary education. However, if the opportunity seems systematically, if unintentionally, weighted towards middle class children, it can be argued that the 'right' is effectively being denied.
73   *Ibid.*, at p. 10.
74   See J.W. Durnford and S.J. Toope (1994), 'Spousal support in family law and alimony in the law of taxation', *Canadian Tax Journal*, **42**, pp. 1–107.
75   It is noted in *Brighter Futures, op. cit.*, note 7 above, at p. 39 that the federal government has commissioned a series of discussion papers dealing with child custody and support. They will be used as a basis for negotiations between the federal, provincial and territorial governments concerning family law reform. For an excellent critical survey of the contemporary legal situation concerning child support in Canada, see C. Rogerson (1990–91), 'Judicial interpretation of the spousal and child support provisions of the *Divorce Act, 1985* (Part One), *Canadian Family Law Quarterly*, p. 155.
76   To make the figures more human, it is helpful to consider that UNICEF estimates that in 1991, the *per capita* contribution of Canadians to overseas development assistance was US\$ 92. The comparable US statistic was US\$ 44. See 'Too Many Canadian Kids …', *op. cit.*, note 11 above. In a September 1993 speech to the UN General Assembly, the Canadian Prime Minister, Kim Campbell, renounced the 0.7 per cent target, calling it 'unrealistic'.
77   *Brighter Futures, op. cit.*, note 7 above, at p. 44. Canada is by no means alone amongst industrialised countries when it comes to the proportion of development assistance dedicated to the basic needs of children. UNICEF estimates indicate that no more than 10 per cent of total official development assistance disbursements has been directed to nutrition, water, primary health care and education (including family planning). See 'Too Many Canadian Kids …?, *op. cit.*, note 11 above.
78   *Brighter Futures, op. cit.*, note 7 above, at pp. 3–36.
79   *Ibid.*, at p. 42.
80   *Ibid.*, at p. 44.
81   Yaclav Havel (1990), 'Introductory Statement by the President of the Czech and Slovak Federal Republic' before the World Summit for Children, 30 September 1990.

4   Children and the Convention: The Danish Debate

Linda Nielsen* and Lis Frost**

Denmark ratified the UN Convention on the Rights of the Child in July 1991, the ninety-fourth country to do so. The general view has been expressed in Denmark that, of course, it complies with the Convention's provisions. However, serious consideration was given to making a reservation on Article 37 about young people in prison, since the special juvenile prisons for persons between 15 and 18 years-old had been abolished, which meant that young persons might be imprisoned together with adult prisoners. But, after a debate in the Danish parliament, agreement was reached to establish special detention centres for juveniles, with the result that Denmark made no reservations. The process and the ratification has also led to a debate about living conditions for children in Denmark. This debate was initiated *inter alia* by the Danish Centre of Human Rights,[1] and has centred on: the child's right to a father and a mother; the right to identity including the right to know genetic parents; violence against children; compulsory removal of children; and children's right to self-determination and to be heard.

When, in January 1995, the Danish Government was examined in Geneva regarding its observance of obligations according to the UN Convention on the Rights of the Child, a number of other topics were considered relevant.

RIGHTS OF DANISH CHILDREN EXAMINED BY CHILDREN'S RIGHTS COMMITTEE

The Danish report was prepared by the Ministry of Justice in cooperation with other ministries handling fields of special importance for children. It

*University of Copenhagen.
**University of Århus.

was discussed by the Committee in April/May 1994 and then in January 1995 with representatives from the Danish Ministry of Foreign Affairs, the Ministry of Justice, the Ministry of the Interior, the Ministry of Social Affairs and the Ministry of Education. In the concluding observations of 27 January, the Committee gave a written summary of its examination of the Danish Government's compliance with the UN Child Convention, including a number of positive aspects as well as principal subjects of concern, suggestions and recommendations.[2]

Among the positive aspects, the Committee thanks the Danish Government for the report and expresses its satisfaction with the constructive dialogue held with government representatives. Furthermore, the Committee thanks the Danish Government for the precautions it has taken in order to improve and protect children's rights, including the passing of the bill prohibiting possession of child pornography material. The Committee is also positive towards the government bill on custody and access (now enacted, see below). Finally, the Committee appreciates that the Danish Governmental Commission on Children put forward a programme in 1994, with the aim to assist exposed groups of children. Also the establishment by the Government of the Children's Council, the governmental City Committee, and a proposal from this Committee regarding assistance and advice to refugees and immigrant children. Finally, the Committee appreciates a document prepared in June 1993 by the Danish Government about human rights and democracy, which is considered to be of importance for international development support, including development support regarding children.

The Committee also raises a number of principal subjects of concern, suggestions and recommendations which in large part do not concern the topics mentioned in this article. One of the principal subjects of concern is Article 40 of the convention about a child's right, when sentenced for a punishable offence, to have the decision heard by a higher, competent, independent and impartial authority or by a court. Denmark has made a reservation concerning this article, especially because, according to the Administration of Justice Act, it is not possible to have the question of guilt heard by a higher court in all criminal cases. Especially in cases tried by a jury, but also in minor criminal cases, the possibilities of having the case heard again are limited. Furthermore, the Committee is dissatisfied with the precautions Denmark has taken to make the principles and decisions of the UN Child Convention widely known to children and adults (Article 42). On this point, the Committee severely criticizes the Government's precautions. It is true that in 1991 the Government appropriated 1 million DKK for an information campaign regarding the UN Child Convention, including the preparation of three publications for children and one publication for adults, but during the hearing, several members of the Committee pointed out that there is a need for lasting and systematic precautions.

Moreover, the Committee is critical of Danish legislation and administrative practice regarding children seeking asylum, especially concerning interview and treatment of applications for the reunion of families (article 10 and 12 in the UN Child Convention). The criticism is centred around the facts *that* children who enter the country together with their parents are normally not heard by the asylum authorities; *that* according to Danish legislation it is difficult for the parents of unaccompanied refugee children to obtain residence permits in Denmark, and *that* the handling of such cases takes a long time (the average being 20 months from entry into Denmark until a decision is made). The Committee was furthermore critical of Denmark's failure to comply with the 'non-discrimination' provision in the UN Child Convention article 2 regarding children seeking asylum and refugee children, especially the right to education as compared with Danish children. Also the Committee is concerned with a number of conditions that exist for children in Denmark, i.e. *that* 15 per cent of all Danish children are socially threatened; *that* one-fifth of all Danish families with children are one-parent families; *that* the number of industrial injuries and diseases due to employment is high for youngsters between 15 and 25 years; *that* the number of suicides by teenagers is relatively high in Denmark; and *that* incidents of sexual abuse of children, violence against children, including violence in their own home, occur. One point of criticism was that normally it is not a punishable offence in Denmark for an adult to pay children between 15 and 18 years of age to have intercourse with him/her, unless this involves his/her own child, an adoptive child, a stepchild or a child entrusted to him/her for the purpose of training or education. Neither is prostitution punishable in Denmark; however, a pimp's activity will be subject to penalty. The Danish attitude is based on the principle that young prostitutes should primarily be helped by social legislation, not penal provisions. The Committee recommends that the Danish Government control the conditions regarding adoptive children in Denmark more thoroughly.

The Committee is dissatisfied that the provisions and principles, guaranteed in UN Child Convention articles 3, 12, 13 and 15, have not been sufficiently introduced into legislation. The criticism was primarily attached to the failure to comply with article 12, securing that every child capable of expressing views about his/her own condition has the right to do so and to have his/her views taken into account, keeping in mind that child's age and maturity. The Danish legislation has the opposite point of departure, as persons under the age of 18 years have no autonomy (see below regarding custody). Finally the Committee points to possible disagreements between the Danish provisions securing sperm- and egg-donors' anonymity on the one hand, and article 7 and 8 securing the child's right to know its parents and the right to keep its identity, including citizenship, name and family relations on the other (see below on donor anonymity).

As has been stated, Danish legislation generally meets the demands of the UN Child Convention, but there are still imperfections regarding children's rights which the Committee has pointed out and which Danish society will have to work at removing.

A CHILD'S RIGHT TO A MOTHER AND A FATHER

The right of children to keep close and meaningful contact with both parents even after they have stopped living together is a question of perennial concern in Denmark. Research from the Danish Institute of Social Research has shown that it is best for both children and adults, if parenthood can 'survive' separation between the parents. The research also shows that the pattern for contact between the child and its parents, which is laid down just after the *de facto* separation, is usually decisive for the contact and access in the years to come. Often – too often – however, children lose contact with one of their parents after separation or divorce, particularly when the conflict between the parents is so bitter that the children are used as a weapon in it. Article 18 of the Convention and Article 9 are of special pertinence in this respect.

The Danish legislation on parental rights: existing law

Danish law aims to place all children, whether born in or out of wedlock, in the same legal position vis-à-vis their parents in terms of inheritance and maintenance, but not of custody. The paramount consideration in all decisions regarding children is the welfare principle: cases have to be decided according to the best interests of the child. The purpose of the legislation is to secure the maximum possible close contact between children and both parents. In Denmark the proportion of children born to unmarried parents is very high because of the great number of unmarried cohabitants.[3] The present Minor's Act has been changed by Act No. 387 of 14 June 1995 on custody and access, coming into force on 1 January 1996, but the basic principles described below have been maintained.

Married parents both have parental rights.[4] When a divorce or separation is granted, the question of whether the parents should have joint custody or that one of them should have sole custody is decided by agreement of the parties concerned or by the court. The parents may agree upon joint custody or agree that one of them shall have sole custody. If the parents cannot reach agreement, the court will decide the question of custody, applying the principle of the best interests of the child.[5] In determining the issue the question of which party was responsible for the breakdown of the marriage is irrelevant. The court can only order that custody be given to one parent, being unable to order joint custody, since that would depend on an agreement between the parents. If the question of custody has been determined by the court on legal separation, the issue need not be decided again on divorce. A custody decision may, however, be altered by a subsequent judgement if circumstances have changed to such an extent that it is necessary, in the interests of the child, to transfer custody to the other parent. Such alterations are rare in practice.

A child born to a mother *cohabiting* with the father is considered to be a child born outside marriage,[6] and the mother has sole custody. However unmarried parents may agree upon joint custody. If the parents wish to end the cohabitation, either party may request that joint custody ends. They may also agree that one parent shall have sole custody. If the parents disagree, the court can decide which parent should have sole custody, applying the principle of the best interests of the child.[7] If the parents have agreed upon joint custody they have equal rights, should the issue of custody subsequently need to be decided by a court – for example, when cohabitation ceases. Where the mother has sole custody, the father can have custody transferred to him against her wishes, applying the best interests of the child.[8]

Custody gives the parents a duty to care for the child and a right to make decisions about a child's upbringing according to the child's best interests and needs. This includes decisions about education, medical treatment and other everyday decisions.[9] A parent who has no custody usually has a right to visit the child. Where parents cannot agree on access arrangements, the County Governor can determine the issue. Parents who frustrate access arrangements can be fined or even imprisoned. The bailiff may also, on request, enforce access rights, unless this is seen as contrary to the welfare of the child. In Denmark free family counselling is offered by the County Governor in disputes over custody or access rights.[10] The counselling is given by different professionals, including persons employed at the County Governor's office, psychiatrists, psychologists and welfare officers.

The debate on parental rights

The debate on the existing law and practice as regards custody, access and so on, and in particular as regards comparisons with the UN Convention, has been extensive. For example, the Fathers' Union has claimed that it is unjust that cohabiting fathers do not automatically share parental rights. The Danish Centre of Human Rights is concerned whether this provision is contrary to Article 18 of the Convention because the father's access rights fail to provide him with the responsibility and right to influence the upbringing and development of the child. The provision may also be contrary to Article 2. Thus, the Centre favours the granting of parental rights to fathers of children born out of wedlock. This is also seen as a fair solution in cases where the parents subsequently cease to cohabit, since it would give fathers equal chances of obtaining custody. Joint custody for children, whether born in or out of wedlock, is seen as being more in accordance with both the Convention and current family patterns.

The Danish Centre of Human Rights also argues that the parent without custody but with rights of access should also have rights to have information about matters affecting the child's life, such as illnesses and schooling, unless this is contrary to the best interests of the child. This is seen as a way both of fulfilling the principle in Article 18 of the UN Convention and as a likely means of decreasing conflicts between the parent with custody and the parent with access (see the new Act on custody and access described below). Moreover, the Centre argues that the parent with rights of access should have the right to protest against, but not a right to veto, the custodial parent's intent of moving to another country with the child.

The sanctions against a custodial parent who undermines the rights of the visiting parent are sometimes seen as inadequate, partly because of the difficulties of enforcement. Lawyers and experts with knowledge of children and great practical experience in these cases have expressed concern that the current Danish law may be said to favour the custodial parent who obstructs access rights, with the result that the custodial parent is often able to succeed in cutting off the contact between the child and the other parent. There has been a call for speedier action and more efficiency in the use of sanctions.

In our opinion, giving stable cohabitants with children equal parental rights may be seen as essential. In can be unfair for a cohabiting father who has taken an active part in the care for, and the upbringing of, his child to be denied the opportunity to obtain custody because of what he may see as a 'formality'. However, from the child's perspective, there may be no need for automatic joint custody between the cohabitants. For a child who is living with both its parents, contact is established through everyday life. How close the contact will be depends on the extent to which the parents – including the father – are engaged in the child's life and care, and not primarily on the legal construction of parenthood. From the child's viewpoint there is consequently no absolute need for automatic joint custody during cohabitation. Neither is there a need for joint custody in cases where there is no cohabitation when the child is born, or if cohabitation ceases in connection with the birth of the child. Joint custody does not secure close contact between the child and both parents, and there is no legal authority to settle disputes about custody between the parents when they have joint custody.

Other arguments in the debate have concerned equality. There are several variations of this theme, one of which is equality between children born of unmarried parents with children born of spouses. An argument in favour of granting joint custody automatically between the parents is an assumption, sometimes put forward, that the legal position underlines and strengthens the factual position – the interest in the child. However, the closeness of the connection between the legal position and the emotional attachment is questionable: it is uncertain to what extent the legal construction secures factual interest. Another theme is equality between cohabiting fathers and married fathers. In this case the father has an opportunity to make a special agreement about joint custody, or to obtain joint custody via a more extensive agreement – that is, the marriage contract.[11] In this way he obtains joint custody together with a number of other legal effects.[12] A third equality theme is that between fathers and mothers. However, most cohabitants agree upon joint custody and, if they do not, this is often due to the father's lack of interest or a difficult and conflictual relationship between the father and mother making cooperation difficult, or the mere fact that it is a casual relationship and she does not know him well enough. Thus, in our opinion the mutual agreement is an instrument balancing considerations for the mother against considerations for the father.

The expansion of the rights for the non-custodial parent seems adequate as a means of limiting the tension between the custodial parent and the parent with access rights. However, in our opinion, the right of a non-custodial parent to protest against the custodial parent moving to another country seems to go too far. It seems neither realistic nor fair to bind a person to stay in his or her present environment. Nevertheless, where the custodial parent frustrates the rights of the visiting parent, quicker and more efficient action is called for, although this should always take account of the child's best interests. A Norwegian case where the non-custodial parent, because his rights to access had been obstructed, obtained custody of a seven year-old child who had only infrequently visited him seems to take the concept of 'punishing' the recalcitrant parent too far. While the parent who obstructs access rights is undoubtedly demostrating a lack of tolerance and feeling for the child's needs, it is the child who is likely to be the loser if custody is taken away from a parent in a well functioning relationship with that child.

A new Act on custody and access has to some extent taken the critical debate into account. A bill of 22 February 1995 proposed a number of amendments to the Minor's Act, and a new Act on Custody and Access was passed on 14 June 1995, coming into force 1 January 1996. The Act does not change the basic principles of custody and access, described above (existing law).

NEW ACT ON CUSTODY AND ACCESS

In the Act of 14 June 1995 a number of amendments have been made regarding custody and access rights.[13] Automatic joint custody, based on the child's interests, for unmarried cohabiting parents in a *stable* relationship, although considered, is excluded from the current Act because it is not thought possible to distinguish between cohabiting mothers and single mothers where the contact with the father may be absent or negative. However, agreements on joint custody for cohabitants need no longer be approved by the County Governor but only reported in connection with the recognition of paternity. When the present Childrens Law Reform Commission finishes its work on considering legislation on paternity, the intention is also to consider reviewing this provision on custody for cohabiting couples.

The legal conditions for joint custody have also been considered, but the Act settles that there should exist agreement on all the principal issues concerning the child – including residence, schooling and religion. To change the law might necessitate the introduction of regulations enabling the authorities to make decisions where parents disagree on such questions as schooling. It is also thought to be unrealistic to force parents to cooperate.

Access rights are not perceived to be as fundamental as the question of the child's residence. Accordingly, the Act introduces a right for the parent with custody but without care of the child to request access and, in case of dispute, to have the County Governor establish its frequency.

The legal position for the unmarried father is also strengthened. This is to promote the child's interests and is particularly directed at long-lasting cohabitations, where it may only be a matter of chance that the parents have not agreed on joint custody. The transfer of custody to the unmarried father after termination of cohabitation is made easier so that the parents' position is assimilated.

A new rule has been introduced enabling the County Governor to decide on contact other than access rights between the child and the non-custodial parent, such as telephone conversations and correspondence. Schools, kindergartens, social security and health-care professionals have now got a duty to pass on information about the child to the non-custodial parent. In exceptional circumstances this right may be taken away from the non-custodial parent at the request of the custodial parent.

Finally, it is emphasized in the Bill on custody and access that it is the opinion of the Law Reform Commission that the present regulation on custody for unmarried parents is not in conflict with Article 18 of the UN Convention.

THE CHILD'S RIGHT TO IDENTITY

The right to identity is found in the UN Convention (Articles 7 and 8). This right has been debated in Denmark in relation to the right for the child to know his or her genetic parents in the case of artificial insemination by donor or egg donation.

Existing law on donor anonymity

Artificial insemination by donor has been practised systematically in Denmark since the 1960s. Today, the technique of artificial insemination by donor and donation of human eggs is undertaken in several public hospitals as well as in private clinics. Insemination is also undertaken on a totally private basis, and appeals for semen donors may be found in the newspapers. There is no legislation in Denmark dealing with the civil aspects of sperm donation, and it is estimated that about 500 children per year are conceived by this means.

Administrative provisions operated through the central Danish cryopreservation facility for sperm ensure that this process is only undertaken anonymously. Legislation form 1992[14] prohibits the donation of fertilized human eggs while permitting the donation of unfertilized ones. The legal motives (found in the explanatory memorandum) specify anonymity as a precondition to the donation of unfertilized human eggs, and provisions about donor anonymity regarding egg donation have now been included in administrative regulations.[15] As a consequence, the donor child is not entitled to obtain information about his or her genetic mother or father.

The debate on donor anonymity

The Danish Council of Ethics 1989 report debated the question of anonymity.[16] The Council was divided on the question, the majority being in favour of retaining the principle of anonymity and a minority wanting openness both as to the fact that donation of semen had taken place and to the identity of the donor. A Danish Ministry of Health working party issued a report in 1992,[17] addressing the question of donor anonymity regarding artificial insemination by donor (AID), which favours keeping the principle of anonymity in consideration of both the donor and the child. The donor is said to be acting from altruistic motives, helping other people to achieve pregnancy and produce a child, and typically does not wish to be regarded as the father of any child conceived through the insemination. He is therefore seen to have a claim of protection later in life against any human and legal consequences extending beyond his expectations at the time he participated in the act of conception as a semen donor. In respect of the child, the working party simply emphasizes that the child's upbringing and family attachment should take place under conditions as close to normal as possible. The report rejects arguments stressing the importance for the child to know its origin, stating that different considerations must be balanced, and, as so often happens, they cannot all be maintained at the same time. It is estimated that the advantages of anonymity exceed any possible harmful disadvantages.

The Danish Centre of Human Rights has advocated that donor anonymity be abandoned. Three types of arguments are used – a procedural argument, a human rights argument and a social argument.

First, it is stressed that the child's right to be informed of the name of the donor should be settled according to either the Civil Service Act or the Public Administration Act. In cases where the name of the donor is included in documents which are part of a case with a public administrative authority – for instance, a public fertility clinic – the request for access of information should be met, although exceptions may be made if consideration for the person or others weighs heavily against it.[18] According to the Centre similar regulations are in force where the donor's identity is registered in a private clinic. This follows from a special legislation concerning access to information in health care,[19] according to which the question of access should be evaluated in each specific case, and the regulation cannot form the basis of a practice where the names of the donors are not provided (though asked for) without such specific evaluation. This leads the Danish Centre of Human Rights to conclude that the provision about anonymity in the administrative regulations,[20] and the present practice which secures donor anonymity for semen donors, is not in accordance with the regulations of access to information in the Danish legislation. If information about a donor's identity still exists, the Centre concludes that the child can probably claim to obtain information about the name of the donor. It is, however, acknowledged that this is a questionable interpretation of the Danish legislation.

Second, the Centre also refers to the European Convention on Human Rights which protects the right to privacy and family life. This is seen to be the case even if donor anonymity is not a case of interference by public authorities, but rather the imposing of a positive obligation on the state.[21] Reference is made to the *Gaskin* case,[22] where it was decided that a system which keeps information confidential without a specific evaluation in each case is not in accordance with the European Convention.

Third, the Centre concludes that the current regulation and practice is not based in the child's rights but in the interests of the donor. Moreover, it criticizes the perception of what is understood by a family life 'as close to normal as possible' as being too narrow.

In a consensus conference arranged by the Danish Technology Board in 1993[23] the importance of trust and openness in the family and the emotional strain attached to family secrets and taboos was emphasized. In a new 1995 report, the Danish Council of Ethics approached this issue again. A majority proposed to the Minister of Health that donor anonymity be abandoned. The question of anonymity may be addressed in a forthcoming bill on artificial procreation.

It is possible to adopt one of at least six positions regarding donation and anonymity:[24]

1   that no information at all be made available to donor children;
2   that there should be openness as to the fact that donation has taken place;
3   that some non-identifying information be provided;
4   that any information be made available provided that it is with the donor's consent;
5   that all identifying information be made available at the request of the person born as a result of fertility services;
6   that the donor should be considered the legal father of the child.

In our opinion no legal consequences, such as obligation of support towards the child, inheritance and so forth, should follow from donation. We are, however, in favour of openness as to the fact that donation has taken place. This is primarily based on the accepted premise that a healthy and genuine parent–child relationship should be built upon trust and truth. Information concerning the donor's medical and genetic characteristics may also be of interest, especially if the importance of genetic origins of certain diseases increases in the future.

The difficult question is whether the child should be entitled to information about the donor's identity. If the donor consents, the child should be allowed information about his identity, but if he does not, this entitlement should not exist unless the donor consented at the time of the donation. Seen from the child's viewpoint and his or her wish to know its roots, the principle of anonymity may seem unfair. It may also cause the child psychological problems regarding his or her sense of identity later in life, which seems to make anonymity a very severe decision to take on the child's behalf, especially as it is not only taken before the child is born but also has consequences long after the child's maturity. In our opinion, this argument should override the concern about not getting enough donors if anonymity is abandoned. If this turns out to be a problem – and, based on Swedish experience, this is probable – it would be unfortunate, but the interests of existing children must have first priority. Abandoning anonymity will also correspond with the legal situation in Denmark for adopted children who are entitled to know the identity of their biological parents. It will be of great interest to see what experiences can be drawn from the Swedish legislation which abandoned donor anonymity in 1985.

The risk of 'procreative tourism',[25] where a ban in one country may lead to persons seeking infertility treatment in other countries, is a matter of concern but should, in our opinion, not be decisive, as this argument would lead to always accepting the 'lowest common denominator' which, in these areas of procreation and infertility treatment, may be very low. The risk of a 'black market' where persons unwilling to accept the non-anonymity principle turn instead to unauthorized insemination will also be low, since the standards observed on such matters as HIV tests will inevitably be lower or even non-existent. At this stage we are, however, of the opinion that a child should always have the information that donation has taken place, and that information about the donor's identity should be kept in records to make it possible for the child to obtain this information when adult, if he or she so desires. This would also be in accordance with the Children's Rights Committee's remarks about the UN Child Convention articles 7 and 8 (see introduction above).

VIOLENCE AGAINST CHILDREN

Article 19 of the UN Convention states that the Contracting Parties are obliged to take all appropriate measures to protect the child from all forms of physical or mental violence, injury or abuse, neglect or negligent treatment, maltreatment or exploitation, including sexual abuse, while in the care of parent(s), legal guardian(s) or any other person who has the care of the child. Article 34 singles out sexual abuse and Article 39 gives the state an obligation to take all appropriate measures to promote the physical and psychological recovery of the child victim.

There are no precise statistical data showing how often children are exposed to physical and mental violence and how severe this violence is. However, since it may be assumed that adult use of violence against the child mostly takes place in the family, only family violence is discussed here. The problem is addressed in three different legal areas in Danish law: in family law, social welfare law and criminal law.

A family law perspective

In the past, parents had a statutory privilege to use violence towards their children but this was abolished in 1866, and the general provisions on violence in the Criminal Code have been applicable to parent–child relationships ever since. Nevertheless, in legal practice it has been accepted that the custodial parent and the spouse or cohabitant of that parent may use a limited amount of physical punishment in raising children. It should be emphasized, however, that the approach to the use of violence has become increasingly restrictive, and in 1985 a new provision stating that custody implies an obligation to protect the child against physical violence and mental cruelty and other kinds of humiliating treatment was enacted.[26] Today, the courts are supposed 'only' to accept a few slaps in the face or a spanking that does not leave physical marks as a non-criminal act, and to regard the use of implements as criminal. It should be noted that very few cases are taken to court, which means that it can take a long time before a change in practice becomes clear and known to parents, authorities, neighbours and so on.

A social welfare law perspective

All people have a duty to report to the city council if a child is being neglected or humiliated by parents or others who raise the child, or if a child is otherwise living under circumstances that are threatening to her or his health and development.[27] The provision is stronger than provisions about secrecy and is also applicable, for instance, to medical practitioners, social workers and lawyers who obtain knowledge about the child's situation through their work. Furthermore, the city council has a general obligation to keep an eye on the conditions in which children are living.[28]

If the social service system (the city council) somehow learns about violence against the child, it has to take action.[29] The council can, for instance, give practical parenting training or other support in the home. It can offer family treatment or similar support; it can offer the whole family a stay in an institution; or it can propose that the child or young adult be placed in some sort of boarding school, institution or a foster family. If the parents are without the necessary economic means the council can give economic support to resolve a crisis, for instance by paying for therapeutic treatment. If this is insufficient to change the situation, and the child is still suffering from violence exercised in the family, or if the (step)parents do not cooperate, the city council can use coercive measures as described below under 'Compulsory removal of the child'. If the child is being, or has been, exposed to criminal offences, such as sexual abuse, the matter must be reported to the police and taken to court.

A criminal law perspective

Most of the cases about family violence against children that are taken to court involve different kinds of sexual abuse.[30] Sexual abuse of children mainly takes place in the family and the abuser is usually either the biological father or the stepfather of the child. Probably more than 2 per cent of all minor girls are victims of sexual abuse in the form of sexual intercourse or similar sexual offences. The maximum penalties range from four to ten years' imprisonment, depending on the age of the child and the relationship between the child and the adult. A biological relationship demands a more severe penalty than other relationships.[31] When an offence is reported to the police, for instance by the social services, they take over the investigation of the matter, question the child and the adults involved. By contrast, the role of social services is to support the child and the family.

Sexual offences are public crimes. The burden of proof is placed on the state and the victim is not a party, but a witness. In fact the abused child is normally the Crown witness. It has often been said that the investigation of the case and the court trial is an additional burden to the child. In many situations the child cannot rely on the parent who normally makes decisions for the child or helps the child making decisions on personal matters because the abuse is often exercised by the parent in question or a person living together with him or her. Therefore, the child needs some professional support and, as with other victims, he or she has a right to a lawyer.[32] The lawyer has limited powers such as a right to be present during police questioning of the victim and a right to see the reports. On the other hand, the lawyer cannot advise the child how to answer questions and cannot witness police interviews with the accused. If the prosecution counsel decides to go to court the lawyer has to prepare the child, and tell him or her what is going to happen and so on. If the police want to question the child the social authorities must be informed, and if the child is below the age of 15 a representative of the authorities has to be present.

The procedure in relation to police interviews with the child differs between jurisdictions and cases. Most interviews take place at the police station but may also be in the home, a day care centre or in school. Over the years it has increasingly become the practice to tape or videotape the questioning process, especially when the child is very young. The child can refuse to answer questions and, in principle, the person with custody can also deny the child the right to answer questions from the police. The interview with the child is normally supplemented by examinations from children's experts, gynaecologists and so on. In court the child is obliged to testify, but he or she can often be exempted from this by the court on the grounds, for instance, that the abuser is a close relative, a step-parent or the like. Once the case has been opened it is probably rare for the child to refuse to testify. If the accused is convicted the court also decides the penalty which, in most cases, is one to three years' imprisonment. Furthermore, the convicted abuser usually has to pay nominal damages (around D.kr. 30,000) to the child.

The debate on violence against children

The starting-point in Danish law is that parents are obliged to take care of their children and are capable of so doing and that they want to do their best out of love for their children. In most situations, this corresponds with reality. At the same time we all know that some parents hurt their children badly and that they are not always able or willing to protect the children against, for instance, a violent or abusive step-parent. The problem is what to do about it. Some groups have suggested that the criminal law system is so damaging to the child and the family, especially when the case deals with sexual violence, that sexual abuse should be decriminalized, or at least that the social authorities should think twice before reporting it to the police. But most professionals (and others) believe it to be important that the criminal law system demonstrates that sexual abuse is a grave crime that will not be accepted by society. It is important to bring the abuse to an end, which means that the abuser must be removed from the family home. To place the abused child outside the home will quite often exacerbate the situation for the child, since the rest of the family will tend to create a barrier against the outer world to which the placed child now belongs and to see the child as a traitor. On the other hand, it is commonly held that punishing the abusive parent does not solve the problem. It is very important that the social service system and children's counsellors, psychiatrists, family therapists and the like cooperate in teaching the family members how to prevent sexual abuse.

The Children's Rights Commission proposes that action be taken with the aim of terminating violence against children, but does not specify which actions the committee has in mind.

Against this background the provision in the Minors' Act (1985), stressing that violence against children is unwise obviously came as a disappointment to the professionals who had hoped for a clear prohibition against the use of violence rather than a statement of intentions where it was even emphasized that the purpose was not to change legal practice. The new Act on custody described above, does not change the legal situation on this point. As things stand, parents are obliged to protect their children against violence but at the same time they themselves can use some violence so long as they do not infringe the provisions in the Criminal Code. This paradoxical situation definitely ought to be changed in favour of the child.[33] Even though there are problems of control and of criminalizing 'internal' family affairs, a ban will probably be in accordance with majority opinion, and the 'social engineering' effect of legislation in this area seems valuable.

COMPULSORY REMOVAL OF THE CHILD

The Convention stresses that parents are obliged to take care of their children, and it follows from Article 9 that a child may be separated from his or her parents against their will only if a competent authority has determined that this will be in the best interests of the child. A little more than 1 per cent of all Danish minors are placed outside their own home under the Social Welfare Act. In 1992 the total figure was 13,753 children. Of these, only 783 were placed outside the home by coercive measures; 38 per cent were placed in families and 23 per cent in residential institutions; 77 per cent of the children were between 7 and 17 years old.

Whether or not intervention by the authorities in the family sphere is legitimate is an ongoing debate. For some, the starting-point is, and has been, that the law should protect the family – and thus the parents – against the state and the authorities, because the family is the best environment for the child. Others have taken the opposite point of departure – namely that the law should protect the child against the parents and that the rule of law benefits the parents but often is contrary to the interests of the child. In 1992 the Social Welfare Act was changed with the purpose of finding a compromise between defending the family from illegal intrusion into its private life on the one hand and of providing legal protection for children and young people with irresponsible, negligent, feckless parents on the other. The principal changes led to more precise grounds for compulsory removal, more explicit demands in relation to the social worker's consideration of the case, better possibilities of legal aid and more self-determination for the mature child/young person.

The Child and Young Person's Board under the city council can decide that a child be placed, for instance, in a foster family, residential institution, boarding school or social–pedagogical community if it is essential to consider the child's special need for support.[34] The decision requires the consent of the parent with custody and the young person who has reached the age of 15. The young person has thus become a party in its own case which is of great importance since almost 40 per cent of all children placed outside the home are between 15 and 17 years old. If the young person refuses to give consent he or she can only be placed outside the family home if the criteria for using coercive measures are fulfilled. A consent from the parent with custody is no longer enough.

Compulsory placing is only legal when there is an obvious risk that the health or the development of the child will be seriously damaged because of:

1 insufficient caring for, or treatment of, the child;
2 violence or other serious excesses;
3 abuse problems, criminal behaviour or other severe social difficulties for the child; or
4 other problems for the child in terms of behaviour or adjustment.

Both the parent with custody and the young person are entitled to a lawyer, and the lawyer for the young person is always without charge. If the young person consents but the parent with custody rejects the placement, the Board can decide to place the child outside the home if the placement is considered to be essential to the young person's special needs and if the problems cannot be solved within the home, even if none of the above-mentioned criteria are fulfilled. Decisions about compulsory removal may be appealed to an administrative body and to a court.[35] The young person has a right to appeal on his or her own.

The basis of a decision on compulsory removal is a plan made by the social worker who 'prepares' the case.[36] The plan must include the purposes of the placement, the expected duration, special demands in relation to caring, treatment, education and so on, and what steps will be taken to support the family during the placement outside the home and after the child is rehabilitated with the family. The parent with custody, as well as the young person, has a right to be informed about the content of the plan before they decide whether to consent or reject a decision about such a placement. The placement outside the home is seen as a temporary measure, and a completely new decision must always be made after one year.

Over the years there has been much debate on the implications of a removal from home on the relationship between the child and its parent. The Danish policy is, and has long been, that contact between the parents and child is important, that foster parents/institutions should cooperate with the parents as well as with the child and that the placement shall be enforced with as much respect as possible for the integrity of the family and for the child's right to privacy. The parents do not lose parental rights when the child is placed outside the home, and they still have the legal competence to make decisions about the child's personal matters. This is mainly of importance in relation to bigger issues such as choice of school, religious confirmation, work and so on. How to arrange everyday life such as whether the child should be home for dinner, can go to the cinema, can bring a friend home to stay overnight and suchlike can be decided within the foster family or institution.

The parents and the child have visiting rights and the right to contact during the child's stay outside the home.[37] The concept 'parent' includes legal parents no matter who has parental rights. The Child and Young Person's Board is obliged to ensure that the relationship between child and parents is maintained and to do something about it if the parents fail. The visiting rights include those of the child to visit the parents as well as those of the parents to visit the child. The right to maintain the relationship also includes telephone and letter contact. If the parents have an agreement or a decision from the County Governor's Office about ,a visiting right for the parent without custody, the agreement or decision is supposed to be followed.

It can also be necessary to regulate the contact for parents with parental rights. First, parents have to follow the rules of the house and they have to respect the child's new life with its activities and obligations. The Board can decide the proportion and the exercise of visits and of letter and telephone contact if, for example, the foster parents cannot gain respect for their reasonable demands, such as seeing parents only when they are sober and not in the middle of the night. The purpose of imposing conditions for the contact is always to take care of the child and to see that the purpose of the placement is followed. Such decisions meet the criteria in the Social Welfare Act, and the above-mentioned rights of appeal are applicable.

If seeing the parents is damaging to the child, it may be necessary to take more severe steps and even to break off the relationship out of consideration for the health and the development of the child. A need to break off the parents' contact with the child does not necessarily imply that the child cannot contact the parents. It can, for instance, be important for the child to write a letter to the parents. Another, milder, reaction is to allow the parents and the child to meet under the supervision of a community representative. A more severe decision can be to change the placement of the child and not inform the parents about the address of the new placement. Such very severe decisions are made by the city council for a specific period. It can also be decided, without court order, to control letters, telephone calls and other kinds of communication between child and parent when the child has been placed in a residential institution.[38]

The debate on compulsory removal of the child

The changes in the Social Welfare Act in 1992 were intended as a response to the criticism that had been going on for years, but the debate continues. The following points are still being made.

- Too few children are placed outside the home, and the authorities act too slowly when it is obvious that the child is suffering from parental negligence, abuse and the like.
- Too many children are placed outside the home. The authorities ruin family life without having much to offer.
- Children in families from another cultural background are removed too quickly because the authorities are prejudiced and misinterpret what is going on in the family.
- The child should have a right to a lawyer without regard to its age and his or her parents' attitude towards a placement.
- Plans for the placement of the child were meant to be an important contribution towards creating legal safety for the child and the parents. They were meant to ensure that the purpose of placement – to improve the welfare of the child – was not lost sight of. But the plans are often not made, or are made after the placement or are unrealistic, unsatisfactory, imprecise, and so on.
- More precise provisions in relation to control over telephone calls, letters and such like are needed when the child is placed in a foster family and not in an institution. This is important for the cooperation between parents, foster family and child – for the benefit of the child.

These views show that the opinions on what is good and bad law and good and bad social work differ very much in this area. Indeed, they often contradict each other. They probably also show that it is extremely difficult to hit the target – namely, the child's welfare. But, while there are many pros and cons to the first points, the same cannot be said about the last one: the authorities *do* have a legal obligation to make plans for children, and this is an obligation which ought to be fulfilled immediately.

CHILDREN'S RIGHT TO BE HEARD: THEIR RIGHT TO SELF-DETERMINATION

Article 12 of the Convention states that any child who is capable of forming his or her own views should have the right to express those views in all matters concerning the child, and that the child in particular should be heard in judicial and administrative proceedings affecting the child.[39] In Denmark, children and young people below the age of 18 are under guardianship, and the person with parental rights is obliged to take care of the child and can make decisions for him or her on the basis of his interests and needs.[40] There is no specific obligation to discuss matters with the child before making the decisions. Although there is no general provision in Danish law that is comparable with Article 12, provisions dealing with specific situations have been enacted in the last decade. The majority of these provisions relate to the child's family life and include custody, visiting rights, placement outside the home and adoption.

Custody

A child who has reached the age of 12 has a right, but is not obliged, to express his or her views to the authorities before a decision is made about custody or visitation rights.[41] The authorities may also consult with smaller children. The discussion can take place in court, at the judge's or the local governor's office or elsewhere, and no special procedures have to be followed. In most cases the parents will not be present, but an expert on children will be there.[42] The authorities can refrain from the interview if it is damaging to the child. The authorities can also omit the interview if it is thought to be of no significance to the decision in the case in question. When parents agree upon who is going to have custody, whether it is joint custody or sole custody, the child is not heard because their agreement normally will be followed. In practice, this means that children are seldom heard when parents are undergoing a separation or divorce. As 90 per cent of all separations/divorces are administratively granted, this implies that they agree on the conditions such as who is going to have custody. Also, as joint custody between unmarried parents is always based on agreement, the child is not heard in these situations either.

A special situation occurs when one of the parents abduct the child. Denmark has ratified The Hague Convention on the Civil Aspects of International Child Abduction and the European Convention on Recognition and Enforcement of Decisions concerning Custody of Children and on Restoration of Custody of Children. The ratifications have been followed up by the International Child Abduction Act.[43] When a child has been abducted or wrongfully retained in Denmark, the Danish state assists his or her return, but the child will be heard before the decision is made, if the child's opinion should be taken into consideration because of his or her age and maturity.[44] Contrary to other Danish provisions, the Abduction Act does not mention a specific age limit, as for instance 12 years.

Access

Parents can make their own agreements about visits, letters, telephone calls and so on, and it is generally regarded as best for the child if the parents can work out a solution of their own. In these situations para. 26 in the Minors' Act (Custody Act s.17) is not applicable. It is only applicable if one of the parents asks the County Governor for a decision about the non-custodial parent's rights of access. Before the County Governor's Office makes a decision it is obliged to have a discussion with any child who has reached the age of 12. In reality children older than 12 years decide for themselves whether they want to visit the other parent or not and therefore there is no reason to stipulate an access right when the child clearly expresses that it will not participate. A decision on access rights can in principle be executed by the bailiff, but if the child clearly refuses to comply the bailiff will not enforce the decision because it is seen as damaging to the welfare of the child. The access right is formulated as a right for the non-custodial parent, but this right does not impose a duty on the child to see the parent.

When the Convention was debated in parliament, the question was raised whether the dominant position of the custody-holders and their agreements was contrary to Article 16 on privacy and the Articles 13–15 on the child's freedom of expression, thought, consciousness, religion, association and peaceful assembly. It was concluded that Danish law was consistent with the Convention, because the Articles have to be interpreted in the light of Article 5 which states that the state shall respect parents' responsibilities, rights and duties to provide, in a manner consistent with the evolving capacities of the child, appropriate direction and guidance in the exercise by the child of the rights recognized in the Convention. The starting-point is that parents in general want to take care, and are capable of taking care, of their child and attending to their interests.

The provision in the 1995 Act regarding custody includes a right for the non-custodial parent to obtain information about the child. This may be problematic in relation to the 17 year-old person's right to privacy.

Placement outside the home

Young people participate in cases where removal from the family home is an issue. This constitutes more than a simple right to be heard. The child who is below the age of 15 has no status as such as a party but must be consulted if 12 years old or more.[45] It is a definite right for the child to express his opinion and wishes. The custodian parent cannot hinder the dialogue, but the child himself can refuse to participate. If the child actually has an opinion, and explains it to the social authorities, his viewpoint must be taken seriously. For children below the age of 12 there is a discretion to hear the child. Small children thus have no right to be heard, but if even a quite small child puts forward a thoughtful, relevant viewpoint it should be taken into account.

The child who has been placed outside the home has to respect reasonable limits put up by the foster parents no matter how old the child is. The child has no general right to self-determination, and ordinary decisions that make everyday life function and are a normal part of the raising of children are not even considered to be decisions in the meaning of the Social Welfare Act. There is no formal procedure, no possibility of appeal, no right to a lawyer or the like. If the foster parent cannot gain respect for their decisions, the City Council can decide the proportion and the exercise of visits and letter and telephone contact. Such a decision meets the criteria in the Social Welfare Act and gives the child a right to be heard as just described. The decision may be appealed to the Social Board of Appeal and young persons who are 15 years old or more can appeal on their own. If it is decided for a child in an institution that letters to and from the child have to be opened, this can only take place with the child's consent and he or she has to be present when it is done. Telephone calls can also only be listened to with the child's consent, and the other person has to be told that the conversation is being overheard. There is no age limit for the child and, if the control is rejected, the received letter will be sent back unopened, the written letter will be destroyed and the telephone call will be interrupted.

Most of these very severe decisions are made by a special Committee for Children and Young Persons under the City Council, and its decisions can be appealed. In relation to these decisions the young person is also considered to be a party with a right to appeal without consent from anybody. It is noteworthy that precisely in relation to control of communication and interruption of visits with the parents the young person has no right to a lawyer free of charge. It is also noteworthy that the Social Welfare Act in this respect sets limits to the child's right to be heard and hereby makes exceptions from the general rule in the Social Welfare Act, para. 124 a. As a starting-point the child and young person have a right to express their views before the decision is made, but if the child is below the age of 12 the committee can omit a consultation with the child for no specific reason and the committee can always omit to hear the child's viewpoint if it is thought it will damage the child no matter how old the child is. The restrictive approach to the child and young person's capability to cope with the situation once he or she has been placed is inconsistent with the approach adopted before the decision to place the child outside the home.

A new family: adoption and transfer of custody to third parties

In 1993, 1038 children were adopted in Denmark: 529 of the children were adopted by step-parents, and most of the remaining 509 came from abroad and were adopted by people unconnected to them. Most children involved in a foreign adoption are below the age of three, whereas most of the stepchildren are much older. Thus, in practice, the right for the child to express his or her own views is of considerable importance in relation to family adoptions. It does not make sense to ask a one year-old girl from Colombia whether or not she wants to be adopted. In principle, it is of course of equal importance to consult the child no matter of what country of origin, and the Danish Adoption Act does not distinguish between foreign and family adoptions in this respect.

The Danish Adoption Act is a stronger provision than Article 12 of the Convention, because it gives the child who has reached the age of 12 a right to refuse adoption.[46] The County Governor's Office will only authorize adoption it if is in the best interests of the child and if the older child gives his or her direct consent. The consent has to be given personally to a legally competent authority such as the County Governor's Office, and before the consent is accepted the authority is obliged to inform the child about the meaning and consequences of an adoption. If the child is coming from a foreign country the consent can be given to a recognized authority in the home country. The authorities can refrain from asking the child if it is thought damaging to the child. This part of the provision was passed to protect families where the child is unaware of the fact that one of its psychological parents is not its biological and legal parent and where it could damage the child to hear the truth at the moment of the application for adoption. This approach is not unproblematic in the light of newer research showing that concealment can cause more trouble than telling the truth.

The legal relationship with the biological parents is completely severed when a child is adopted. Sometimes the adults involved want to make a less irreversible move such as a partial transfer of parental rights. A father might, for instance, not be interested in giving up his parenthood. He might want to preserve his rights of access and, at the same time, he may accept that a new man now is the psychological father for the child in its everyday life. Custody can be given to one of the parents and his or her new spouse if all the adults involved agree.[47] The agreement will be recognized unless it is thought to be against the best interests of the child. Since joint custody in this case is based also on agreement, we are outside the scope of the formerly discussed para. 26. The child may be as old as 17, and yet the County Governor's Office is under no obligation to ask the child about its views on this construction. Before an agreement is recognized the adults are called to a meeting at the County Governor's Office where they are told about the legal implications of the custody transfer. Normally the child is not asked to participate in the meeting.

One way of protecting the child and recognizing that he or she is vulnerable and needs legal safeguards is to ensure that the child always has a custody-holder who can make legally binding decisions on behalf of the child. Therefore the Minors' Act (and Act on Custody)[48] imposes a duty on the County Governor's Office to appoint a new custodian if the former custody-holder has died and the minor is therefore without a formal custodian. The Minors' Act, para. 26 (Act on Custody s.29) is also applicable in this situation, and it is very likely that the County Governor will ask even a small child to express its opinion, since the child is not experiencing the same kinds of conflict of loyalty as in situations where the parents are disputing custody.

The debate on the child's right to self-determination and to be heard

Too little attention has been paid to the question of minor's self-determination in the Danish debate. The ratification of the UN Convention may, together with other initiatives, change this situation. It is a difficult matter. On the one hand we know that some children are very mature and capable of making decisions in relation to serious matters by the age of ten and that they would like to make other decisions that their parents undertake on their behalf, for instance in relation to psychiatric treatment, treatment for cancer and blood transfusions.[49] On the other hand, it can be very difficult for a child to be left responsible for impossible decisions on where and with whom to live, on treatment for all sorts of diseases, on parenthood and so on. It has been suggested that the age of majority be lowered from 18 to 15, but it may be more helpful to the child to establish a form of joint decision-making by imposing a duty on parents to inform children on matters of interest for their lives and to discuss possible choices and solutions at a level that corresponds with the child's age and maturity, and thus to listen to the child. In matters where the authorities are involved, such as custody, custody transfer and access, the authorities also ought to hear at least older children, when the adults agree, since the child may have good arguments against an agreement. The idea is not to free the parents – and the authorities – from their responsibilities as decision-makers but to show respect for the child's integrity and to strengthen a listening attitude towards children – to hear what they say.

As pointed out in the introductory remarks, any child who is capable of forming his or her own views according to the UN Child Convention article 12 should have the right to express those views in all matters concerning the child. The Danish legislation has the contrary point of departure, as persons under the age of 18 years have no autonomy. Decisions about a child's condition have been left with the custody holder or the guardian. Only if the custody holder or guardian so wishes are the views of the child taken into account. Danish legislation contains exceptions to this principle, but these are merely exceptions. The Committee has declared its dissatisfaction with this situation, based on the rights of parents and guardians, rather than those of the child, to express themselves and to be heard.

CONCLUSION

It has been emphasized that international treaties, as does national legislation, support the myths that reality is as described by national legislation and international conventions. The signing of an international convention therefore demands that a public follow-up of the realization of the convention's content is taking place in each state.

In more general terms there seems to be an ever-expanding segregation between children and adults in Danish society – part of a general tendency to segregate work from private life and to differentiate the roles of different family members. The goal of securing the child is probably best achieved by securing, first and foremost, safe motherhood. The individualization of social problems seems problematic. Children need to know their roots and traditions, and all children need more proud adults devoting their time to them. It should be emphasized that it is most essential for a child to be born as a loved and wanted human being to parents who emotionally can and will fulfil the task of bringing him or her to adulthood.

There is a perpetual necessity to be very cautious about the living conditions for children in general, especially for weak and vulnerable groups of children. The UN Convention on the Rights of the Child forms an excellent opportunity to reflect on children's rights and to go through legislation and practice to see where improvements can be made. In this respect, it is less important whether or not provisions conflict with the UN Convention, the main point is the wish to see legislation and practice from a child's, rather than an adult's perspective and to make the starting-point of departure and the goal of the analysis the 'welfare of the child'.

In Denmark the recent establishment of a Children's Council may serve as a catalyst for such a principle securing 'the best interest of the child'. The seven-member Council is independent and includes different kinds of professionals and others. The Minister of Social Affairs appoints the chairman and two members, and organizations dealing with children appoint four members. When appointing members it must be ensured that several areas are represented: children's development; children's school, cultural and leisure concerns; children's health; children's special needs; and children's rights. We must wait to see what impact this new organization has on children's rights in Denmark.

NOTES

1   In 1993 the Centre published an anthology about children's rights in Denmark (*Børns rettigheder i Danmark*) and also set up a task group to investigate whether Denmark observes the provisions of the Convention. In addition, the working group investigated whether legislation and practice should be changed in order to secure the protection of children's rights in Denmark in the best possible manner. In 1993 the working group published a report called *Law and Justice about Children* (*Lov og Ret om Børn*), published by the Danish Centre of Human Rights. This provides background material for this paper.

2   List of issues to be taken up in connection with the consideration of the initial report on Denmark. Concluding observations on the rights of the child: Denmark CRC/C/15/ Add33/1995. United Nations, Press Release, Rights of Danish Children examined by Children's Rights Committee: HR/CRC/95/16, 17/1995. Summary Record of the 199th, 200th and the 201st meeting held at the Palais des Nations, Geneva, on 19 and 20 January 1995. Contents: Considerations of reports of States parties, Denmark: CRC/C/ SR/199,200,201/1995. The Danish 'Red Barnet' (Save the Children Organization), which made an alternative report to the Danish governmental report, was – together with the Danish Centre of Human Rights – invited to participate in talks with the committee on 28 April 1994 in Geneva. A representative of the Danish Save The Children Organization, Eva Caspersen, has in a Danish article reflected upon the observance of the UN Child Convention in Denmark (*Juristen* 1995, pp. 275–83: 'Børnekonventionen og dens efterlevelse i Danmark').

3   Approximately 25 per cent of all couples live together without being married. In 1993

47 per cent of children were born outside marriage – the vast majority of which (90 per cent) were born to cohabitants.

4 Minors' Act, s.8 (Act No. 231 of 6 June 1985); Act on Custody and Access (Act No. 387 of 14 June 1995, coming into force 1 January 1996) s.42.

5 Minors' Act, s.10 (Custody Act, s.9).

6 If a man named by the mother acknowledges paternity, his legal paternity can be given recognition administratively by the County Governor. Otherwise the case must be submitted to the court.

7 Minors' Act, s.10; Custody Act, s.9.

8 Minors' Act, s.14 states that the change must be in the best interests of the child. Custody Act s.12 places cohabiting parents in an equal position.

9 Minors' Act, s.7; Custody Act, s.2.

10 Minors' Act, s.27a; Custody Act, s.28.

11 Of course, this is conditional on the mother's consent.

12 The legal effects of marriage and cohabitation is outlined in Linda Nielsen (1995), 'Family law in Denmark' in Carolyn Hamilton and Kate Standley (eds), *Family Law in Europe*, London: Butterworths.

13 The act is primarily based on a report from a Law Reform Commission regarding joint custody, difficulties in visitation and counselling: 'Betænkning nr. 1279/1994 om fælles forældremyndighed, samværsvanskeligheder, børnesagkyndig rådgivning'.

14 Act No. 503 of 24 August 1992. The legislation came into force in October 1992 with a statutory obligation to undertake review and revision if necessary by 1995–96. A new bill is expected to be presented in 1995–96.

15 Provisions on cryopreservation and donation of human eggs (*Bekendtgørelse nr. 392 af 7.5.1994, om nedfrysning og donation af menneskelige æg*).

16 Protection of human gametes, fertilized eggs, pre-embryos and embryos. (*Beskyttelse af menneskelige kønsceller, befrugtede æg, fosteranlæg og fostre*) 1989.

17 Infertility treatment (*Behandling af ufrivillig barnløshed*) 1992.

18 See Civil Service Act, s.4, and Public Administration Act, s.9ff.

19 Act no. 503 of 30.6.1993, which came into force on 1 January 1994.

20 See provisions on cryopreservation and donation of human eggs. (*Bekendtgørelse nr. 392 af 7.5.1994 om nedfrysning og donation af menneskelige æg*).

21 The Danish Centre of Human Rights refers to the court decision from the European Courts on Human Rights of 18 December 1986, in the case of *Johnston* and Others (Publications of the European Court of Human Rights n. 112, Köln, Berlin, Bonn, München: Carl Heymanns Verlag, 1986).

22 Decision of the European Court of Human Rights of 7 July 1989 (Publications of the European Court of Human Rights n. 160, Köln, Berlin, Bonn, München: Carl Heymanns Verlag, 1989).

23 In a report from the conference with the theme of infertility (*Barnløshed. Teknologi-Nævnets rapporter 1993/4*), different aspects of infertility were debated, including essays *inter alia* by Monica Tafdrup Notkin and Linda Nielsen about donation and anonymity.

24 See on the topic of Linda Nielsen (1993), 'The right to a child versus the right of a child' in John Eekelaar and Petar Sarcevic (eds), *Parenthood in Modern Society*, Dordrecht: Nijhoff, pp. 213–21; Linda Nielsen and Derek Morgan (1993), 'Prisoners of progress or hostages to fortune?' in *Journal of Law, Medicine and Ethics*, **21**, (1), pp. 30–43; and Linda Nielsen and Derek Morgan (1992), 'Dangerous liaison? Law, technology, reproduction and European ethics' in Shaun McVeigh and Sally Wheeler (eds), *Law, Health and Medical Regulation*, Dartmouth, pp. 52–7.

25   For a more detailed description see Linda Nielsen (1994), 'Procreative Tourism and the Law', paper presented at the Eighth World Conference of The International Society of Family Law on 'Parenthood in a changing society', Cardiff (to be published in a forthcoming book).

26   Minor's Act s.7, subs. 2 (now Act on Custody and Access, s.2).

27   Social Security, Act, s.20.

28   Social Security Act, s.32, subs. 1.

29   The remedies are described in The Social Service Act, Chapters 8 and 15a. The procedure is laid down in Chapter 18.

30   The following is based on Beth Grothe Nielsen (1991), *Sexual Infringement of Children in the Family*, (*Seksuelle Overgreb mod Børn i Familien*), Åarhus.

31   Criminal Code, s.210, 222 and 223. The general provisions on sexual offences such as rape are, in principle, also applicable.

32   Administration of Justice Act, s.741a, subs. 1.

33   While discussions on the described kind of violence has taken place for several years before the UN Convention was ratified, Article 24(3) has played a more important role in stimulating a debate in Denmark on the circumcision of girls. The phenomenon has become more visible over the last years due to the fact that more people with circumcision as a part of their cultural background have come to live in Denmark. Although it is important to recognize different cultures and seek understanding between people all over the world, we do not consider that this obligation extends to the molesting of girls. To perform female circumcision is without doubt a violation of the Criminal Code, s. 245 and should stay so.

34   Social Welfare Act, ss.33 and 35.

35   Social Welfare Act, ss.128–30.

36   Social Welfare Act, s.66b. A plan also has to be made when the child is placed outside the home with consent from the parties.

37   Social Welfare Act, s.67.

38   Social Welfare Act, s.66(5); cf. s.14(7).

39   For a more detailed description see Lis Frost (1994), 'Children's rights to family life and privacy', paper presented at the Eighth World Conference of The International Society of Family Law, Cardiff, June.

40   Minors' Act, s.7; Custody Act, s.2.

41   Minors' Act, s.26; Custody Act, s.29.

42   Administration of Justice Act, s.450a.

43   See Lis Frost and Ingrid Lund-Andersen (1994), 'Child abduction – a Danish perspective' in Lis Frost (ed.), *International Family Law. A Scandinavian Approach*, Åarhus, p. 99ff.

44   Abduction Act s.16.

45   Social Welfare Act, s.124a.

46   Adoption Act, s.6.

47   Minors' Act, s.13 (Act on Custody s.11).

48   Minors' Act, s.15 (Act on Custody s.14).

49   A consent from the person with parental rights is normally required in relation to medical treatment.

5   The Convention: An English Perspective

*Michael Freeman**

When Lloyd de Mause referred to childhood as a 'nightmare'[1] he wrote in very general terms, but many would claim that childhood as experienced by English children has come close to this description. Of course, things have changed since the graphic portrayals in such Victorian novels as *Jane Eyre*, *David Copperfield* and *The Way of All Flesh*, but these changes in child-rearing and in attitudes have been recent and are, perhaps, not all that profound. It is with this historical understanding in mind that I come to appraise the question of children's rights in England. There are references to the importance of children's rights in English case law[2] from the 1970s onwards. The UK, it is true, has ratified the UN Convention on the Rights of the Child,[3] albeit belatedly, although its support for the Convention was half-hearted, with a number of reservations being entered.[4] An aura of complacency greeted its ratification – the responsible government minister, Virginia Bottomley, saying publicly on several occasions that 'of course' English law went further than the Convention. Here, she was referring principally to the Children Act of 1989,[5] hailed, as has been each previous Children Act, as a 'children's charter'.[6] As we shall see, although certain features of the Act highlight a child's autonomy, other values dominate the Act and, it may be thought, 'trump' children's rights.[7] The judiciary has continued to assert, as did one of its number, Lord Justice Butler-Sloss in the *Cleveland* report,[8] that children are 'persons and not objects of concern'.[9] Yet this principle has not been upheld consistently in practice, even by judges, like Butler-Sloss, who proclaim it most vociferously.

This chapter examines some of the key provisions in the Convention and appraises English law and practice in the light of them. In taking this

*Professor of English Law, University College London, co-editor of the *International Journal of Children's Rights*.

approach my intention is not to endorse the Convention as the final word on children's rights. There are provisions in it, often reflections of international compromise,[10] which could be redrafted to show distinct improvements. But that is not the goal of this chapter: it is to show ways in which English law can be improved in the light of the current world consensus on the status of children. The chapter does not purport to be an exhaustive examination of the issues raised, since each Article of the Convention could occupy a paper in itself. All that is attempted here is to highlight problems, point to short-comings and to suggest improvements and modifications in English law and practice.

THE BEST INTERESTS OF THE CHILD

Article 3 is, together with Article 12, arguably the most important provision in the Convention. It provides in subparagraph 1:

> In all actions concerning children, whether undertaken by public or private social welfare institutions, courts of law, administrative authorities or legislative bodies, the best interests of the child shall be a primary consideration.

It will be observed that the Convention says that the children's best interests are 'a primary consideration', not *the* primary consideration or *the paramount* consideration. It is regrettable that the Convention does not set a standard as high as that found in English law.[11] Where the child's interests are paramount they 'determine' the course to be followed.[12] On the other hand, the *scope* of the provision far exceeds the range of decisions within the remit of English law in section 1 of the Children Act 1989. English law applies the paramountcy principle only to courts and not even to all court decisions. In adoption the child's welfare is only the 'first consideration'[13] (this is in line with the UN standard). In divorce, the child's welfare is not considered at all, although it is the 'first consideration' when matters of money and property are considered[14] – at least that is the theory, for the Child Support Act of 1991 has clearly prioritized the rights of taxpayers over the interests of children.[15] In situations where one parent is trying to oust the other from the family home, because of violence or other molestation, the child's welfare is merely one consideration:[16] the Court of Appeal was quick to point out that the Children Act had not changed the law on this.[17] Even in wardship, where the 'golden thread' is that the child's welfare comes 'first, last and all the time',[18] the courts have found questions relating to children which are not governed by the paramountcy rule.[19]

Outside 'courts of law', as narrowly construed, there are a vast range of tribunals dealing with matters affecting children which are in no way bound by the 'best interests' principle. The *Bulger* case[20] has reminded us that criminal courts are not so constrained: in what sense can the trial processes, which were in no way adapted to the needs of 11 year-olds – and, indeed, the sentence in that case – be said to be impressed by the best interests of the two boys involved? It tends to be forgotten that in many European countries Thompson and Venables, who were aged ten at the time of their crime, could not have stood trial: indeed even in England had they committed the murder of James Bulger six months earlier they would have been presumed conclusively to lack the capacity for criminal activity.[21] Yet the Home Secretary, bowing to public pressure, purported to increase their sentences by executive act.

So far as tribunals are concerned the list is endless, and only a few will be picked out for comment. Tribunals hearing nationality and immigration appeals are not bound by any best interests principle. Tribunals in the education system, hearing appeals on such matters as school choice, school exclusions and special educational needs are not so bound. Nor are social security tribunals, although these may hear appeals from young people of 16 and 17 who are denied benefits.

Outside the courts, the absence of the 'best interests' principle in any number of areas calls out for examination. Perhaps most glaring of all is the way successive Education Acts have shamefacedly refused to acknowledge children's rights in the area of education. The message conveyed by recent education legislation is very clear: the consumers of education are the parents, not the children. Similarly, housing legislation contains no 'best interests' principle: the placement of a child in 'bed and breakfast' accommodation can thus not be challenged by reference to any principle such as that in the Children Act (or UN Convention). This leaves unanswered the question whether a judicial review examining such a decision would be governed by the paramountcy principle. It is an interesting argument, but not one likely to succeed.

Even social services departments' obligations do not necessarily extend to giving first consideration to children's interests. The Children Act requires them to 'safeguard and promote the welfare of children within their area who are in need'.[22] But 'in need' can be, and in practice is, interpreted restrictively.[23] There is a thin line between setting priorities and reinterpreting legislation. The latter is unlawful, but a successful challenge to it would be difficult to mount.

The Children Act requirements have gone a long way towards ensuring that institutions dealing with children act in their best interests. There are duties on community homes, voluntary homes, private children's homes, independent boarding schools,[24] (although the duties as regards these have already been diluted). But these duties – to safeguard and promote the child's welfare – do not apply to maintained schools or to non-maintained special schools. There is no best interests principle either in the health service or in the penal system.

THE CHILD'S RIGHTS OF PARTICIPATION

Article 12 of the Convention requires State Parties to:

> ... assure to the child who is capable of forming his or her own views the right to express those views freely in all matters affecting the child, the views of the child being given due weight in accordance with the age and maturity of the child.

For this purpose, the child is to be given '[t]he opportunity to be heard in any judicial and administrative proceedings affecting the child'.

In formulating this right the Convention goes well beyond earlier international documents.[25] It is the first explicitly to state that children have a right to have a say in processes affecting their lives. Marta Pais has argued that this converts the child into a 'principal' in the Convention, and that this is an act of enormous symbolic importance.[26] Article 12 can be seen as a development from the child liberation philosophy of the 1970s,[27] and it is in line with the House of Lords *Gillick* decision in 1985.[28] In Lord Scarman's words, 'parental right yields to the child's right to make his own decisions when he reaches a sufficient understanding and intelligence to be capable of making up his own mind on the matter requiring decision'.[29]

The initial impression is thus that English law complies with Article 12, and there is much in the Children Act to reinforce this perception. A child, admittedly after leave (perhaps an unnecessary and unjustifiable filter), can seek a residence or contact order. Courts making decisions about a child's upbringing, albeit in a limited range of circumstances, are required to have regard to the 'ascertainable wishes and feelings of the child concerned' in the light of that child's age and understanding.[30] Local authorities, before making any decision concerning a child whom they are looking after or are proposing to look after, are required to ascertain the wishes and feelings of that child, so far as this is reasonably practicable.[31] There is a range of provisions in the Children Act allowing a child of sufficient understanding to make an informed decision the right to refuse to submit to a medical or psychiatric examination or other assessment in the context of a child assessment order, emergency protection or similar protective measure.[32]

It is, however, worth examining this example, itself a logical progression from the *Gillick* ruling, to see how the judges have interpreted it. When this is done we encounter an interpretational backlash, as judges confront what they see as the reality of the problem. The result of a number of cases is that the *Gillick* principle does not seem to confer upon a competent child a power to veto over treatment, but merely allows him (or her) to give valid consent to such treatment.[33] A girl of 15, if competent within the terms of the *Gillick* test, can thus consent to an abortion but, should she refuse consent, her pregnancy can nevertheless still be terminated.[34] While the consent of a *Gillick*-competent child cannot be overridden by those with parental responsibility, except by the court, the Court of Appeal ruled in *Re W* (a case of a 16 year-old anorexic girl who tried to starve herself) that *refusal* to accept treatment by such a child can be overridden by someone who has parental responsibility. The Master of the Rolls, Lord Donaldson, did, however, concede that 'such a refusal is a very important consideration in making clinical judgments and for the parents and the court in deciding whether themselves to give consent'.[35] Lowe and Juss have said that 'in this way ... the court fuses the principle of child autonomy with the practice of intervention'.[36] This may be so. But what does it leave to child autonomy? It is hardly surprising that, in *South Glamorgan C.C.* v. *W and B*,[37] a first-instance judge should hold that, despite the statutory right of veto in s.38(6) of the Children Act (and, presumably, also that conferred by s.43(8), referred to above, s.44(7) and Schedule 3, para. 4), the court could exercise its inherent jurisdiction to override the child's refusal.

These cases show a judiciary unable to digest the implications of the Children Act – and, it should be added, the UN Convention. And it leaves the law in a mess. Significant questions are raised, not least what children can do if they believe that they are unfairly deemed to be incompetent. That they can seek a specific issue order from a court is hardly a satisfactory answer, but it is the last resort.

The Children Act is quite positive on Article 12, but not consistently so. Whereas it offers considerable scope for the representation of a child's wishes and feelings in the public welfare area,[38] when it comes to private law disputes such as divorce, it is difficult to see where, if at all, the wishes and feelings of the child are considered or can be represented. The child is not independently represented: the emphasis on the guardian *ad litem* in public law is quietly overlooked in such private law disputes.[39] It seems to be forgotten that the child may need independent representation as much when his or her parents are at war as when there is some conflict between them and the local authority – for example when abuse or neglect is alleged. There is, it seems, no voice for the child in divorce.[40] In relation to divorce, the Children Act is parent-centred, rather than child-centred, legislation.

Whether this would improve under new proposals for divorce[41] may also be doubted.

But then it might be asked why children should be able to express their views at the juncture of a divorce when the law provides no mechanism for them to have a say at home. In English law, as in virtually every other legal system, parents do not have to ascertain or have regard to their children's wishes before making decisions, even major ones, which affect the child. In Finland the Child Custody and Right of Access Act of 1983 states that before a parent who has custody

> ... makes a decision on a matter relating to the person of the child, he or she shall, where possible, discuss the matter with the child taking into account the child's age and maturity and the nature of the matter. In making the decision the custodian shall give due consideration to the child's feelings, opinions and wishes.[42]

The Scottish Law Commission is also attracted to this idea. It considered that there might be a value in such a provision 'even if it was vague and unenforceable' for it could have an influence upon behaviour.'[43] There is considerable force in this argument. If parents were expected to take their children's opinions and wishes seriously, they would probably demand similar attention to the rights of children to participate given by public authorities. And this, despite the Children Act, certainly does not happen at present.

A clear example of this failing occurs in the field of education. There is a certain irony in this, for one of the aims of education is to enhance the capacity for decision-making and yet, in crucial areas, participation in major decisions is removed from those most affected by those decisions. Article 12(2) provides that children should be given an opportunity to be heard in judicial and administrative proceedings affecting them, but such provision is egregiously absent from school exclusion procedures, in the procedures for choosing a school and in school choice appeals and in the entire discussion over such matters as the school curriculum. English education law bears little resemblance to the participatory model spelled out in Article 12, but when attempts were made during the passage of the Education Act 1993 to incorporate a right of the child to be heard in line with this Article, the government minister in charge came close to calling the idea 'dotty' and condemned it as 'politically correct'. The irony in this is that the 1993 Education Act is the first major children's legislation passed since the UK ratified the Convention, yet the government scorned an obvious opportunity to bring the law into line with international obligations.

ABUSE AND NEGLECT

Article 19 requires State Parties to:

> ... take all appropriate legislative, administrative, social and educational measures to protect the child from all forms of physical or mental violence, injury or abuse, neglect or negligent treatment, maltreatment or exploitation including sexual abuse. ...

English law, both criminal and civil, clearly targets abuse and neglect.[44] Parents who abuse or neglect children may be prosecuted,[45] and protective measures using emergency protection[46] and care and supervision orders are available.[47] The linchpin of the protective system is 'significant harm'.[48] A care or supervision order may be made if a child is suffering significant harm or is likely to suffer significant harm if no order is made, and this is attributable to the quality of parental care not being what a reasonable parent could give or the child being beyond parental control. The Children Act extended the ambit of care to include suspicion that a child is at risk.[49]

There have been other statutory changes recently which have made it easier for children's accounts of abuse, in particular of sexual abuse, to be brought before a criminal court.[50] US research findings[51] indicate that the introduction of these innovatory techniques to assist the abused child to give evidence are not working successfully – for example, prosecutors are reluctant to use them for fear that juries will believe they have a weak case. There is no replicating evidence in England, but a suspicion that similar patterns of underuse would be found here too. The lesson is clear: changing laws (in this case procedures) changes nothing unless you also convert those who are to operate the new laws or administer the processes to their value. It has also become more difficult to prove abuse in the civil courts, as the courts, in a well-meaning effort to protect innocent parents, have increased the standard of proof.[52]

But laws also achieve little without the injection of resources: one of the lessons of the English struggle to conquer child abuse is of the failure to address the resources question. Social services departments are consistently reporting that they have children on child protection registers with no social worker allocated to them.[53] Reports of inquiries into child deaths have constantly reiterated the need for greater resources to target families at risk.

Article 19, though, goes beyond abuse in its narrow and accepted sense. It pledges states to protect children from 'all forms of physical ... violence'. English law, however, permits parents and others to use 'reasonable chastisement'.[54] The provision in the Children and Young Persons Act 1933 which criminalizes wilful assault on a child, specifically excludes physical punishment.[55] The Newson studies point to its prevalence in England and to the fact that the use of an implement or its threat remains common.[56] Five European countries have prohibited all physical punishment of children (Sweden in 1979; Finland in 1984; Norway in 1987; Austria in 1989 and Cyprus in 1994).[57] A recommendation of the Council of Europe Committee of Ministers in 1985 hoped that Member States (the UK is one) would 'review their legislation on the power to punish children in order to limit or indeed prohibit corporal punishment, even if violation of such a prohibition does not entail a criminal penalty'.[58] Yet, in England, one of the controversies of 1993–94 concerned the 'right' of a childminder to smack children, with prominent government ministers support that right.[59]

The Children Act, while it continued the progress towards outlawing corporal punishment outside the home (though apparently without extending the ban to child-minders) did not take up the issue of physical chastisement by parents. And yet nothing is a clearer statement of the position that children occupy in society, nor a clearer badge of childhood, than the fact that children are the only members of society who can be hit with impunity. There is probably no more significant step that could be taken to advance both the status and protection of children than to outlaw the practice of physical punishment. Much child abuse is, we know, punishment which has gone terribly wrong. England thus continues to allow moderate and reasonable physical chastisement but Sweden in its Parent and Guardianship Code outlaws not just the hitting of children but 'other injurious or humiliating treatment' as well.[60] Is it too much to hope that England will follow the lead of Sweden and the other European countries that have declared the hitting of children to be unacceptable? For how much longer will what has been called 'the English vice'[61] continue? When will the UK legislature bow to the inevitable and accept that the legitimization of violence against children is unacceptable in a civilized society?

FREEDOM OF EXPRESSION

The Convention states that the child shall have the right to 'freedom of expression' (Article 13). This right is to include

> ... freedom to seek, receive and impart information and ideas of all kinds ... either orally, in writing or in print, in the form of art, or through any other media of the child's choice.

The only restrictions (Article 13(2)) are to protect the rights and reputations of others (the law of defamation, for example) and to protect national security and public order as well as public health and morals. The Convention states that the child's right to freedom of expression *includes* the forms of expression listed, but it is therefore not exhaustive of them. The 'freedom to hold opinions and to receive and impart information and ideas without interference by public authority'[62] in the European Convention on Human Rights is thus arguably also embraced within Article 13.

There are a number of ways in which English law fails to sustain this freedom. Governmental intrusions on school curricula, limiting teaching about homosexuality,[63] forbidding 'the pursuit of partisan political activities by pupils' and the 'promotion of partisan political views' in the teaching of any subject in the school,[64] restricting sex education[65] are all potentially breaches of Article 13.

The insistence by schools on the wearing of school uniforms may also be considered to be a breach of Article 13. English courts have upheld headteachers' insistence on the wearing of uniforms, in one case agreeing with a headteacher who sent home a girl who wore trousers (she had had rheumatic fever, but no doctor's letter was offered in support of her mother's decision to send her to school so dressed).[66] The European Commission in the *Stevens* case in 1986 rejected a mother's application which alleged that the rules on school uniform breached her and her son's rights under the European Convention. But it admitted that 'the right to freedom of expression may include the right of a person to express his ideas through the way he dresses'.[67] In this case, the Commission considered that it had not been established on the facts that the child had been prevented from expressing a particular 'opinion or idea by means of ... clothing'. What, then, of a child refused permission to wear a CND badge, an earring signifying homosexuality or a kippah proclaiming a commitment to Judaism? In 1969 the US Supreme Court upheld school students' rights to wear black armbands to protest the Vietnam war. 'It can hardly be argued', it pronounced, 'that either students or teachers lose their constitutional rights to freedom of speech or expression at the schoolhouse gate.'[68] English schools regularly breach both the letter and spirit of this principle and have hitherto got away with it, although there is a strong, arguable case that the Convention would find many of their practices unacceptable. It is also difficult to see how they could be defended in terms of Article 13(2) of the UN Convention.

FREEDOM OF THOUGHT, CONSCIENCE AND RELIGION

The Convention requires State Parties to respect the right of the child to freedom of thought, conscience and religion.[69] Freedom to demonstrate religious beliefs may be subjected only to such limitations 'necessary to protect public safety, order, health or morals or the protection of the rights and freedoms of others'. The European Convention on Human Rights lays down a similar right, although it does so in stronger terms emphasizing the right to change religion and to 'manifest religion in worship, teaching, practice and observance'.[70]

Nowhere does English law articulate similar norms. To conform with the UN Convention there ought to be statutory confirmation of the rights set out in the Convention. Schools which deny Muslim children the opportunity to pray on Fridays or insist upon Jewish children attending schools on Saturday clearly breach the UN Convention. English education law, which gives parents a right to withdraw their children from religious worship and instruction in schools and even allows them to request special lessons in a particular religion, also breaches the Convention because it does not give children themselves similar rights.[71] The continuing reluctance of UK governments to approve funding for voluntary-aided Muslim schools – while allowing this for Church of England, Catholic and Jewish schools – is a breach of both the 'religion' Article (Article 14) and of Article 2.[72] The imposition by the Education Reform Act of 1988 of collective worship 'of a broadly Christian character' may result in breaches of Article 29 for it can hardly be said to inculcate respect for the child's cultural identity and values, in cases where the child belongs to a minority group.[73] Demands by some,[74] allegedly in the cause of children's rights, to ban circumcision of male babies clearly also fly in the face of the freedom of religion article. The UK government has resisted the weak arguments proffered to outlaw the practice – as indeed has every other government today. It has been banned in such formerly 'rights-conscious' countries as the Soviet Union and Nazi Germany. Is further comment necessary?

Children in care may not be brought up 'in any religious persuasion other than that in which [they] would have been brought up if the order had not been made'.[75] On one level this is right, but what of the child in care who does not wish to be brought up in the religion of his or her family, perhaps associating it with the abuse to which he or she has been previously subjected? Or the child who does not wish to be brought up in any religion? In theory, the *Gillick* case should cater for such children, provided, of course, they are deemed both to have sufficient understanding of the issues and to have sufficient maturity and intelligence to have considered them rationally. Certainly, regulations under the Children Act[76] should satisfy this requirement, but in practice the Christian ethos of many UK child-care organizations may not make this particularly easy.

It may be noted also that wards of court are, at least in theory, also denied freedom of religion, since the court has the power to direct this.[77] In practice, it is doubtful whether the problem exists. Nevertheless, it ought to be made clear by statute that the powers of the wardship court, in effect the inherent jurisdiction of the High Court,[78] cannot be used in derogation from the principle set out in the UN Convention on the Rights of the Child.

FREEDOM OF ASSOCIATION

The Convention recognizes the right of the child to freedom of association and to freedom of peaceful assembly, subject only to restrictions necessary in a 'democratic society in the interests of national security or public safety, public order, the protection of public health or morals or the protection of the rights and freedoms of others'.[79]

The refusal of UK schools to allow union activity or, for example, CND meetings or anti-apartheid meetings or meetings to celebrate a particular national day of an ethnic group within a school breaches this Article. The UK has passed a new Education Act almost annually in recent years. Is it too much to hope that the next one will encode some basic rights for schoolchildren? Similar problems arise in the context of local authority care: it is known that the National Association of Young People in Care (NAYPIC) has had difficulty organizing in some areas. Again, it has to be stressed that local authorities which obstruct such activity are in breach of the UN Convention.

It is doubtful whether UK public order legislation, in particular the restrictive Public Order Act of 1986 and the new Criminal Justice and Public Order Act of 1994, satisfies the Convention. The offence of 'disorderly conduct' in the 1986 Act is wider than the exceptions allowed in this Article. Certainly, the police could interpret it, and have interpreted it, to restrict gatherings by young people. The new powers in the 1994 Act, for example, in relation to 'raves',[80] and the new offences of aggravated trespass and trespassory assembly, will confine assembly by the young even further.

THE PROTECTION OF PRIVACY

Article 16 of the Convention states:

> No child shall be subjected to arbitrary or unlawful interference with his or her privacy, family, home or correspondence, nor to unlawful attacks on his or her honour and reputation.

A child's privacy is largely controlled by parents or other caretakers, and the physical privacy that parents can offer is also largely related to their income and other resources. The poor have never had much privacy: their lives have always been more public than that of more affluent people. The privacy provision cannot, therefore, be entirely disentangled from another Article in the Convention which proclaims the right of every child to an adequate standard of living.[81] Children condemned to live in bed and breakfast accommodation, perhaps because local authority housing is sold to potential Tory voters as in the City of Westminster,[82] have neither an adequate standard of living nor any degree of privacy. It may also be added that they are hardly likely to have the opportunities for play and recreational activities set out in the Convention[83] or, indeed, to find the right to education,[84] guaranteed by the Convention, of much import.

A child's privacy is interfered with in a number of ways. Within the home this may be difficult to provide for, but in institutions, where there is widespread abuse of privacy, English law has done far too little to protect the freedom guaranteed by Article 16. Even where attempts have been made – for example, by Regulation under the Children Act –[85] there is growing evidence that these attempts are frustrated in practice. The right to private correspondence is not protected in all institutions which house children and young persons. In some residential institutions children cannot even use toilets in complete privacy and there may be communal bathing facilities only. There are also institutions in which young women's menstrual cycles are monitored by staff. In some children's homes – notably, but not exclusively, secure accommodation – closed-circuit video cameras and two-way mirrors are used to observe children. This may be done without their knowledge, let alone their consent.

There are many other ways in which a child's privacy is invaded and to which all too little attention has been given. For example, the growing UK practice of advertising children for adoption with exposure of biographical details and the use of a photograph is a clear breach of Article 16. Whether the practice should be stopped is another matter. If adoption or another form of permanent placement is in the best interests of the child concerned, it may be thought unduly legalistic to insist upon this 'lesser' right and therefore sacrifice a 'greater' one. This Convention does after all, in Article 21, mandate those countries which permit adoption to 'ensure that the best interests of the child shall be the paramount consideration' (a provision with which, as we shall see, English law does not currently comply). At the very least it must be hoped that the current 'advertising' practice would be subjected to sustained scrutiny and reasoned debate.

ADOPTION

As already indicated, English law falls short of its Convention obligations in relation to Article 21, the adoption article.

First, the 'best interests' of the child is only the 'first consideration' in adoption proceedings in England.[86] The Convention requires them to be the 'paramount' consideration. 'First' suggests, as is indeed the case, that there are other considerations, such as the rights of biological parents: 'paramount' suggests, by contrast, that the best interests of the child should be determinative. If the report of the Inter-Departmental Review on Adoption is implemented, English law will be brought into line with the Convention,[87] but there are no immediate plans for this to be done.

Second, the Convention requires that the 'persons concerned [should] have given their informed consent to the adoption on the basis of such counselling as may be necessary' (Article 21(a)). In England, counselling is not always available and, where given, is often offered after the adoption has taken place. Furthermore, English law (unlike that in Scotland[88]) has never required the consent of the person most concerned, namely the child. Again, the recent Adoption Review will, if and when implemented, remedy, at least partially, this defect. However, its proposal that the age of 12 is the appropriate age for consent[89] is unduly cautious: a child can clearly express a desire for or against a particular adoption at a much earlier age than this. I would advocate fixing the age at no higher than seven years old. A transplant to a new family is too important a step to contemplate against the wishes of a child able to express wishes and feelings about its desirability.

Third, there is the issue of intercountry adoption. This was one of the more controversial areas covered by the Convention, with some countries, notably Venezuela, being understandably unhappy with the whole concept.[90] It needs to be said that if other provisions in the Convention were universally fulfilled (adequate standard of living,[91] adequate health care for mothers and children[92] being the most obvious examples), there would be little need for intercountry adoption. But in the foreseeable future, and particularly in the light of the upheavals in Eastern Europe in the late 1980s and early 1990s, there will be a felt necessity to rescue children from orphanages and bring them to more prosperous and stable countries such as the UK. However, English law does appear insufficient to assist the process of intercountry adoption – the *Luff* decision, in particular, showed an insensitivity to the needs of Romanian orphans.[93] But where intercountry adoption is allowed, it is clear that English law and practice falls short of the Convention obligation to ensure that the safeguards and standards are 'equivalent' to those existing in the case of national adoption. With the implementation of the Hague Convention on the Protection of Children and cooperation in respect of intercountry adoption of May 1993 this should change. But we must wait and see.

HEALTH AND HEALTH SERVICES

The Convention states that:

> States Parties recognise the right of the child to the enjoyment of the highest attainable standard of health and to facilities for the treatment of illness and rehabilitation of health.[94]

States are to 'strive to ensure that no child is deprived of his or her right of access to such health care services'. The UK sets no standards, as such, for children's health services, nor is there any sense that the allocation of resources within the National Health Service reflects the needs of children. There are also known to be wide regional variations in health-care provision. Furthermore, poverty is strongly associated with increased risk to child health,[95] so that full implementation of this Article requires sustained measures to eradicate child poverty. Yet, the incidence of child poverty has increased steeply during the 16 years of the Conservative administration: in 1979 one in ten children was living in a low-income family; today poverty hits one in three.[96]

However, part of the problem lies in the fact that the health of children, indeed, of the population generally, is the responsibility of unelected health authorities whose power to purchase services is now shared with fund-holding general practitioners (GPs). As the number of such GPs and the types of health care they may purchase increases, the balance of purchasing power is shifting away from the health authority. But there is no way of knowing whether GPs have the same values regarding health as health authorities or whether either of them shares the values of the general public. A recent study by Bowling,[97] however, indicated that doctors gave much greater priority to reducing mental illness than was given by the public. Do they target child health as the public would wish them to do? We have no way of knowing.

In particular, Article 24 requires a number of measures. It requires measures to be taken to diminish infant and child mortality.[98] This has declined in the UK, but the decline has slowed,[99] is slower than many comparable countries and is high in comparison with, for example, France, Italy and Sweden.[100] The UK has the highest post-neonatal mortality rate of seven European countries as reported in a 1990 study.[101] The Article also requires an emphasis on primary health care. There is concern that recent changes in the delivery of health services may work to the detriment of this, particularly as regards children.

The Article further requires measures to tackle the 'dangers and risks of environmental pollution'.[102] There is evidence of an association between respiratory illnesses in children and the degree of pollution in the areas where they live.[103] More could be done to cut air pollution. Much more could be done to tackle smoking now that the evidence of the effects of passive smoking is incontestable. Smoking could be banned in public places; cigarette advertising could be stopped, including sponsorship of sporting and other events; taxation on tobacco products could be vastly increased; and more could be done to discourage young people from smoking. The right to a smoke-free environment must trump[104] the so-called freedom of smokers to destroy themselves and others. Questions must also be raised about nuclear installations in light of the growing evidence of a clear association between them and childhood leukaemia.[105] An EEC Directive of 1980[106] was supposed to be implemented by 1982: the UK was not fully in compliance with this in the early 1990s (there were promises of full compliance by 1993) but it is doubtful whether, in the north of England in particular, air quality is satisfactory.[107]

Article 24 also requires appropriate pre- and postnatal health care for mothers. There are regional variations here, as well as class differences, and little doubt that more could be done. Health education is also inadequate; neither is it included in the National Curriculum.[108]

Article 24 also contains one of the most controversial provisions in the Convention. In paragraph 3, States Parties are required to take 'all effective and appropriate measures with a view to abolishing traditional practices prejudicial to the health of children'. The UK has legislation prohibiting female circumcision[109] which was the principal target of the provision, but it cannot be said that the legislation is working very effectively. There have been no prosecutions in England. France takes a more heavy-handed approach to the problem, and parents there have been imprisoned for performing such acts on their daughters. The problem might be better resolved by means of education, but there is little evidence of any such campaign among the communities concerned in the UK.

A number of children's rights advocates, including Alice Miller, Penelope Leach and Peter Newell, continue to associate infant male circumcision with the practice of female genital mutilation,[110] although there is no evidence that this practice, properly carried out, is prejudicial to the health of male babies. Other traditional practices have been targeted at various times: for example, the Yoruba practice of making excisions in the faces of male children was the subject of a well publicized prosecution in 1974,[111] although there is little doubt that the practice continues. Ear and nose piercing arguably also falls within the purview of this Article but, in a world where children are victimized in so many more harmful ways, it hardly warrants attention.

A CONCLUDING COMMENT

This survey has shown that complacency about children's rights in England is totally misplaced. It has directed attention to some of the areas where legislative change is required, where practice needs to be better monitored, where greater thought has to be given to protecting the interests and furthering the rights of children.

Progress towards these ends needs a structure. The development of such a structure is beyond the scope of this chapter, but I offer the following tentative suggestions.

1   The UN Convention should be incorporated into English law:[112] breach of a provision of the Convention should be an infringement of English law with all the implications that this would have.
2   The concept of a child impact statement should be introduced.[113] All legislation, including subsidiary and local, should be accompanied by an assessment of its effect on children. This should apply also to health plans, education innovations (the National Curriculum for example) and other policy changes.
3   The UK should follow the example of Norway[114] and other countries[115] which have introduced the concept of an ombudsman for children. Such an office would be information-gathering, complaint-receiving and litigation-initiating. It would also monitor UK compliance with the Convention and publicize areas where law and practice fall short of the ideals and norms in the Convention.

The structure sketched here would give some teeth to the Convention in the UK. The Convention has to be seen as a beginning, but it will not have an impact on the lives of children until the obligations it lays down are taken seriously by legislatures, governments and all others concerned with the daily lives of children – in reality, by all the nation's adults.

NOTES

1   Lloyd de Mause (1976), *The History of Childhood*, London: Souvenir Press, p.1.
2   For example, *M* v. *M* [1973] 2 All ER 81, the first decision to hold that access to a parent is a child's right.

3   See B. Walsh (1991), 'The United Nations Convention on the Rights of the Child: A British View', *International Journal of the Law and Family*, **5**, p. 170.

4   Notably on immigration and citizenship.

5   On which see M.D.A. Freeman (1992), *Children, their Families and the Law*, London: Macmillan.

6   This was particularly so as regards the Children Act 1975.

7   See L. Fox Harding (1991), 'The Children Act 1989 in Context: Four Perspectives in Child Care Law and Policy', *Journal of Social Welfare and Family Law*, 179, p. 285. *Cf.* M. Freeman (1992); 'In the Child's Best Interests? Reading the Children Act Critically', *Current Legal Problems*, **45**, p. 173.

8   *Report of Inquiry into Child Abuse in Cleveland*, Cm. 412, London: HMSO 1988.

9   For example, in *Re B* [1992] 2 FLR 1,5.

10 See D. Johnson (1992), 'Cultural and Regional Pluralism in the Drafting of the UN Convention on the Rights of the Child', in M. Freeman and P. Veerman (eds), *The Ideologies of Children's Rights*, Martinus Nijhoff, p. 95.

11 See Children Act 1989, s.1(1).

12 *J* v. *C* [1970] AC 668, 710 *per* Lord MacDermott.

13 Adoption Act 1976, s.6.

14 Matrimonial Causes Act 1973, s.25(1) (added by amending legislation in 1984).

15 Though based on a report called *Children Come First*, London, HMSO, Cm. 1264, 1990. This is not negated by the amending Child Support Act 1995.

16 Matrimonial Homes Act 1967, s.1(3).

17 *Gibson* v. *Austin* [1992] 2 FLR 349. See also *Pearson* v. *Franklin* [1994] 1 FLR 246.

18 *Per* Dunn J in *Re D* [1997] Fam. 158.

19 See, for example, *Re C* [1991] 2 FLR 168.

20 On which see G. Sireny (1994), 'The James Bulger Case', *The Independent on Sunday*, 13 and 20 February.

21 Ten being the age of criminal responsibility.

22 The Children Act 1989, s.17.

23 See S. Barber (1990), 'Heading off Trouble', *Community Care*, **840**, p. 23, and in the context of housing, L. Clements (1994), 'House Hunting', *Community Care*, 28 July– 3 August, p. 20.

24 See ss. 61, 64, 67, 86, 87.

25 Where the emphasis was on rights as protection or the furtherance of welfare. But Article 12 does not say that a child has the right to be listened to. See K. Kufeldt (1993), 'Listening to Children: an Essential for Justice', *Int. J. of Children's Rights*, **1**, p. 155.

26 Marta Pais (1991–92), 'The U.N. Convention on the Rights of the Child', *Bulletin of Human Rights*, pp. 75, 76.

27 See, in particular, R. Farson (1978), *Birthrights*, Harmondsworth: Penguin and J. Holt (1975), *Escape From Childhood*, Harmondsworth: Penguin.

28 [1986] AC 112. In Scotland this ruling now has statutory force: see Age of Legal Capacity (Scotland) Act 1991.

29 *Ibid.*, p. 189.

30 Children Act 1989, s.1(3)(a).

31 *Ibid.*, s.22(4).

32 *Ibid.*, in ss. 43(8), 44(7), 38(6), Sch. 3, para. 4.

33 *Re R* [1991] 4 All ER 177; *Re W* [1992] 4 All ER 627.

34 Although the judges denied that, in practice, this could happen because doctors would not allow it to happen.

35   *Re R, op. cit.*, note 33, pp. 639–40.

36   N. Lowe and S. Juss (1993), 'Medical Treatment – Pragmatism and the Search for Principle', *Modern Law Review*, **56**, pp. 865, 870.

37   [1993] 1 FLR 574.

38   See Children Act 1989, s.41.

39   See J. Roche (1991), 'Once a Parent Always a Parent?', *Journal of Social Welfare and Family Law*, p. 345. More generally see *The Future of Children*, **4** (1), 1994.

40   Perhaps even less if the proposals on divorce procedure from the Lord Chancellor's Department in *Looking To The Future*, Cm 2799, London: HMSO, 1995, are implemented.

41   *Looking To The Future* is an adult-oriented report.

42   See M. Savolainen (1986), 'More Rights for Children', *Journal of Family Law*, **25**, pp. 113, 117.

43   Scottish Law Commission (1990), *Parental Responsibilities and Rights*, Discussion Paper, London: HMSO, para. 2.1 *et seq*, 2.60 *et seq*.

44   Children Act 1989, s.31(2).

45   Under the Children and Young Persons Act 1933, s.1.

46   Children Act 1989, s.44.

47   *Ibid.*, ss.33, 35.

48   On which see M. Adcock, R. White and A. Hollows (1994), *Significant Harm*, London: Significant Publications. I discuss the concept in D. Freestone (ed.) (1990), *Children and The Law*, Hull: Hull University Press, p. 130 and in A. Levy (ed.) (1994), *Refocus on Child Abuse*, London: Hawksmere, p. 17.

49   *Cf. Essex C.C.* v. *T.L.R.* (1978) 9 Fam. Law 15.

50   Criminal Justice Acts 1988 and 1991. See also the Dept. of Health's *Memorandum of Good Practice*, London: HMSO, 1992.

51   E. Gray (1993), *Unequal Justice*, London: Macmillan. On the need for a 'support person' for child witnesses in criminal proceedings see J. Morgan and J. Williams (1993), 'A Role for a Support Person for Child Witnesses in Criminal Proceedings', *British Journal of Social Work*, **23**, p. 113.

52   *Re M* [1994] 1 FLR 59; *Re P* [1994] 2 FLR 751.

53   In relation to which see C. Jones and T. Novak (1993), 'Social Work Today', *British Journal of Social Work*, **23**, p. 195 and M. Walton (1993), 'Regulation in Child Protection – Policy Failure?', **23**, p. 23, *British Journal of Social Work*, p. 139.

54   See P. Newell (1994), in A. Levy (ed.), 'Beyond Child Abuse: A Child's Right to Physical Integrity', *Refocus on Child Abuse*, London: Hawksmere, p. 93.

55   See Children and Young Persons Act 1933, s.1(7).

56   For example, J. and E. Newson (1968), *Four Years Old in an Urban Community*, London: Allen and Unwin. See also their *The Extent of Parental Physical Punishment in the UK* (1986) (91 percent of boys, 59 percent of girls hit with an implement by the age of 7). See now *Children and Violence* (GulbenKian Foundation, 1995).

57   Germany is committed to this reform too and it is possible that Switzerland, Poland and Canada will follow the Nordic lead.

58   Recommendation 85(4) para. 12. (26 March 1985).

59   On the litigation see *L.B. of Sutton* v. *Davis* [1994] 1 FLR 737. See *The Guardian*, 28 September 1994; *The Times*, 3 December 1994 on the governmental support for smacking and the new guidelines.

60   See P. Newell (1989), *Children Are People Too*, London: Bedford Square Press, pp. 70–86 on Sweden and its legislation.

61   See I. Gibson (1978), *The English Vice*, London: Duckworth.

62   See Convention, Article 10.

63   Local Government Act 1988, s.28 (homosexuality is defined as a 'pretended family relationship'). See further D.T. Evans (1993), *Sexual Citizenship*, London: Routledge, ch. 5. It is possible that Thatcher herself was behind 'Clause 28' (see N. De Jongh, 'Moral Education and the Child's Right to an Open Future', *The Guardian*, 8 April 1988).

64   And see G. Haydon (1993), *International Journal of Children's Rights*, **1**, p. 213 (child's rights to an open future).

65   Sex education is now compulsory in maintained secondary schools (Education Act 1993, s.241). But teaching about HIV, AIDS and STDs has been removed from the National Curriculum and parents can withdraw their children from any sex education other than that covered by the National Curriculum. On the dangers of withdrawal from classes see A. Weyman (1993), 'The Fourth "R"', in *Concern*, no. 86, p.3.

66   *Spiers v. Warrington Corporation* [1954] 1 QB 61.

67   *Stevens v. United Kingdom* [1986] 5 EHHR 137.

68   *Tinker v. Des Moines School District* 393 US 503 (1969).

69   In Convention, Article 14.

70   See Convention, Article 9(1).

71   It also breaches the discrimination Article because substitute lessons (in the child's religion) must be paid for.

72   Prohibiting discrimination. It is thought that such status is more likely to be granted since the Education Reform Act 1993.

73   Minority Rights Group (1994), *Education Rights and Minorities*, London: MRG.

74   Particularly Peter Newell and Penelope Leach (see note 110 below).

75   Children Act 1989, s.33(6)(a).

76   Children's Homes Regulations 1991, r.11. See also *The Children Act Guidance*, vol. 4, paras 1.121–1.124.

77   It can take a decision on any matter of significance relating to the child.

78   There is no real distinction between wardship and inherent jurisdiction now.

79   Convention, Article 15(2).

80   Criminal Justice and Public Order Act 1994, ss.63–67.

81   Convention, Article 27.

82   As in the City of Westminster (se revealed in *The Independent* on 23 January 1994).

83   Convention, Article 31.

84   Convention, Article 28 (on the goals of education see Article 29).

85   See, in general, *The Children Act Guidance*, vol. 4, part 1

86   Adoption Act 1976, s.6.

87   Department of Health (1994), *Review of Adoption Law: Report To Ministers of Interdepartmental Working Group*, London: HMSO, para. 7(1).

88   See Scottish Law Commission, *Legal Capacity and Responsibility of Minors and Pupils* (Edinburgh: HMSO, 1987).

89   Dept. of Health, *op. cit.*, note 87, above, para. 9.5.

90   For a rather different perspective see E. Bartholet (1993), *Family Bonds*, New York: Houghton Mifflin

91   Convention, Article 27.

92   Convention, Article 24(2).

93   [1992]1 FLR 59. On the new Convention see N. Cantwell (1993), 'The UN Convention on Children's Rights', *Int. Children's Rights Monitor*, **10**, p. 22.

94   Convention, Article 24(1).

95   DHSS (1980), *Inequalities In Health* (the Black Report) London: DHSS; G. Davey

Smith *et al.* (1990), 'The Black Report on Socioeconomic Inequalities in Health 10 Years On', *British Medical Journal*, pp. 301, 373.

96   See C. Woodroffe and M. Glickman (1993), 'Trends in Child Health', *Children and Society*, **7** (1), p. 49, and Department of Social Security (1994), *Households Below Average Income: A Statistical Analysis 1979–1991/2*, London: HMSO. And these figures do not take account of hidden poverty experienced by children (and their mothers) when income is not shared fairly within the family.

97   A. Bowling, *Local Voices in Purchasing Health Care. An Exploratory Exercise in Public Consultation in Priority Setting*, London: St Bartholomew's Hospital Medical College, 1992.

98   Convention, Article 24(2)(a).

99   World Health Organization Regional Office for Europe (1992), *Health For All Indicators*, Eurostat/PC, WHO.

100   See Woodroffe and Glickman, *op. cit.*, note 96 above, p. 50.

101   See J. Bradshaw (1990), *Child Poverty and Deprivation in the UK*, London: National Children's Bureau.

102   Convention, Article 24(2)(c); see also P. Pevato (1994), *International Journal of Children's Rights*, **2**, p. 169 on the child's role in environmental protection.

103   Children's Legal Centre (1989), 'Children and the Environment', *Childright*, no. 59, p. 9.

104   The expression is Ronald Dworkin's: see R. Dworkin (1978), *Taking Rights Seriously*, London: Duckworth.

105   V. Beral (1990), 'Leukaemia and Nuclear Installations: Occupational Exposure of Fathers to Radiation may be the Explanation', *British Medical Journal*, **300** (6722), p. 411. Also, Health and Safety Executive (1993), *Investigation of Leukaemia in the Children of Male Workers at Sellafield*, London: HMSO.

106   Directive on Radiation Safety Standards, 80/836, O.J.L. 246, 17 September 1980.

107   See European Community Directive 80/779/EEC (1980).

108   This is set out in the Education Report Act 1988, s.3.

109   Prohibition of Female Circumcision Act 1985. Guidance was issued under the Children Act in 1991 to alert social workers and others to the problem: Department of Health, *Children Act Guidance*, vol. 8, para. 1.7.16. But see L. Eaton (1994), 'Short Cuts', *Community Care*, 21–27 July, p. 16.

110   See A. Miller (1990), *Banished Knowledge*, London: Virago, pp. 135–40; P. Leach *et al.* (1994), *Children First*, London: Michael Joseph, p. 204; P. Newell (1991), *The UN Convention and the Rights of The Child in the U.K.*, NCB 1991.

111   *R.* v. *Adesanya, The Times* 16 and 17 July 1974.

112   Spain and Sri Lanka have done this.

113   I first developed this concept in 1987 at the Brian Jackson Memorial Lecture entitled 'Taking Children's Rights Seriously': see M. Freeman (1988), 'Taking Children's Rights Seriously', *Children and Society*, **1**, pp. 299, 316–317. See more fully M. Rosenbaum and P. Newell (1991), *Taking Children Seriously*, London: Calouste Gulbenkian.

114   On which see M.G. Flekkøy (1991), *A Voice for Children*, Jessica Kingsley.

115   Costa Rica, New Zealand and Sweden.

6 The Relevance of the Convention on the Rights of the Child in Holland

*Coby de Graaf**

INTRODUCTION

In the current Dutch debate on the approval of the Convention on the Rights of the Child, there is little discussion on the compatibility of Dutch legislation with the Convention itself. However, while the atmosphere is one of enthusiasm about the usefulness of the Convention, it is a usefulness perceived as more relevant for other nations than for Holland.

In fact, children's rights in the Netherlands fall obviously short of the Convention's standards, even taking into account that the language of its Articles permit various interpretations. From the perspective of the Convention, the legal position of children in Holland is far less satisfactory than the government appears to believe. The lack of serious effort within government circles to compare current legislation with rights in the Convention promises little improvement in the legal position of children. The government seems to believe that little need improvement.

Concerns about children's specific problems in a welfare state[1] do not seem to be addressed. Instead, the discussion reveals a fear of children's rights, which may explain the neglect of the question as to whether or not current legislation meets Convention standards. Is this fear of children's rights actually suppressing the very discussion of their necessity? The lack of discussion about the compatibility of legislation, together with the reservation about the Convention raised by the government, would seem to underscore this question. In particular, the three reservations the gov-

*University of Amsterdam.

ernment has expressed – on social security (Article 26) and on the legal position of children in criminal law (Articles 37 and 40) – show this clearly.

Apart from the doubt, also expressed by a majority of members of parliament, as to whether the wording of these Articles made these reservations necessary at all, for one of the most prosperous countries in the world to make a reservation on children's right to social security constitutes a very shameful act. Although the social security systems of most other countries lag far behind the Dutch system, it is only Holland that has so far made such a reservation.[2] Clearly, the real source of this reservation lies in the political consideration of a government currently engaged in heavy debate on scaling down the Dutch social security system, particularly for young people. However, general opposition in parliament to this reservation raises serious doubt as to whether it will be upheld.

In a way, the Dutch discussion about approval of the Convention parallels the way the Convention itself was established. During the drafting process, lower standards concerning child labour and children in armed conflicts were accepted than already existed in international humanitarian law. In Holland, also, the outcome of the discussion has been determined by political pressure. This seems principally to happen when material – social and economic – interests are the issue. Where civil and political rights are at stake, states tend to be more generous, perhaps because there is no price tag attached.

Be that as it may, once the Convention is ratified the possibility of appeal cannot be excluded. Although the Convention itself has no provision for individual complaints, in the Dutch system a direct appeal based on the Convention is possible; this depends on the formulation of the relevant Article and the judge's decision whether this Article has so-called 'direct applicability'. In the explanatory memorandum of the Dutch approval law on the Convention, 'direct applicability' is explicitly stated, despite the fact that most regulations give prescriptions for the government. As an example of this 'direct applicability', Article 9 of the Convention has been mentioned, dealing with the right of the child to family life – the direct equivalent of Article 8 of the European Convention on Human Rights.

In this chapter we will investigate three bills – together covering the traditional fields of juvenile law – on family law, child protection law and criminal law and their compatibility with the Convention Articles 9 and 40. The fact that changes in all these fields have been proposed shows that the whole area of juvenile law is currently adrift. The question which must be addressed is whether the rights of children as set out in the UN Convention have been taken into account in these bills. An investigation of their content – separate from an evaluation of Dutch legislation in the approval bill on the

Convention – is of importance: are these proposals compatible with the Convention, particularly with Articles 9 and 40?

FAMILY LAW AND ARTICLE 9 OF THE CONVENTION

Article 9 aims to protect the right of the child as regards family life – the right of the child to stay with his or her parents. An earlier text of the Convention was clearer in this respect because it contained a separate paragraph which embodied the provision that:

> The State Parties to the present Convention recognise that the child should enjoy parental care and should have his place of residence determined by his parents, except as provided herein.[3]

This paragraph was deleted on the grounds 'that its contents were covered elsewhere in the Convention'. But of even greater significance is the fact that Article 9 itself was very nearly not passed. It was inserted as a result of strong pressure by the US representative who initiated a revision of the text. An earlier version only looked to the right of parents as regards family life, and was clearly misplaced in a Convention on the rights of the child – a fact which was acknowledged by the representatives of various countries. This history also explains the use of the phrase in the present Article 9 that 'a child shall not be separated from his or her parents against their will'. From the view point of the right of the child, the wording 'against their will' is obviously both ambiguous and incorrect. Is it therefore a relic of the earlier text written from the perspective of the rights of the parents? The Dutch legislature nevertheless starts from the wording 'against his or her will', which is a plausible interpretation because this Article would otherwise lose a great deal of its value.

In Article 9, paragraph 3, it is stated that the child has the right 'to maintain personal relations and direct contact with both parents on a regular basis'. Although this right is explicitly recognized in art. 1:161a of the Dutch Civil Code, it is difficult to see how this right can be enforced by children. The child does not have the formal right – as do the parents – to request a court settlement. A child of 12 years or older has, according to art. 162a, so-called 'informal' access to the court, meaning that the court can make an *ex officio* decision, according to this Article, when the court deems this to be the wish of the child. This implies that the child may approach the court in a non-formal way – even by telephone without written application – but it also implies that the court has a discretion whether or not to investigate the matter. The court is under no obligation to decide on the issue of a minor's wish to visit the parent with whom he or she does not reside or a minor's wish to end the access obligation.

This 'informal' access to the court, only adopted in December 1990, was recently evaluated by the Scientific Research and Documentation Centre (WODC) of the Ministry of Justice. In this investigation it appeared that only 12 children had initiated this kind of legal action to solve a problem concerning parental access. To explain this limited use, the researchers blame ignorance of the adopted law and children's loyalty conflicts towards their parents, which play an important role in situations of divorce and parental access. Of particular interest is the reason given by those judges interviewed for the small number of minors who had availed themselves of this 'informal' access. They suspect that it is related to the small number of formally arranged parental access arrangements for older children. Such an arrangement for parental access usually precedes the use of the 'informal' access provision. Yet most parents realize that contact with older children is difficult to enforce by formal arrangements, and this is also observed by the WODC in its evaluation.

It is also important to note that judges involved disagree with the 'informal' procedure. They object to the fact that much work usually done by attorneys now has to be done by the court's officials. They are also concerned about the independence of the courts because, without a child's representative, they are responsible for representing the interests of the minor against those of the parents. The evaluation also reveals that some of the judges would not refuse a request from a child younger than 12 years. Further investigation of these judges' arguments is recommended, because they have more experience of the problem and greater concern for children's rights than the Dutch government whose response to the survey was that a formal procedure would probably only aggravate the children's loyalty conflicts. Is this argument sufficiently strong to justify the conclusion that the provision of art. 162a needs no change, except perhaps concerning the age limit of 12 years?

One can also argue that a court's decision can help the child overcome his or her loyalty conflicts. Children are not able to influence the circumstances of their parents' divorce, and it is noteworthy that the argument that it will aggravate family relationships always arises when children's rights are at issue. In divorce procedures, the parents' actions create a general atmosphere of tension. It seems only fair to give children adequate legal support to act for themselves in situations over which they have no influence. The priority of the parents' rights to family life can be seen even more clearly from the way children's rights to family life have been neglected in the procedure of art. 161a itself. The legal criteria on which the court can refuse parental access are strictly formulated and accentuate the parents' rights to the detriment of those of the children. Take, for example, the criterion that access should not seriously damage the mental and physical development of the child. What is meant by 'serious' damage? Is *any* damage serious enough?

But here also, with regard to the procedure of art. 161a, in which children form the 'main issue' between the parent's claims, it seems that the judge is more sensitive to the interests of children than is the legislator. A good example of this is the decision of the Dutch Supreme Court in the *Hendriks* case, Hendriks, relying upon his right to family life embodied in Article 8 of the European Convention on Human Rights, claimed parental access to his son. The court considered that the interests of the father, in relation to his claim to parental access, should be considered, but that the interests of the child have priority. The European Commission, to which the father appealed, was divided about the propriety of the conclusion reached by the Dutch Supreme Court. The majority, however, agreed with the Dutch decision, concluding

… that the interference with the applicant's right to respect for his family life, being proportionate to the legitimate aim pursued, was justified under para. (2) Art. 8 as being necessary in a democratic society for the protection of the rights and freedoms of another person, namely the child concerned.[4]

In the new bill on family law, the contents of art. 161a are repeated. Materially the rule is not changed at all, but the circle of persons entitled to access to the child has been enlarged. Family members such as grandparents, step-parents and the biological father – if he has any kind of actual family life with the child – are given the right of access to the child. It is remarkable in this respect that no attention has been paid to the possibility of visiting rights between brothers and sisters. In practice, such demands are common.

The enlargement of the right of access is in accordance with the Dutch jurisprudence on Article 8 of the European Convention. However, the enlargement of rightful claimants on access to the child will only increase the type of tension within family relationships of which the government seems to be so afraid. This can be expected despite the fact that the criteria for the judge to refuse access here are wider-ranging than in cases of parental access on the part of both of the parents. The judge can also refuse access here, when it is thought not to be in the child's interests and when a child of 12 years or older makes an objection. The regulation of informal access of children to the court in art. 162a is unaffected by the new bill.

Are these provisions covering the demand of the child's participation to be found in Article 9 of the Convention? There is good reason to doubt this. First, there is the age limit of 12 years. From the *travaux préparatoires*, it is clear that, while the basic working text as adopted by the 1980 working group spoke of 'a child of pre-school age', in subsequent discussions there was a vociferous demand to delete this, which indeed has happened. That means that it concerns children of all ages and that the provision of Article 9, paragraph 2, applies to all children too. Second, it may be asked if the Dutch legal provision of art. 162a implies participation. Participation surely means something more than merely 'being heard', as the explanatory memorandum with the approval bill is suggesting. We reach this conclusion if we compare the wording of Article 9 with that of Article 12, where it is laid down that the child shall be provided the 'opportunity to be heard in any judicial and administrative proceedings affecting the child'. The difference between these two formulations is significant and justifiable, considering the different decisions which have to be taken. In Article 9, concerning decisions affecting the child directly in his family life, the child has the right to participate in the procedures. In other cases, 'the judicial and administrative proceedings' of Article 12, the right to be heard is the rule. In this respect it is interesting to note that in administrative procedures the Dutch legislator was more generous, since here it is proposed that minors can act for themselves if they can be considered to be reasonably capable of promoting their own interests.

CHILD PROTECTION AND ARTICLE 9 OF THE CONVENTION

Article 9 is intended primarily to protect the right of the child against intervention by the state. Thus it is particularly important to state clearly what are the criteria for state intervention in the family. It is also important to look at child protection law – more specifically the regulations governing the circumstances for putting a child into care. In this area, too, significant legal changes have been proposed. We will look first at the existing Dutch law and the ground for state interference formulated within it.

This ground appears to go beyond the criterion of Article 9, 'abuse or neglect'. Under the existing child protection law, steps can also be taken in cases when actual abuse or neglect are not yet the issue, but there is a fear or expectation that it might occur. The use of Article 9 may lead to a narrower interpretation of this ground, underlining the tendency to give priority to keeping the child within his or her own family. In Holland there is a more critical attitude towards state intervention, and the increasing doubt that the putting children into 'care' brings beneficial results certainly plays a role in this. As Goldstein *et al.* have written:

> ... the law does not have the capacity to supervise the fragile, complex interpersonal bonds between child and parent. As *parens patriæ* the state is too

crude an instrument to become an adequate substitute for flesh and blood parents.[5]

Articles 16, 18 and 25 of the Convention confirms this attitude towards the important function of the family for the child, and the Dutch parliament also accepted this value assumption.

In the new bill, revising this child protection measure, the ground for state intervention is formulated in a different way, but the criterion is not refined; materially it stays the same. The child protection measure has been heavily criticized because of the central position of the juvenile court in it. The court not only has to 'judge' but is also charged with the responsibility of the execution of the measure. The amendments which have been proposed to separate these functions may also influence the legal position of children.

Children have been granted informal access to the court which in this case means that they can address the court without a lawyer representing them. The access, however, is only possible for decisions which are taken after the measure itself has become a fact. There is no provision for children to protest the measure itself. A difference is that the court here has the obligation to decide on the child's request. In this respect the access to the court in this category is less informal than in the provision of art. 162a. On the other hand, children do not have the right to appeal to a higher court and, here again, for children under the age of 12 there is no legal provision at all. Although at least some kind of 'participation' is envisaged here it cannot be claimed that the provision is sufficient to satisfy the Convention.

It is important to note that, in a recent decision of a higher Dutch court, a child's appeal against a decision of a children's court magistrate was accepted, the higher court being influenced by the age of the child (he was almost 17), the seriousness of his deprivation of liberty and the necessity of an urgent review of the earlier decision.

PENAL LAW AND ARTICLES 37 AND 40

The drafting of the text of these Articles in the Convention was a difficult task, in which once again the US representative played a significant role. On the issue of juvenile justice in particular 'there were days of complicated and lengthy meetings by the drafting parties' as Cynthia Price-Cohen has revealed.[6] During this process the Dutch representative was also active in introducing proposals to amend the text of the various former versions – in particular of the present Article 37. These amendments can be easily understood if we consider the Dutch juvenile justice system, which also underlies the reservations which the Dutch government has suggested on this Article.

The issue at stake here is whether a reference to an age limit – 18 years – should be provided for the application of the juvenile justice system. Such a reference is not appropriate to the Dutch system since it allows for adult law to be applied to children aged between 16 and 18 years.

This particular issue was a major concern during all the deliberations. In the course of the drafting process the original provision that children should be detained in separate institutions from adults had been toned down. The phrase 'unless it is considered in the child's best interest not to do so' had been added to an earlier draft of the text providing the basic rule about separate deprivation.[7] The objection of the US representative against special criminal treatment of all children below the age of 18 years, without any differentiation, played a decisive role in this. As was stated by this representative:

> ... it was understood that the United States maintained its right to make a reservation on this point and it was implicitly understood that a child committing an offence which, if committed by an adult, would be criminal could be treated as an adult.

During the drafting process, in the first reading, several proposals had been made to replace the still so far accepted draft text of this part of Article 27. For obvious reasons a provision that a child should be separated from adults 'unless it is considered in the child's best interest not to do so' was not satisfactory. It is difficult to defend the notion that an adult penal treatment can be 'in the child's best interests'. The wish to punish children who commit serious crimes in the same way as adults is comprehensible, but to pretend that an 'adult' punishment can be in the best interests of the child is not defensible. At this stage of the drafting process the proposal of the Dutch representative to add to the text 'unless it is considered in the child's best interest not to do so' the phrases 'or it is unnecessary for the protection of the child' was accepted.[8] However, in the second reading, due to the fact that the dispute over the entire Article intensified, this addition disappeared; the provision stayed in its original formulation, as is also clear in the text of the present Article 37. As the *travaux préparatoires* puts it: 'it became obvious that there was a total lack of consensus' – to the extent that it was decided to appoint an open-ended drafting group. The revised text which resulted from this was almost the same as the present Article 37. The US and Dutch representatives, joined by the UK representatives, made it clear that they reserved the right for their respective governments to make reservations on the issue of the application of a special criminal treatment of all children below the age of 18 years without exception. While this line may be disagreed with, at least their attitude was consistent. A more interesting question is how countries with a less progressive system of juvenile justice will handle this prescription.

Conversely, in respect of Article 40, the Dutch government is not at all consistent. In the new bill revising youth criminal law, Article 40, which obviously supplies guarantees of a fair trial, has been used for a completely opposite goal. The government justifies the settlement of legal offences by the police, by means of Article 40 which says:

> States Parties shall seek to promote the establishment of laws, procedures, authorities and institutions specifically applicable to children alleged as, accused of, or recognised as having infringed the penal law...

and, in particular:

> Whenever appropriate and desirable, measures for dealing with such children without resorting to judicial proceeding, providing that human rights and legal safeguards are fully respected.

On the other hand, the government felt obliged to propose a reservation on the same Article 40. Was this necessary to create the legal possibility for the police to 'punish' children for minor offences?

What in fact has happened is that attitudes towards crime have hardened. This can be concluded from the bill on revision of juvenile criminal law and also from the bill changing the compulsory education act. In the first bill the scope for punishing young people between the ages of 16 and 18 by means of the adult penal law has been widened. Where, in the present system, two criteria are involved – the personality of the offender and the seriousness of the crime – in the new bill just one of these conditions is sufficient for the application of adult criminal law for the young offender. In addition, a third criterion has been added – the circumstances in which the crime was committed. In respect to compulsory education it is proposed to punish children who play truant, which means that truancy becomes a criminal offence. To summarize: the possibility for the police to punish before judgment, more opportunities to punish, as in the case of truants, and heavier punishments, because of the wider application of the adult penal system, all demonstrate a toughening of the penal climate in the Netherlands.

To evaluate these developments in the light of the Convention, it must be concluded that the widening of the scope to punish children results in a violation of the Convention, in particular of Article 40 – precisely that same Article previously used by the Dutch government to justify the introduction of the possibility for the police to punish children.

CONCLUSION

The way in which the Dutch government values the Convention is primarily politically determined. The reservation which has been made in the approval Bill in respect of social security is unnecessary, while in the new bills on family law and on child protection law, where the Dutch legal system is clearly not compatible with the Convention, no comment is made. We cannot consider these proposals as a serious attempt to discuss the existence and the necessity for children's rights. Only in the field of criminal law has the Dutch government been consistent, at least in respect of the first part of Article 37. In respect of Article 40, it might even be concluded that the Convention has been abused. This has happened despite the clear and un-equivocal text in the explanatory memorandum accompanying the approval law, which states that those existing legal rules, incompatible with the Convention's Articles, have to be changed so that any incompatibility is removed.

Why, it may be asked, does the Dutch government not make a more critical evaluation of Dutch legislation in the light of the Convention? The answer lies in the current dominant Dutch tendency to try to satisfy as many demands of different groups of persons with their different claims as possible, in the hope of achieving a consensus – consensus 'not as a middle but as an end', as was recently said by a leading Dutch journalist.

In this process the position of children who usually do not operate as a pressure group – a notable exception being 'the national committee of active pupils' (LAKS) – is, by its very nature, weak. Clearly, the predominant political climate does not favour children and their rights: this is indisput-able if one looks at Dutch legislation. Yet, is there a possibility that the Convention will improve the status of children's rights in the Netherlands? In Holland the relevance of the Convention lies principally in its direct implementation. Once it has been approved by the Dutch parliament and has come into force, the Convention is directly applicable: it is up to the court to decide whether the Convention is applicable in a particular case or not. In this respect the government's inattention may cost it dearly. The Convention can give children more rights than the government expects in the same way that, as we saw earlier, the European Convention on Human Rights influ-enced Dutch jurisprudence and legislation. A number of members of parlia-ment have made this observation in their reaction to the government's approval bill on the Convention. Much work therefore has to be done by lawyers and others concerned about the rights of children, and upon these efforts will depend whether the Convention will have a positive influence or only create more right-holders, as Stephen Parker has warned.[9] This warn-ing is of particular importance here, where the tangible rights of children are at stake. Adults may be able to live with illusions, but to give children no more than the opportunity to dream would be tragic.

NOTES

1   See Miek de Langen (1992), 'The meaning of human rights for children' in M. Freeman and P. Veerman (eds), *The Ideologies of Children's Rights*, Dordrecht: Martinus Nijhoff.
2   See the information from the Journal of DCI the Netherlands, 3e jrg, no. 2, June 1993.
3   S. Detrick, J. Doek and N. Cantwell, *The United Nations Convention on the Rights of the Child, A Guide to the 'Travaux Préparatories'*, Dordrecht: Martinus Nijhoff.
4   ECRM-report 8 March 1982, Applic. no. 8427/78.
5   J. Goldstein, A. Freud and A. Solnit (1980), *Before The Best Interests of The Child*, New York: Free Press, p. 12.
6   Concerning the drafting process see Cynthia Price-Cohen's lecture in *Rights of the Child*, cahier 2, Centre for the Rights of the Child, University of Gent, 1991–92.
7   S. Detrick, *et al.*, *op. cit.*, note 3 above, p. 465.
8   See the proposals of the representative of the United States and the Dutch observer in S. Detrick *et al.*, *op. cit.*, note 3 above, p. 467.
9   Parker in Philip Alston and Glen Brennan (eds) (1991), *The UN Children's Convention and Australia*, Canberra: Human Rights and Equal Opportunity Commission, p. 16.

7 Controversies and Dilemmas: Japan Confronts the Convention

*Yukiko Matsushima**

There is a parable that goes like this. While a mother and her child were walking through a forest, a ferocious bear suddenly appeared. How did they react to the situation? If this were to happen in Europe or the USA, the mother would stand facing the bear with her back to the child. She would fight the bear to protect her child or encourage him to run away. However, if this happened in Japan, the mother would squat down with her back to the bear and embrace the child, never leaving him. If the bear ate her, she would want her child to be eaten also.

Although parental affection is the same worldwide, the ways of expressing it differ from country to country. The feeling that no mother could die isolated from her child demonstrates the strong unity between mother and child. Every parent feels this unity, yet in Japan this feeling sometimes goes so far as to deny a child's individual identity. A unique problem in Japanese family law is this failure to recognize the opinion or rights of the child. Today, Japan is struggling to transform the relationship between parents and children into one of partnership rather than one of unity or harmony within the family structure.

INTRODUCTION

The United Nations Convention on the Rights of the Child has been ratified by 170 countries.[1] The awareness of people worldwide of the importance of the rights of the child is ever increasing.

Japan became a signatory to the Convention on 21 September 1990, and the proposal for its ratification was submitted to the Diet in March 1992. After much discussion, the Japanese Diet ratified the Convention on 29 March 1994, and it came into effect on 22 May 1994.

*Professor of Law, Dokkyo University.

125

From the legal point of view, the House debate mainly concentrated on the following topics: educational issues (Articles 28 and 29); the rights of children to express their opinions (Article 12); the status of illegitimate children (Article 2); adoption (Article 21); right of access (Article 9(3)); joint custody and parental responsibilities (Articles 18 and 27(4)); juvenile justice (Articles 37, 39 and 40) and other related items.

During the last debate it became evident that the government considered that it would be unnecessary to reform existing laws concerning children.[2] The government explained that this was due to the fact that the Convention follows the beliefs of the Japanese Constitution, which is based on respect for fundamental human rights. However, there have been many suggestions by academics, legal practitioners and non-governmental groups for the reform of existing laws.

The reason why it took the government a long time to ratify the Convention was that it would greatly influence national law in Japan. The question of direct applicability of the Convention in domestic judicial proceedings is of utmost importance, particularly in the light of the increasing opportunities to sign the Human Rights Conventions. However, there has been little discussion on this point, partly because there have only been a small number of judicial proceedings in which this point has become a material issue, and partly because the Japanese Constitution provides a long and open-ended list of fundamental rights which seemingly make it unnecessary to resort to the Conventions.

Initially, the government signs treaties which must then be approved by the Diet before they are ratified by the government. They are incorporated into the Japanese legal system without transforming national law. Since the Constitution provides that treaties to which Japan is a party should be observed faithfully[3] and, as the approval of the Diet is needed, it is generally agreed that international treaties are superior to national law. Therefore, before ratification, all laws, and the application of those laws, are reviewed. If there is a conflict, the national law is changed.[4]

In Japan, the German *Pandecten* system of civil law is used and legal precedents are built round the interpretation of the relevant code. Although, in practice, the lower courts are bound to follow the judgements of the Supreme Court, in principle they do not strictly form precedents as in common law. However, the judgements of the courts undoubtedly play a significant role in applying a 'general' law to a specific real-life situation. The courts take into account what is considered to be the 'done thing' in today's society and supplement the deficiencies of an abstract code with a search for justice in an individual case. I hope that the Japanese approach to precedents will be appreciated by those who practise common law; otherwise some of the arguments currently made in Japan might be misunderstood.[5]

The purpose of this chapter is to provide an overview for those readers who are not particularly familiar with children's rights under Japanese law. Therefore, in the first part, I will summarize the legal rights of parents and children under Japanese civil law including the history of family law, the legal status of children, parental rights, and the protective function of the family court. Then, in the second part, I will describe, as objectively as possible, controversial children's rights issues with regard to the Convention, including cruelty, discrimination against illegitimate children, rights of children after divorce and juvenile justice. I shall occasionally make references to the relevant Articles of the Convention, and summarize majority (and sometimes minority) academic opinions on important issues with regard to current legal problems in the area of the child's rights in Japan.

LEGAL RIGHTS OF PARENTS AND CHILDREN UNDER JAPANESE CIVIL LAW

Historical background

The history of Japan's present Civil Code dates back to the Meiji Restoration in the mid-nineteenth century. The Meiji government came to power in 1868 and immediately started to modernize the country by replacing the feudal system, based on Confucian political philosophy, with a strong Western-style government whose powers were to be centralized and concentrated in the hands of the Emperor. In terms of both domestic and foreign policies it was necessary to create a modern legal system. Domestically, the legal system needed to be unified and modernized in order for the new government to control people nationwide. Externally, the prevention of colonization by Western superpowers and the abolition of unfair treaties which were imposed on Japan provided the two principal reasons for having an effective legal order.

The Civil Code (*Meiji-Minpo*) enacted in 1898 is, with certain modifications, still in force today. It was based on the German *Pandecten* system and contained property law provisions which were designed to be compatible with the development of capitalism, and two chapters on family and inheritance provisions which reflected the paternalistic *Iye* (extended family) system[6] of society at the time.

Under the old provisions of the Civil Code the purpose of family law was the maintenance of the hierarchical *Iye* system. For example, a first son was, in principle, the sole heir to the family property. The head of a family had full responsibility for the children's maintenance, and at the same time governed over children and could even oust disobedient children. However, as the capitalist economy developed and families became smaller, the focus of the relationship between parent and child shifted from the principles of *Iye* to the individual parent and child themselves. Family law thus originally came to exist for the benefit of parents who exercise total control over their children.

After the Second World War, new provisions of the Civil Code came into effect in 1948, abolishing the *Iye* system and taking away various feudalistic rights of the head of a family. The focus of family law changed from parental rights to parental 'responsibilities'. Today it is generally considered that the law of parents and children exists for the benefit of children. However, there are still some provisions that 'favour' parents and one of the problems to be solved in their interpretation is how to protect the welfare of the child.[7] Nearly half a century later, the Civil Code has once more come under review.[8]

Outline of the law of parents and children

As in many other countries, relationships between parents and children are based either on natural blood relations or on adoptive relations. The former is further divided by the existence or non-existence of a marital relationship between parents with the consequence that a child born to them is either legitimate or illegitimate. Generally, Japanese family law places a heavy emphasis on biological connections in parent–child relationships.

Under the Civil Code a child born during marriage is presumed to be legitimate. A child born within 200 days of, or 300 days after the dissolution of, marriage is presumed to be conceived during the marriage.[9] Art. 772 of the Civil Code was designed to achieve the establishment of the child's legal status at a very early stage, and to stabilize the family relationship. Accordingly, the presumption of legitimacy also applies to a child born to a married woman and a man other than her husband so long as the child is born during the woman's marriage. Only a husband is allowed to challenge this presumption within one year from the time of his knowledge of the child's birth, and the law requires strict proof of certain conditions before the presumption can be rebutted. However, there are exceptions to this strict requirement in interpreting the Code in case law. For instance, if it is impossible for someone to father a child, by reason of impotence or a long separation, the presumption does not apply, and any interested party can bring a lawsuit to challenge the father–child relationship.

Legal marriage is only established after registration in the *Koseki* (family registration system). The courts have ruled that, where a couple fails to register their marriage despite the fact that they have led a *de facto* married life, that marriage is legally effective as a common law marriage and carries the same legal consequences as normal marriage. However, these precedents do not apply to inheritance rights nor to the legitimacy of the couple's children.

A child born to an unmarried couple is illegitimate. In this case, a relationship between the father and the child is created either through voluntary acknowledgement by the father's registration in the *Koseki*, or mandatory acknowledgement through court proceedings brought by the child or his legal guardian during the life of, or within three years of the death of, the father.[10] A relationship between a mother and a child could also be established by voluntary or mandatory acknowledgement, but the Supreme Court has held that the act of delivery is a conclusive fact.[11]

The relationship between parent and child could also be created by adoption. There are two types of adoption in Japan: special adoption and ordinary adoption. In special adoption a baby or young child under six years of age is adopted by a family, and all relations with the child's natural parents are severed.[12] In ordinary adoption a child, or even an adult, is adopted. The concept of adult adoption is peculiar to Japan. In this case, a person or a couple in their twenties or thirties is brought into a childless family in order to continue that family's name or lineage, support the parents and inherit property.[13] I will describe the ordinary adoption of minors in more detail later.

Parental rights

There are two categories of parental rights: custody, and rights to administer the property of a child. The former rights include:

1 parental rights and responsibilities to have custody of and to educate a child;
2 rights to determine the residence of a child;
3 rights to punish a child 'to the extent that is necessary'; and
4 rights to approve the vocation of a child.

The latter rights include:

1 parental rights and responsibilities to administer the property of a child; and
2 rights to represent a child in a legally effective act concerning the child's property (except where there is a conflict of interest between the parent and child).[14]

The parental rights of a minor (a child under 20) are exercised jointly by both parents so long as they are married. On the other hand, it may not always be realistic to expect a divorced or unmarried couple to act jointly and, if that is the case, only one parent may exercise parental rights. In the case of an illegitimate child it is usually the mother who is given parental rights. If the parents are divorced, they agree between themselves or, failing an agreement, the family court decides to whom will be given parental rights. It is possible to divide parental rights between a mother and father: for example it is possible to give custody of the child to the mother and property administration rights to the father. Should there be any abuse of parental rights, the family court may order the removal of parental rights from the parent who has abused them.

If a minor has no parent, a guardian will be appointed. A guardianship is regarded as supplementary to parental rights, but the main difference is that the former may be subject to stricter supervision by the state.[15]

The protective function of the Family Court

I now turn to the special and important functions of the Family Court in protecting a child. The Family Court, established on 1 January 1949, has been a forum for resolving many matrimonial conflicts and dealing with juvenile offenders.[16]

It also plays an important role in adoption. Article 21(a) of the Convention provides that 'State Parties ... shall ensure that adoption of a child is authorised only by competent authorities ...'. In Japan, art. 798 of the Civil Code requires the permission of the Family Court for the adoption of a minor except where the minor is the direct descendant (for example, a grandchild) or the stepchild of the adoptive parent.[17] Where an adoptive child who is over 15, or an adoptive or natural parent, or the legal representative of an adoptive child who is under 15, makes an application for adoption, a judge of the family court questions the parties including adoptive and natural parents, focusing on the welfare of the child. In many cases, a probation officer of the Family Court conducts an additional investigation. Proceedings at the Family Court cover a wide range of matters, including the purpose of adoption, suitability of the adoptive parents, family environments and compatibility of the adoptive parents and child, as well as the wishes of the child where the child is capable of making a relevant judgement. If the family court decides that an adoption is contrary to the welfare of a child, it may refuse to grant the necessary permission.[18] The role of the Family Court in 'special adoption' proceedings, established in 1987, is particularly indispensable in protecting the welfare of a child, in that special adoption has the drastic effect of severing all family relationships between the natural parents and an adopted child.[19]

With regard to Article 9 of the Convention, more than 90 per cent of all divorces are settled by the parties' agreement,[20] and any questions concerning children are left to be agreed on by the parties themselves. If the parties cannot agree as to who should have custody of a minor child, the matter is resolved through mediation conducted at the Family Court. The court considers how the child's best interests can be served and may take into account his or her wishes if he or she has the ability to decide for him or herself (from around the age of 10 years). The Family Court can also change parental rights at a subsequent date or remove them from a parent, for example on the grounds of cruelty. Child maintenance may also be determined by the court.

With regard to Article 37 of the Convention, the equally significant role of the Family Court in dealing with juvenile offenders is discussed at the end of the chapter.

CONTROVERSIAL CHILDREN'S RIGHTS ISSUES WITH REGARD TO THE CONVENTION

Cruelty

Article 19(1) of the Convention provides protection for children from abuse, neglect and exploitation by their parents. Cruelty against children tends to occur behind closed doors, and victims are usually not able to report the fact to the outside world. Consequently, it is not entirely clear how often child abuse occurs. According to a report by the Child Guidance Centre[21] published in June 1989, there were about 1039 reported cases of child abuse in six months. Of these cases, the most common type of abuse involved was child neglect, such as failing to feed the child properly or leaving the child in unsanitary conditions (37.9 per cent), followed by physical violence (26.5 per cent), desertion (22 per cent), and sexual abuse (4.6 per cent).[22] Child abuse is more widespread in city areas and is increasing every year. In many cases the parents lack the ability to raise a child and are not even aware that they are abusing their child. Some parents have no stable employment or have a low income and tend to consider that they can treat their child in any way they like. These parents would repeat the abuse soon after the child is returned from protective facilities, unless in the meantime their lives have stabilized and they have been re-educated as to their responsibilities as parents.

There are three possible remedies for child abuse:

1   criminal sanction,
2   removal of parental rights, and
3   enforcement of child welfare laws.

Here, I would like to focus on the removal of parental rights, although options (1) and (3) are equally important. Suffice it to say that criminal sanction against a parent who abuses his right is not always in the best interests of the child who may well need a continuing relationship with the parent.

Art. 834 of the Civil Code provides that the Family Court may declare the parental rights of a parent lost where he or she abuses them or fails to exercise them properly. Child abuse is no doubt a ground for such a declaration. This procedure, however, is subject to limitations and, according to the Annual Report of Judicial Statistics in 1990, the declaration was granted in only 10 cases out of 130 applications. The reasons for this number being so small are as follows. First, the Family Court has no power to order that the child should live separately from the parent. Thus even after the removal of parental rights, the daily life of the child often remains unchanged and the declaration may be rendered meaningless. Second, the petition for the removal of parental rights may be made either by a relative of the child, or by a public prosecutor or by the president of the Child Guidance Centre, all of whom are often reluctant to resort to such a drastic course of action. In particular, it is the policy of the Child Guidance Centre to help parents and children rebuild their relationship as a family, and it tries to avoid at all costs categorizing parents as failed parents through legal proceedings. Third, art. 834 of the Civil Code lacks flexibility in that it only provides for the *total* removal of parental rights. This 'all-or-nothing' approach produces reluctance in the minds of decision-makers.

Thus, it has been suggested that new measures should be introduced enabling the Family Court to remove parental rights in stages[23] – a view which I share. The new procedure should include temporary suspension of parental rights and will be flexible enough to pave the way towards a solution for certain aspects of child abuse.

Discrimination against illegitimate children

Article 2(1) of the Convention prohibits discrimination against any child. During the debate of the last Diet, one of the most controversial matters was discrimination against illegitimate children – a discrimination still existing in Japanese society and its legal system. I shall summarize the main points below and then consider the problem of the *Koseki* and inheritance in detail later.

The debate focused on these two points:

1   In recording a child in the *Koseki*[24] and *Jumin-hyo* (residents' cards),[25] a distinction is made between legitimate and illegitimate children (although the *Jumin-hyo* system has been reformed very recently).
2   When a parent dies, an illegitimate child will only be entitled to inherit half of that to which a legitimate child is entitled.

With regard to the first point, the government took the view that the mere fact that the *Koseki* and *Jumin-hyo* record whether or not the child is legitimate does not constitute an unreasonable discrimination against the illegitimate child, since the *Koseki* and *Jumin-hyo* simply record the facts. As to the second point, the government argued that the Article 2 of the Convention cannot be interpreted to cover inheritance and thus does not conflict with the proviso to art. 900(4) of the Civil Code which provides the inheritance share of the illegitimate child. However, these government responses do not redress the discrimination which illegitimate children encounter every day.

Other differences between legitimate and illegitimate children are their treatment for the purposes of tax and social security. Under the Income Taxation Act a widow is entitled to certain exemptions, while a single mother who has lost her partner is not. Inevitably, therefore, a single mother pays higher income and residence taxes than a widow. Moreover, single mothers pay higher national health insurance premiums and national pension insurance.

The disadvantages of having, or being, an illegitimate child do not stop there. In Japan the illegitimate child is discriminated against socially in terms of entry into private schools, and marriage or employment opportunities. This social discrimination and the legal disadvantages seems to discourage people from having children outside marriage; indeed, the number of illegitimate children born in Japan is very low, being only 1.03 per cent of the total number of newborns (1989), compared to Sweden's 49.9 per cent (1987), Denmark's 43 per cent (1985), France's 26.3 per cent (1988), the USA's 21 per cent (1984) and the UK's 19.2 per cent (1985).[26]

In 1979 an attempt was made to abolish the distinction between legitimate and illegitimate children, but the law was not reformed because public opinion favoured the maintenance of the distinction.[27]

Problems concerning the Koseki *and* Jumin-hyo

In January 1994 one couple's attempt to name their first son *Akuma* (Devil or Demon) caused great controversy. The parents rejected the recommendation of the city registry for *Koseki* that they should change the name because it would be harmful to the child. Although under the law relating to the *Koseki* Register, there are no restrictions on the parents' right to name their child, the registry refused to register the name on the grounds that it was an abuse of that parental right. The parents sought to have the registry's refusal quashed by the family court.[28] For nearly a whole year the child remained nameless. Finally the parents named their son *Aku* (using different Japanese characters, the meaning of which is totally different from Devil) and the registry accepted it. This case highlighted several issues: the limits of parents' right to name their child, how far the state should interfere in family matters, and the importance of *Koseki* in Japan.

Since the Meiji era, the *Koseki* has proved most useful for successive governments. The essence of the *Koseki* system is the national registration of every citizen, their blood relationships and permanent residence. Since every member of a particular family is thus registered, it enables central government to extend its control nationwide. The *Koseki* has played a key role in the effective administration of conscription and collection of taxes. It is said that the *Koseki* is more comprehensive and efficient than any other similar system in the world, such as those based on birth and marriage certificate systems. The *Koseki* also plays an important role as the established proof of a Japanese person's nationality.

When a child is born, his or her birth must be reported within 14 days by registering the fact under the *Koseki*. In the *Koseki* it is compulsory to register the name of the child, the date of birth, the name of the child's natural parents and their family relationships.[29] In the last respect, a distinction is made between a legitimate and an illegitimate child. For example, if a child is a first-born legitimate daughter or a second-born legitimate son, she or he is registered as 'first daughter' or 'second son'. If a child is illegitimate, he or she was simply

registered as 'male' or 'female'. In the *Jumin-hyo*, a legitimate child was registered as 'first son' or 'first daughter', while an illegitimate child was simply
registered as 'a child' (the *Jumin-hyo* system has been reformed very recently).

A few years ago, before the reform, a lawsuit was brought in respect of the
registration system in the *Jumin-hyo*.[30] The question arose out of the marrying
couple's wish that the wife should not change her surname after marriage
(which is incidentally one of the most controversial topics in the reform of the
Civil Code). This is not allowed under the current law, and the parties chose
not to register their marriage. Their child was accordingly illegitimate under
the law and the *Jumin-hyo* recorded the child simply as 'a child', clearly
indicating the illegitimacy. The parties argued that the differential language
used in the *Jumin-hyo* would further discriminate against the illegitimate child
and would thus violate the equal protection and basic human rights provision
in Articles 13 and 14 of the Constitution and the Convention on the Rights of
the Child. However, on the 23 May 1991 the Tokyo District Court held that the
present law is not unconstitutional because it is based on reasonable grounds.
This means that since there is a distinction between the legitimate and illegitimate child under the present law, the differential treatment as embodied in the
language used in the *Jumin-hyo* is not unconstitutional. Although the parties'
claim was dismissed, this case gave impetus for reform.

As of March 1995, the Ministry of Home Affairs abolished the previous
system of recording in the *Jumin-hyo*. Henceforth both legitimate and illegitimate children are to be registered simply as 'a child'. However the *Koseki*
system has remained unchanged. Insofar as this distinction helps maintain
discrimination against the illegitimate child, it must be urgently abolished.
The reform in this respect would not by any means affect the authenticity of
the *Koseki*, as it has not caused any disturbance or inconvenience in the *Jumin-
hyo* system.

Problem of entitlement to inheritance of an illegitimate child

The proviso to art. 900(4) of the Civil Code provides that an illegitimate child
is entitled to inherit only half the amount to which a legitimate child is
entitled. The first case which challenged the constitutionality of the proviso
came before the court a few years ago.[31] In that case, the plaintiff whose father
had predeceased her, inherited a proportion of the assets of her grandmother.
However, because the plaintiff's father was an illegitimate son of her grandmother, she could inherit only half of what the legitimate children inherited.[32]

The family court rejected her argument that the grandmother's estate should
be divided equally among all children regardless of legitimacy, so she appealed.
On 29 March 1991 the Tokyo High Court gave a judgment, declaring art. 900(4)
constitutional, and held that the question of entitlement to succession is one of
state policy and thus for the legislature to determine. The High Court approved

the decision of the family court. The traditional view of the court was that, apart from some legislative problems, the distinction between the legitimate and illegitimate child was constitutional because its purpose was to protect legal marriage and to maintain social order. The plaintiff's final appeal to the Supreme Court was recently dismissed (for further details, see below).

However, in another case, on 23 June 1993 the Tokyo High Court decided for the first time that the proviso to art. 900(4) was unconstitutional.[33] The case was brought by a 38 year-old piano teacher, an illegitimate child whose father had died intestate, against his legitimate child, who was the other heir to the father's estate under the law. She demanded an equal share of their father's estate.

The grounds for the judgment are very detailed but can be summarized as follows: 'Article 14 of the Constitution prohibits discrimination based on race, creed or social status. The phrase "social status" refers to social positions that are determined at birth.' The proviso to art. 900(4) of the Civil Code is a discrimination in economic and social relations based on social status. Art. 900 is intended to encourage and respect proper marriages and to protect family relationships based on lawful marriage, and these purposes must still be respected. However, at the same time the individual dignity of illegitimate children must be equally protected. The Court concluded that, in today's society, where people have a variety of views as to the value of marriage, any attempt by the government to restrict the birth of the child outside marriage is futile and that the proviso no longer has any reasonable basis. The Court further noted that in recent years the strong tendency among other nations is to enact laws that ensure equal rights between the legitimate and illegitimate child. The Court also stated that any conflict between the idea of protecting the family relations based on lawful marriage and the idea of protecting the individual dignity of the illegitimate child must be resolved in such a way that both ideas remain valid. The Court said that its ruling was particularly true in the light of the spirit of art. 24(1) of the International Covenant on Civil and Political Rights, and art. 2(2) of the Convention on the Rights of the Child, which was shortly to be ratified in Japan.

The Tokyo High Court also gave a judgment on 30 November 1994 on the same issue.[34] These judgements accord with the general trend of today's academic opinions.

However, the Supreme Court of Japan reversed this trend by its judgment on 5 July 1995, holding by the majority of 10 to 5 that the difference between legitimate and illegitimate children concerning their respective rights under intestate succession *was* constitutional.[35]

The judgment of the Supreme Court can be summarized in the following terms. First, art. 14(1) of the Constitution prohibits discrimination which is not based on any reasonable grounds. However, the Court held that so long as there are reasonable grounds, it is not unconstitutional to distinguish on the basis of legitimacy. Further, the provision of the Civil Code concerning intestate succession is only one of many provisions governing the law of succession, which it merely supplements. Since only lawful and not common law marriages are recognized under the Civil Code, it is inevitable that there should be some distinction in the treatment of legitimate and illegitimate children.

With regard to the rationale behind the proviso to art. 900(4) of the Civil Code, the Court stated that it was intended as a compromise between the conflicting interests of legitimate and illegitimate children. In light of the fact that the Civil Code only recognizes lawful marriages, the proviso distinguishing between legitimate and illegitimate children is based on reasonable grounds; accordingly, the Legislature did not exceed its discretion. Therefore, the Court held that the proviso was constitutional.

However, it may be noted that among the 15 judges of the Supreme Court, five expressed dissent to the majority judgment. They took the view that, even in the interest of protecting legal marriages, it was unnecessary to discriminate by law against illegitimate children who are not responsible for their own illegitimacy. They thought that the proviso was unconstitutional, particularly in light of art. 26 of the International Covenant on Civil and Political Rights and art. 2(1) of the Convention on the Rights of the Child. Even among the majority, two of the judges expressed an opinion as to the desirability of law reform and another two registered doubts as to the reasonableness of the proviso. Law reform in this area is eagerly awaited.

In July 1994, the Law Commission of the Ministry of Justice made a proposal to abolish the proviso to art. 900 (4) of the Civil Code so that, on intestacy, an illegitimate child would become entitled to a share equal to that of a legitimate child.[36] This has become one of the central issues of debate because of the various changes that have occurred in this area of law. The increased awareness of law reform may be the result (i) of the decision of the Tokyo High Court in June 1993 declaring the proviso unconstitutional, (ii) of the recommendation of the Human Rights Committee addressed to the Japanese government in October 1993 as to the incompatibility of the proviso with art. 26 of the International Covenant on Civil and Political Rights, and (iii) of the ratification by Japan of the International Convention on the Rights of the Child in March 1994. It is becoming socially unacceptable to retain a provision which discriminates on the ground of legitimacy. It is hoped that appropriate law reform will finally be made by the Diet in 1996.

Rights of a child after the parent's divorce

Custody

Article 18(1) of the Convention provides that primary responsibility for the upbringing of children rests with both parents. Thus, even after divorce, parents should continue to fulfil their parental responsibilities jointly.

However, as to the custody of the child, Japanese law, unlike that of the USA or some other countries, does not allow joint custody. Therefore, only one of the parents becomes the custodian of the child.[37] In practice, in more than 70 per cent of cases, custody is given to the mother.[38]

The procedure for divorce by consent in Japan is unique in that all that is necessary is the consent of both parties to divorce and the registration of this in the *Koseki*. In the case of divorce by agreement, even when the custody of the child is at issue, the child is frequently only used as a pawn in determining the amount of matrimonial relief and division of property. Moreover, in practice, Japanese divorce cases tend to be extremely acrimonious. This means that, unless the parties could show a more mature attitude to divorce, joint custody would not work effectively even if it were to be introduced now since, if all decisions are to be made jointly, it would not only cause the child considerable inconvenience but also might disturb his or her emotional stability (particularly in the case of a small child) if he or she had to go back and forth between his or her parents.

However, an even more serious problem in many cases may be the fact that the father who has lost custody tends to abandon his parental responsibilities altogether. Some even forget about their child. In order to prevent that from happening, and in order for the child to feel loved and needed by the father, it is essential to establish some form of joint parental rights or rights of access by a non-custodial parent after divorce. Today, in Japan, family styles are changing as is seen in the emergence of nuclear families and the increasing economic independence of working women. As lifestyles change and the number of children born in a family decreases,[39] young fathers are becoming more interested in helping to raise a child. Sooner or later there will be many parents who want to share parental responsibilities even after their divorce.[40]

Access

Article 9(3) of the Convention provides rights for a child who is separated from one or both parents to contact them. In Japan there is no provision in the Civil Code expressing the access right. However, the right has been recognized in case law. Art. 766(1) of the Civil Code states that custody and other 'necessary matters' for a child should be determined at the time of divorce by consent, and the Supreme Court has ruled that access to a child after divorce is one of these matters.[41] In reality, however, a survey shows that in 61 per cent of divorce cases there was no contact between father and child, in 11 per cent of the cases fathers originally had some contact but gradually lost it, and in only 26 per cent of all cases did fathers still maintain contact with their children.[42] This is partly due to the reluctance on the part of the custodial mothers to let the children see their fathers, as some wives prefer to sever all contact with their ex-husband once they are divorced by reason of the husband's violence, adultery or desertion. Conversely, some parents force their children to see them against the children's will.

Access should be decided in the best interests of the child and should not be dependent on the egoism or self-interest of the parent. Until now the right of access has been mainly parent-oriented. However, the child's desire to meet a parent after divorce should also be an established right.

The Law Commission of the Ministry of Justice made a proposal to include an explicit provision concerning access.[43]

The child's right to express his or her views

Article 12(1) of the Convention provides the right of a child to express his or her views. It is important to consider the child's opinions regarding education and any matters relevant to their daily lives. In this instance, I will discuss Article 12(1) in relation to cases of divorce. At present, when the child is 15 years old or over, the family court has a legal duty to listen to the statement of the child before making decisions as to custody.[44] Moreover, even when the child is under 15 years of age, the probation officers or the family court mediators frequently consult the child.[45] In family court practice, children over 10 years old are to be asked their opinion. Therefore, in these cases it can be said that the child's view is considered.

However, in divorce by consent, which amounts to 90 per cent of all divorces, there is no system to check the child's opinion. Therefore, it is desirable, even in cases of divorce by consent, that it is referred either to the family court or some public service in order to ensure the child's welfare. The Bar Association has also suggested that an independent system of a 'special representative' should be established; this representative would safeguard the child's interests during mediation, litigation, or even at a consensual divorce settlement.[46]

In any event the child's wishes should be more respected in determining custody, and commonly held assumptions in Japan, such as 'young children are always better off in their mother's care', or 'children's views are trifling', should be abandoned.

Enforcement of child maintenance payments

Article 27(4) of the Convention provides enforcement measures to secure child maintenance from the parents. The most serious problem facing the mother who has custody of the child is how to ensure maintenance payments for the child. According to a report in 1988, as many as 75.4 per cent of the mothers have never received any payments from their ex-husband. Even among the remaining 24.6 per cent of the single mothers, 14 per cent of them constantly received the payments, whereas 10.6 per cent of them received payments only in the past.[47]

Among the divorces which were mediated by the Family Court in 1990, only 51.7 per cent of the decisions imposed some sort of payment towards the cost of the child's upbringing. The method of payment was usually a fixed monthly payment. The most common rate of payment was 20,000 to 40,000 yen (£120–240) per month per child.[48]

However, in many cases, the money is never paid, due to the ineffectiveness of the means of enforcement and, in cases of divorce by consent, the fact that no enforcement can be provided. The creation of some reforms of assurance and enforcement of payment towards the upbringing cost are therefore urgently needed. For instance, the parties could be required to sign and file an agreement setting out the obligations of each party as to payment. As to establishing a strong enforcement process, it may be effective to create a system, as in Sweden, whereby the state pays the cost of the upbringing of the child on behalf of the parties, or one of the parties, who must then repay it as a loan to the state.

Such a new system needs to be capable of effective enforcement, in order to ensure the recognition of the principle that the parents have common and primary responsibilities for the upbringing of the child. These are issues which are being considered by the Law Commission.

Juvenile justice

Articles 37, 39 and 40 of the Convention set out the structure for juvenile justice together with other UN regulations and guidelines. The Article places importance on the attainment of the right to defence and the prevention of criminal sanctions in dealing with juvenile offences. The Convention recognizes that criminal trials and punishments not only fail to deter juvenile offenders but also prevent their rehabilitation and are not in the interests of society as a whole.

The 1948 Juvenile Act was enacted on similar principles. Under the Act the Family Court is given jurisdiction to hear all juvenile cases independently of other courts, and different criteria are applied in making a decision. The purpose of a hearing is not to decide what is a proportionate punishment to the crime or wrongful conduct, but to consider what is the most effective way of reforming the offender, taking into account his family background and personality. The hearing is not open to the public and is conducted 'in a kind and non-aggressive manner'.[49]

Juvenile delinquents are classified into three categories:

1   those aged 14 or over and under 20 who have committed a punishable offence;
2   those under 14 years of age who are not punishable according to Article 41 of the Criminal Code; and

3   those under 20 years of age who have not yet committed an offence but are likely to do so in the near future.

All cases in category 1 and some cases in category 2 are referred directly to the Family Court by the police or prosecutors. The remainder are dealt with in accordance with the Child Welfare Act; and some of these may still end up in the Family Court. The Family Court investigates facts, conducts a hearing and eventually determines an appropriate means of dealing with the juvenile. Those means include non-commencement of the proceedings or dismissal of the case, sending the case to the Child Guidance Centre,[50] appointment of probation officers, sending the offender to a protective or juvenile offenders' institution or, in the worst cases, sending the case to a prosecutor for normal criminal proceedings.

In practice, however, more than 70 per cent of the cases are terminated by way of non-commencement of the proceedings or dismissal. This is because most offenders show strong possibilities for reform during the course of the proceedings or the investigation by the Family Court, and the judges tend to conclude that further proceedings are unnecessary. In resolving juvenile matters this way, the Family Court probation officers perform indispensable counselling and casework functions.

However, the environment surrounding the juvenile justice system has been changing since the 1960s. Recently the number of juvenile offences reached the highest figure since the Second World War, with some particularly serious offences committed in the late 1980s. This has led some to argue for tougher sanctions for juvenile offenders and for lowering the age limit for criminal liability. Consequently, the welfare aspect of the Family Court in protecting the interests of juveniles is gradually being replaced by the criminal justice function. The Family Court probation officers are also losing their independence and expertise by being forced to cope with a considerable number of cases with more speed and mechanical efficiency.[51]

There are new problems emerging from some court decisions in dealing with minor offenders. For instance, a typical case is the 'High School Girl Murder'.[52] On 25 November 1988 several teenagers kidnapped a schoolgirl, who died after 41 days of repeated rape and abuse. The defendants put the girl's body in an oil drum filled with cement and abandoned it at a construction site. The principal defendant (then 17 years old) was sentenced to 17 years' imprisonment. Another case was the 'Otaka Ryokuchi Park Murder'.[53] Six youngsters who had just met each other kidnapped a couple from a park in order to steal valuables from them, murdered them and buried their bodies in a nearby mountain area. The principal defendant (then 19 years old) was sentenced to death. The others were also sentenced to life or 17 years' imprisonment. In both these cases, unusually severe punishments were imposed on the offenders, taking into account the cruel nature of the acts committed. These decisions have been criticized for merely scapegoating the particular offenders and failing to address the underlying reasons for the crime – the kind of reasons which continue to cause more youngsters to offend. It should not escape our attention that juveniles today live in much harsher environment that in the past as a result of rapid industrialization, the breakdown of traditional family units, school education being infected with the business world's competitiveness, and the disappearance of playgrounds and a sense of community. It is this deterioration of the living environment which should be a major cause of our concern.

Another example is the 'Ayase Mother and Child Murder'.[54] On 16 November 1986 a 36 year-old mother and her 7 year-old son were strangled to death in their apartment in Ayase, Tokyo. Some cash was stolen. Three teenagers (15 and 16 years old) confessed, during police interrogation, to having committed the crime. They subsequently claimed innocence, and further investigation revealed sloppiness in the original police investigation. Doubt was also raised as to whether there could be any safeguard for the rights of juveniles when faced with a biased judge at the Family Court. Another case[55] occurred in 1988 where a policeman intentionally made a false allegation that two teenagers (16 and 17 years old) assaulted him and interfered with his execution of public duty. The accused boys' supporters, including their lawyers, later successfully proved to the court that those allegations were unfounded and that there had been no delinquent behaviour on their part. In these cases, juveniles were left defenceless in the hands of the police authority without any legal or other assistance at the first stage of criminal investigation.

Although there has been considerable movement towards the introduction of criminal procedure, it must be remembered that the juvenile justice system often requires different policy considerations. It is important to prevent juvenile proceedings from becoming criminal prosecutions. It is thus widely acknowledged that the rights of juveniles should be protected at an earlier stage, for example by ensuring legal representation or assistance when questioned by the police.

At the same time the Family Court should try to restore its casework function and the probation officers' expertise in counselling. Furthermore, too much attention should not be paid to the violent appearance of each offence, since it is the living environment of the offenders which needs to be improved.

CONCLUSION

Parents and children in Japan tend to be much closer to one another than in other countries. Parents tend to feel that they and their children are a single 'unit', and distinctions between individuals often become blurred. This sense of unity on the part of parents often leads to excessive control over their child and inhibits the development of respect for individuals. It is ironic that while parents seek so earnestly to protect their children they actually strip them of their rights as individuals.

Traditionally a child has been regarded as an object of protection by society, and not regarded as possessing independent rights. Japan constantly finds that its ancient 'national harmony' or 'family harmony' philosophy conflicts with modern law concerning individual rights. It is to be hoped that the Convention will lead to more discussions towards the establishment of the clear legal structure of family relationships which will, in turn, educate the Japanese people into the view that the rights of every family member should be equally respected.

Japan is a consensus society. Because of this, law reforms seem to be very slow – often even impossible – to achieve. Many important law reforms in the past have been made as a result of pressure from foreign countries. For example, as a result of the ratification of the Convention on the Elimination of All Forms of Discrimination Against Women, the Nationality Act was reformed in 1984. Now a child whose mother or father is Japanese can claim Japanese nationality. Previously this was only a paternal right.

Therefore, the Convention on the Rights of the Child is also likely to facilitate the process of reform for the acknowledgement of the rights of the child. I am confident that the Convention will make a strong impact in diversifying and improving the status of the child in Japanese law and practice.

NOTES

1   UNICEF Japan Office (1994), 'Jido no Kenrijoyaku' *Update*, no. 34, 8 June.
2   See the minutes of the 126th Diet foreign affairs committee meeting, vol. 7, 11 May 1993, p. 2.
3   Constitution, art. 98(2).
4   However the traditional view is that not all provisions in a treaty are directly applicable to the court; see, for example, Ken Fujishita (1991), 'Jido no Kenri ni kansuru Joyaku to Minji Horei ni tsuite', *Minji Geppo*, **46**, (4), May, pp. 11–12. Some progressive scholars believe that human rights treaties are always directly applicable but this debate has not yet been resolved.
5   The most important English textbooks on Japanese Law are: Hiroshi Oda, *Japanese Law*, London: Butterworths (1992); Hideo Tanaka, *The Japanese Legal System*, Tokyo: University of Tokyo Press (1976); Yoshiyuki Noda (1976), *Introduction to Japanese Law*, Tokyo: University of Tokyo Press.
6   About *Iye*, see Fujiko Isono (1988), 'The evolution of modern family law in Japan', *International Journal of Law and the Family*, **2**, pp. 183–202.
7   See Akira, Yonekura (1992), 'Shinkengainen no Tenkan no Hitsuyosei', *Gendaishakai to Minopogaku no Doko* (the last volume) Tokyo: Yuhikaku, pp. 359–407.
8   Moves are now underway to reform the Civil Code provisions that apply to marriage and divorce. In December 1992 a subcommittee of the Ministry of Justice's Legislative Council produced an outline of its proposed reforms. For details, see Yukiko Matsushima (1994), 'Japan: Reforming Family Law', *University of Louisville Journal of Family Law*, **32**, (2), pp. 359–67; Yukiko Matsushima (1995), 'Japan: Continuing Reform in Family Law', *University of Louisville Journal of Family Law*, **33**, (2), pp. 417–21.
9   Civil Code, art. 772.

10   Civil Code, art. 787.
11   Judgement of the Supreme Court, 27 April 1962, *Minshu*, **16**, (7), p. 1247.
12   About special adoption, see Minoru Ishikawa (1989), 'Reform of the adoption law in Japan', *The Japanese Annual of International Law*, (32), pp. 67–72.
13   The average of adult adoption in the last few years is more than 70 per cent of the whole adoption, see Ichiro, Kato (1989), 'The adoption of majors in Japan' in John Eekelaar and David Pearl (eds), *An Aging World; Dilemmas and Challenges for Law and Society*, Oxford: Clarendon Press, pp. 161–6.
14   Civil Code, art. 820–826.
15   Recently some have even argued for an abolition of parental rights altogether and for the unification of parental rights and guardianship which should be merged into general guardianship.
16   According to the report by the Supreme Court Secretariat in 1993, the number of family court organizations is: 50 courts, 201 branch offices and 79 sub-branch offices. The staff of the family court is: 350 judges, 1200 court clerks, 1500 family court probation officers, 50 medical officers, 50 nurses and 2350 other members (mediators, etc.).
17   Critics argue that the family court should also be involved in cases concerning the adoption of a stepchild: see the minutes, *op. cit.*, note 2 above, vol. 13, 26 May 1993, p. 12.
18   In fact about 10 per cent of all applications for the adoption of a minor have been refused or withdrawn.
19   Civil Code, art. 817-2–817-9.
20   There are three types of divorce systems in Japan: divorce by mutual consent, divorce by mediation in the family court and divorce by judgement under art. 770 of the Civil Code in the ordinary court. Statistically, about 90 per cent of divorce cases in Japan are decided by mutual consent, 9 per cent of divorces are resolved at the family court and the remaining 1 per cent are solved at the ordinary court. In 1993 the divorce rate was 1.53 in 1000, at total of 189 000 divorces in the year.
21   The Child Guidance Centre (*Jido Sodanjo*) is a public institution which supervises various aspects of child welfare. It is set up in each prefecture and selected cities.
22   For the facts of child abuse cases, see the report by the Japan Bar Association (1990), 'Shinken wo Meguru Hotekishomondai to Teigen', *Jiyu to Seigi*, **41**, (1), January.
23   *Ibid.*
24   The *Koseki* is a registration system under which every family, husband, wife and unmarried children, is registered with the government. Birth, marriage, divorce and death are recorded as is the relationship between each person. This carries great legal and social significance in Japan. Recently, criticism from young scholars against the *Koseki* system has increased. They advocate the modification of the family registration system to an individual registration system.
25   *Jumin-hyo* are residents' cards in which people's present address and everyone in the household is mentioned. Their relationships based on the *Koseki* are also mentioned.
26   See Shuhei Nonomiya (1992), 'Hichakushutsushi no Syusseisu, Jinkoshizansu, Ninchisu', *Hogaku Seminar*, **37**, (1), (January), p. 29.
27   A survey showed that 48 per cent of the people surveyed were in favour, as opposed to 16 per cent who were against it.
28   Judgement of the Tokyo Family Court, Hachioji Branch on 31 January 1994, *Hanrei Jiho* (1486), pp. 56–61.
29   Family Registration Law, art. 13.
30   Judgement of the Tokyo District Court, 23 May 1991, *Gyoseijiken Saibanreishu*, **42**, (5), p. 688.

31   Judgement of Tokyo High Court, 29 March 1991, *Hanrei Times* (764), p. 133, *Jurist* (1002), p. 22.
32   In Japan it is not common for the deceased to leave a will, and the estate is usually distributed in accordance with the rules of intestate succession. Under the law of succession, a surviving spouse always become an heir. The priority of their heirs are; children, then lineal ascendants, and finally siblings. The share of each heir would depend upon the composition of the beneficiaries. For example, if the beneficiaries are a surviving spouse and children, they will each inherit a half of the estate, and the share of the child is divided equally among all the children (Civil Code art. 900(4)). A common-law wife has no right of inheritance.
33   See *Hanrei Jiho*, (1465), pp. 55–65; also Shuhei Ninomiya and Yonezawa Koichi (1993), 'Hichakushutsushi Sabetsu wa Kuzureta', *Hogaku Seminar*, **38**, (9), (September), pp. 53–61.
34   Judgement of the Tokyo High Court on 30 November 1994, *Hanrei Jiho* (1512), pp. 3–10.
35   Decision of the Supreme Court on 5 July 1995 (appeal case of the decision by the Tokyo High Court on 29 March 1991), *Saibansho Jiho* (1150), pp. 1–7, *Jurist* (1074), pp. 208–15. This is the first decision by the Supreme Court in this area and some academics are worried about that the decision might discourage the trend of reform.
36   See the Family Law Reform proposal by the Ministry of Justice, *Jurist* (1050), p. 217.
37   Civil Code, art. 819.
38   According to the demographic statistics published by the Ministry of Health and Welfare in 1989, in 71.3 per cent of all cases a wife exercises all parental rights over a child.
39   The average number of birth rate is 1.5 for each couple in 1993.
40   The proposal for the 1994 United Nations International Year of Family also refers to joint custody of a child after divorce.
41   Judgement of the Supreme Court on 6 July 1984, *Kasai Geppo*, **37**, (5), pp. 35–9.
42   Report by Nihon Jido Mondai Chosakai (1986), 'Rikon to Boshikatei'.
43   See the Family Law Reform proposal by the Ministry of Justice, *Jurist* (1050), p. 216.
44   The Rule of the Family Court Proceedings, art. 54.
45   See debate 'Ko ga Ibasho wo Erabu made', *Case Kenkyu*, (227), May 1991, pp. 23–55.
46   See Shizuko Sugii (1991), 'Bengoshi ga Mita Kodomo no Genjo; Rikon to Kodomo no Kenri', *Jiyu to Seigi*, **42**, (2), February.
47   National survey on the single-mother family household by the Ministry of Welfare in 1988.
48   Annual Report of Judicial Statistics for 1990, vol. 3 Family Cases by General Secretariat, Supreme Court.
49   Juvenile Act, art. 22(1).
50   *Supra* note 21.
51   For example, the 'Guideline in dealing with juvenile matters', drafted under instruction from the Supreme Court, has been criticized as being too efficiency-oriented.
52   Judgement of the Tokyo District Court on 12 July 1990, *Hanrei Jiho* (1396), pp. 15–41.
53   Judgement of the Nagoya District Court on 28 June 1989, *Hanrei Jiho* (1332), pp. 36–49.
54   Dismissal at the Tokyo Family Court on 12 September 1989, *Hanrei Jiho* (1338), pp. 157–162.
55   Decision at the Osaka Family Court on 29 March 1988, *Shonenho Tsushin*, (36).

8 Implementation of the Rights of the Child in the Mozambican Context

Luis Filipe Sacramento and Ana Maria Pessoa

INTRODUCTION

This chapter first reviews Mozambican law applicable to children and offers a comparison of domestic legislation, including the new Mozambican Constitution and the Mozambican Declaration of the Rights of the Child ('Declaration') with the UN Convention on the Rights of the Child. We offer a critical perspective of how the state has attempted to move from the codification to the realization of rights, principally through programmes targeting specific populations, efforts to end the armed conflict, and economic and social policies. We assess these attempts against the backdrop of the ongoing war and its implications for the success or failure of child-care policies. Finally, we review recent steps to promote compliance with the norms delineated in the Convention and we prescribe the role of the state and its institutions and local, as well as international, communities with regard to the implementation of children's rights in Mozambique.

PROTECTION OF THE CHILD WITHIN THE NATIONAL LEGAL FRAMEWORK

This section provides an overview of the protection accorded the child within the country's legal framework. We have grouped some of the most fundamental rights of the child into three categories: political, economic and social rights.

Political rights

Equal protection irrespective of race, religion, ethnic origin, age, etc.

Equal protection is a constitutional principle. Art. 66 of the recently approved Constitution ensures that in the Republic of Mozambique all citizens enjoy the same rights and are subject to the same obligations, regardless of colour, race, sex, ethnic origin, place of birth, religion, level of education, social position, civil status of parents, or profession. Art. 56(4) of the Constitution restates this principle and further establishes that a child may not be discriminated against, especially on account of his birth.

As early as 1979, the principle of equal rights for all children was proclaimed in Principle One of the Mozambican Declaration of the Rights of the Child, (which was approved by Resolution 23/79 of 26 December 1979). Statements of that same principle can be found in the earlier Law 2/77 of 27 September 1977 which instituted uniform and non-discriminatory criteria for health and medical assistance, and in Law 4/83 of 23 March 1983 which introduced the National Education System and defined the fundamental principles of its application. Finally, equal protection is reaffirmed in art. 3(1) of the Labour Law:

> ... all citizens have the right to work, independent of their ethnic origin, sex, religion, race, colour, social position and political opinion.

Right to a name and nationality

The Constitution's Chapter II codifies and regulates the right to a nationality, which is based, to a certain point, on the principles of *jus sanguinis* and *jus solis*. Although the right to a name is not mentioned in the Constitution, such an omission does not indicate a void with regard to this matter in domestic law. Principle Three of the Mozambican Declaration of the Rights of the Child stipulates that '... you have the right to a name by which your parents, brothers, sisters and friends call you and by which you will be known wherever you may be'. Arts 122 and 123 of the Code of Civil Registry stipulate that a first name and family name be provided when registering a birth. Even in the case of an abandoned child, the law guarantees this right whenever it is not possible to determine the existence of a prior registration. For the purposes of birth registration, art. 127 of the Code of Civil Registry defines as abandoned a newborn of unknown parents found anywhere, an insane minor, or a minor apparently of less than 14 years of age found in an uncared-for state. Finally, the Civil Code[1] reinforces the principle stipulated in art. 122 of the Code of Civil Registry, stating that children have the right to use their parents' last name.

The freedoms of expression, thought, assembly, association and religion

The Constitution recognizes and protects these rights for all citizens. Art. 74(1)(2) cover the freedoms of expression and thought. The exercise of free speech in constitutional terms includes the right to information and the right to state one's thought, within the bounds of respect for the dignity of the human being and the interests of foreign policy and national defence. Special emphasis is given in art. 79 to the freedom of scientific, technical, literary and artistic creation as manifestations of the liberty of expression and thought.

Arts 75 and 76 cover the freedoms of assembly and association. It is important to note that forms of association provided for earlier in the regular legislation now have greater significance since they are formally in the new Constitution. Because new types of association can be anticipated that are not already dealt with in existing law, new regulations may be called for.

Art. 78 guarantees each citizen the right to practise or not to practise a religion. Arts 80, 81 and 82 set up the legal mechanisms that safeguard fundamental rights, especially those referred to above.

We recommend that a thorough analysis of current legislation, and the potential to exercise the rights described above, be undertaken to determine whether any amendments or additional legislation are necessary to protect these rights.

Economic and social rights

Right to be treated with understanding and love by family and society

Principle Two of the Mozambican Declaration of the Rights of the Child declares: 'You have the right to grow up surrounded by love and understanding, in an atmosphere of security and peace.' This principle is not expressly stated in the new Constitution. Nonetheless, the right to understanding and love is contemplated indirectly in art. 56(2)(3) of the Constitution, which states that the family is responsible for the harmonious growth of the child and that his or her education will be based on the principles of respect and social solidarity. This right derives not only from the parental duty to sustain and educate the child, but also from the general principles stated in the Civil Code currently in force. Now new legislation should be drafted to give depth and specific meaning to these principles.

Right to a family

Arts 55 and 56 of the Constitution mandate that the state protect the family, motherhood and infancy. This principle is contemplated explicitly in Principle Three of the Mozambican Declaration of the Rights of the Child:

> You have the right to live in a family … When you do not have a family, you have the right to live with a family that will love you like a son or daughter.

Principle Four of the Mozambican Declaration offers, as a general principle of family responsibility towards the child: 'So that you grow up strong and healthy, you have the right to be fed, sheltered, dressed and educated by your family.'

Arts 1576 and 1578 of the Civil Code consider the parents to be one of the sources of legal family relations. Thus, according to art. 1801 of the Civil Code, the children born into a marriage are, as a rule, presumed to be the legitimate children of that family group. Children born outside of the legally recognized family can formally obtain this right through adoption procedures and/or investigation of the illegitimate paternity or maternity.[2] Guardianship and adoption are the legal mechanisms available to guarantee orphaned or abandoned children integration into family atmosphere.[3]

Right to special protection for complete physical, mental and social development

The Constitution and other existing legislation addresses this set of rights in a very generic way. Nonetheless, Principles Three, Four, Five, Seven, Eight and Nine of the Mozambican Declaration repeatedly contemplate these rights. Several articles in the labour law[4] assure the realization of the right of the child to special protection with regard to his or her complete development. Employers are obliged to take steps aimed at furthering the professional, cultural and recreational development of young workers, and to do so in coordination with the unions and the Youth Organization. And, in addition to circumscribing the admission of workers under 15 years of age, special labour rules are stipulated for this group of workers.

Right to health

Arts 54 and 94 of the Constitution and Principle Eight of the Mozambican Declaration affirm the right to health. The Organizational Charters of the Ministry of Health, approved successively by Decrees 1/75, Presidential Decree 75/83 and Ministerial Decree 35/85, state these major principles: the state must organize a health system that benefits all the people; health is a right of the citizen and the duty of the state; preventative medicine has special priority; and health education and maintaining a sanitary atmosphere have a major role. The first two principles are regulated through Law 2/77, which set up the National Health System.

Right to education

As with other fundamental rights, education is a right and duty of every Mozambican citizen.[5] The Constitution obliges the state to organize a national education system and to provide equal access.[6] A national education system (NSE) was earlier mandated by Law 4/83. The major programmatic goals of the NSE are: provision of full access to education; compulsory education; and the opportunity for professional training. With regard to compulsory education, Law 4/83 provides free education to the seventh grade (first and second levels of primary instruction). This goal was fully realized seven years after the promulgation of that law.

The constitutional text permits the community to participate in teaching activity, within the framework of the NSE. The state has long realized the important role of families and communities in the success of education programmes. Art. 66 of Law 4/83 provides that:

… parents, economic and social institutions and popular bodies at the local level contribute to the success of mandatory schooling through promoting the registration of school-age children, supporting them in their studies, and preventing drop-outs before completion of the seven grades of primary education.

Aware of its constitutional responsibility to guarantee the exercise of the right to education, but also aware of the scarcity of resources with which to fulfil such a responsibility, the state authorized the institution of private instruction via Decree 11/90. Private instruction permitted at all school levels and in all types of instruction. However, the institutionalization of private instruction does not mitigate the state's obligation to create mechanisms that guarantee the right to education for all citizens. The decree itself establishes rules by which private instruction may be controlled by the state. In fact, free access to education is reiterated in this decree as a condition of operation of private teaching programmes of the NSE, and they remain subject to inspection to verify that the national curriculum, norms and regulations are observed.

The responsibility to assure compulsory schooling and the eradication of illiteracy falls to the Ministry of Education. The Ministry has begun a programme of special instruction to promote the reintegration into schools of thousands of children who were denied access to education over the past years.

Right to special protection for the physically or mentally disabled

Art. 95 of the Constitution proclaims that 'all citizens have the right to aid in case of incapacity', and further on, 'The State promotes and encourages the creation of conditions for the realisation of this right'. The Ministry of Health, through the State Secretariat for Social Action, must direct, organize, plan and promote the protection, support and social rehabilitation of the physically and mentally disabled. Special rehabilitative schools are now functioning. Decree 11/90 permits the participation by non-governmental entities in this type of instruction.

Protection from abuse, exploitation and abandonment

This right is not mentioned expressly in the Constitution, although it may be derived from several constitutional principles. For example, the child cannot be subjected to abuse; the state and society must protect the orphaned or homeless child, and all citizens have the right to life, to physical integrity and freedom from torture, cruel or inhuman treatment.[7] The Labour Law[8] establishes in arts 158 and 159 a body of rules intended to protect the child from exploitation by an employer. With regard to special protection against abandonment, the Civil Code, the Jurisdictional Statute of Aid to Minors and Law 2053 in the ordinary legislation regulate mechanisms and institutions tending to guarantee that same protection. In addition, the penal law punishes the sexual exploitation of children with imprisonment, whether they are the parents or third parties who incite, encourage or facilitate child prostitution or corruption. The protection given by penal law extends to all minors. For the purposes of the penal law, a minor is any individual under 21 years of age.

We have attempted to give an overview of some general principles of legal protection for the child under Mozambican law. Now we will address attempts to put principles into practice.

IMPLEMENTATION OF THE RIGHTS OF THE CHILD: THE MOZAMBICAN EXPERIENCE

The constitutional principles and the legal instruments referred to above provide the bases for the state's social programme, particularly those programmes designed to protect, aid and ensure the development of the

Mozambican child. This body of law reflects the state's political will in the area of child welfare and is more fully appreciated when one recalls that Mozambique is a recently independent country, still highly underdeveloped, with numerous competing calls on limited resources. As we analyse the implementation of children's rights in Mozambique, at no time should one lose sight of, first, the state of the economy at the time of independence (1975) and, second, the war which began practically at the moment of sovereignty and which intensified when Zimbabwe won its independence (1980). Our evaluation will therefore proceed in two distinct stages: the period from 1975 to 1981, and the period of 1981 to the present.

Background

1975 to 1981

Upon independence, Mozambique was economically impoverished, with a very high rate of illiteracy and a population lacking the most elementary health care and decimated by endemic illness. Thus, the state channelled its resources towards reversing this situation as quickly as possible; actions and programmes were directed towards improving the economy, health and education. As a result of efforts in the economic sector, per capita GNP rose from $170 to $270, and simultaneously, national GNP rose from $1,600,000,000 to $4,774,000,000.

In the area of health, the objective was to attain health care for all through the following actions:

- prioritization of preventative medicine;
- promotion of mother–child health services; extension of the health network to rural areas;
- formation of teams for different levels of care.

To achieve these objectives, the health budget grew from 4.5 per cent in 1975 to 12 per cent in 1981, representing a per capita expenditure from $1.7 to $5.4. The practical consequences were:

- a growth in the health network from 447 units to 1350 units;
- a national vaccination campaign which achieved 96 per cent coverage of all 0–2 year olds between 1976 to 1978;
- a significant increase in access to primary health care;
- a drop in the mortality rate (which in 1981 was at 159/1,000);
- an improvement in family sanitation (in 1980, 47 per cent had a

minimal sanitary infrastructure in their homes against the 3 per cent rate registered at the beginning of the 1970s);

- a substantial increase in infant health care support centres (from six in 1975 to 119 in 1981).

In this same period, 6050 health teams were formed with doctors, nurses, midwives, technicians, medical agents and multi-purpose auxiliaries. In addition, programmes were developed, which increased the population's access to drinking water. Thus in 1980, 15.88 per cent of the population benefited from water.

The state also increased its allocation of resources for education. Between 1975 and 1980, the budget for primary instruction doubled and reached an annual growth rate of 15.6 per cent; the budget for fifth and sixth grades quadrupled, reaching an average annual growth rate of 31.4 per cent; and the budget for secondary school doubled, reaching an average annual growth rate of 16.2 per cent. Illiteracy among people over 15 years old was reduced from 93 per cent to 71.9 per cent. The school network grew from 5325 to 5730 primary schools and from 7 to 35 secondary schools. The number of schoolteachers rose 10,281 to 17,030. All this contributed to an improved standard of living for Mozambicans and, in particular, for children.

It is important to mention that these results were not the fruit of state action alone; the direct contribution of the family and the community must also be acknowledged. This is a valuable lesson, which it is important to disseminate and retain for future actions. It was the community itself which, in many cases, constructed or helped to construct the health station, school, day-care or children's centre, as well as the teacher's, nurse's or health agent's home. The community was instrumental in the mobilization of citizens for health and education actions and programmes. Special mention must be made of the Organization of Mozambican Women for their mobilizing action in the heart of the community, which stimulated the community to become directly involved in all the programmes intended to improve and realize the rights of the child, particularly in the areas of health and education. In sum, the community's assumption of responsibility towards the child certainly contributed to the achievement of many of the results. But this process, leading undoubtedly to the gradual improvement of the Mozambican child's life, was abruptly interrupted by acts of armed banditry.

1981 to 1988

In reality, although natural catastrophes have wreaked great damage on the nation's economy, with devastating consequences for Mozambican children, the war of aggression, which intensified in 1981, is the principal cause of the dramatic present state of Mozambican children.

The direct and indirect effects of this war were felt throughout the country, and all national programmes and policies were disrupted. The war reversed the development process, especially in the education and health sectors, and also exaggerated the negative effects of the already weak economy in the social sectors. In addition, the need to spend greater resources on the country's defence drastically reduced the resources available for those very sectors. All these factors inevitably had serious results for the country's population and in particular for the children. Of a population of over 15 million, the number of dead as a direct result of the war is estimated at 900,000 of which 494,000 were children; the number of orphaned and abandoned children is said to be 250,000; 3.4 million citizens were displaced from their homes; 6.5 million were seriously affected. About 33 per cent of urban family members and 50 per cent of the rural family members are living in absolute poverty. Approximately 1.1 million are refugees in neighbouring countries; 50–60 per cent of the total of displaced persons and refugees are estimated to be children according to a study carried out by the Catholic Refugee Bureau in relation to the 80,000 Mozambican refugees in South Africa in September 1990.

The war has wreaked devastating consequences. Infant mortality (0–5 years of age) is today at 350/1000; the overall rate of infant mortality rose to 200/1000; and, of the nearly 7 million children under 15 years of age, only a small percentage will not have been directly affected by the lack of adequate food or the lack of basic health services. Over 500,000 children are deprived of primary education. Between 1981–1987, 824 health units and 2085 schools were destroyed; in April 1988, it was estimated that 33 per cent of the health network was out of operation, affecting 2.3 million people in the rural zones. In 1989 the internal GNP was 84 dollars per capita. The total cost of the war has now reached over $15 million, which is equivalent to three times the value of the country's external debt.

Nevertheless, despite the national circumstances, we would insist that, with the necessary political will, it is always possible to take action on behalf of children. Fortunately, the state has not remained indifferent to such a serious situation. In the following sections, we review policies and programmes promulgated on behalf of specific sectors of the population, all containing large numbers of children.

Action undertaken on behalf of specific populations

Displaced persons

In 1987 the state launched an emergency appeal to the international community, seeking funds for an emergency programme to address the critical social and economic situation. The emergency appeal garnered support from the international community and permitted the realization of the programme, embracing the areas of health, education, agriculture and food, among others. Even before that date, the state undertook to resolve the most serious problems of the most vulnerable population groups by creating the Department to Combat Natural Catastrophes, mandated to provide those most affected by economic and natural adversity with food, clothing and tools.

The 1989–90 emergency programme increased agricultural production in the family sector. The 1991 emergency programme aimed to increase the number of work implements and the number of seeds distributed to 180,000 and 300,000 displaced families, respectively, over two years. The objective was to enable these families to recommence producing food and thus to reduce their dependence on food aid. Food aid was sought in order that each displaced person would receive the equivalent of 1500 daily calories. This programme includes the supply of domestic utensils, clothing and hygiene products, distributed to displaced people upon arrival at the accommodation centres existing in several of the country's provinces.

In the 1991 emergency appeal, the health goals were to include supplemental food to 250,000 seriously undernourished children, supplies of essential medicines, vaccines and basic medical material to meet the needs of displaced population and the reconstruction of health units and support for displaced children of preschool age. In the area of education, the emergency plan aimed to supply basic school material for 116,000 primary school students who had been accommodated in centres.

Even before the beginning of the emergency programme, the state began to reconstruct destroyed health units and schools. This action was undertaken with the support and the direct involvement of the local communities which, in some cases, had already initiated such activities. Thanks to state action, local community involvement, the positive response from the international community to the emergency appeals and the participation of humanitarian and non-governmental organizations, the reconstruction and refurbishment of the 572 health units and an unspecified number of schools was possible. Specific governmental health and education programmes have been instituted for the displaced population accommodated in centres. Priorities are primary health care, mother–child programmes, nutritional programmes and vaccination. Educational programmes on sexually transmitted illnesses, including AIDS, as well as medical check-ups for preventable illness are provided. A special teaching programme was introduced for those children who have been deprived of schooling for a long time, many of whom may require special psychosocial rehabilitation.

The refugee population

The government instituted multi-faceted actions for the refugee population in neighbouring countries, in coordination with UNHCR and the host governments. The state has paid particular attention to the education and health of the children accommodated in the refugee centres outside Mozambique. Special teaching curricula were prepared, and Mozambican teachers have been sent to refugee camps to train others in the use of the teaching materials. Efforts are made to extend national programmes in the area of mother–child care, nutrition and vaccination. When conditions permit, the state attempts to and has repatriated such populations, in coordination with host governments and the United Nations. Repatriated persons receive identical support to the internally displaced, except that for the former an attempt is made to provide land for farming.

The indirectly affected population

Given its very limited resources, the state has sought to implement various programmes and actions for the general population. Priority has always been given to preventative medicine, to combating epidemics, to mother–child health programmes and to vaccination campaigns. When it became clear that there were areas not covered by the vaccination campaigns, a school health programme was introduced to guarantee the immunization of all students against tetanus and to ensure a regular programme of medical check-ups. Due to a lack of resources, check-ups are not yet available in all of the principal teaching establishments.

In the area of education, the school social action programme was created to provide books and school materials to children of families that do not have the financial means to buy them. In the area of aid for preschool children, the number of centres created after independence did not keep pace with the population growth. The state has provided incentives and support for the creation of schools and kindergartens by the community, at homes or work sites, and by humanitarian or religious organizations.

Unaccompanied children The state maintains a policy of seeking families for orphaned or abandoned children, reverting to residence in institutions only when the possibility of family integration is impossible. The Social

Action Service (SAS) of the Ministry of Health, in coordination with the local community and humanitarian and non-governmental organizations, bring abandoned children and orphans to accommodation centres and immediately begin the family tracing and reunification process. Once these possibilities have been exhausted, foster families, adoption and guardianship are considered. The legal procedural rules were simplified to facilitate adoption and guardianship.

Despite enormous economic and financial strain, the SAS founded at least one orphanage in each of the country's provinces to take care of orphans and unsheltered children who could not be integrated into families. To prevent the child's isolation, the community has been encouraged to participate in the programme of these institutions. Humanitarian and nongovernmental organizations are increasingly involved in these programmes, creating centres for orphaned or abandoned children, principally in rural zones, and seeking always to place such centres at the heart of local community life.

However, because the SAS includes only preschool children, when the child reaches six years of age he or she becomes the responsibility of the Ministry of Education, at which point they are sent to internment centres where the above-listed programmes are not continued. This abrupt transition causes problems of adaptation and integration into the environment. Children very often marginalize themselves and leave to seek solutions to their problems outside the educational establishment. Such a situation contravenes that prescribed in the text of the Constitution and the principles in the Mozambican Declaration of the Rights of the Child and the organic charter of the State Secretariat for Social Action. Mozambique should rethink the mechanisms to guarantee continual, correct and harmonious help for orphaned or abandoned children until they reach the age at which they can integrate themselves into productive activity.

Street children   The growth in the number of street children continues unchecked, and the state does not possess the means to solve this problem in the short or medium term. As a stop-gap measure, the state has been providing incentives for a variety of actions aimed at alleviating the unsheltered situation in which these children live. Action is being taken by the popular organizations such as the *Continuadores* and the Organization of Mozambican Women, as well as by humanitarian, religious and non-governmental organizations. Most programmes avoid the institutionalization of children while offering food, clothing, shelter and recreational activities.

Instrumentalized children   With regard to instrumentalized children – those children who were brainwashed and tortured by the rebel forces – the state has been making additional efforts to speed their recuperation through medical and psychological guidance. In the area of education, these children benefit from special pedagogical help with the gradual involvement of family members and the local community. The state has placed high priority on the rehabilitation of these children and is supported in these efforts by the international community of humanitarian and non-governmental institutions.

Efforts to end the armed conflict

As the government is conscious of the fact that only peace will enable Mozambican citizens fully to enjoy the rights in the Constitution and benefit from improved living conditions, it has been attempting for a long time to put an end to the war. Because the 1984 Nkomati Accord did not serve to end the war, the government began to seek alternative routes to peace and stability. With the participation of several countries, preliminary contacts with Renamo, the rebel forces, were initiated. Such efforts have the support of numerous countries including those of the African continent.

In an effort to extend aid to the most vulnerable populations, including children, affected by wars in Africa, in July 1990 the Council for Ministers of the Organization of African Unity adopted a resolution calling for the establishment of peace corridors. This principle was reaffirmed by the heads of state and government at UNICEF's World Summit for Children, which took place in New York in September 1990. The government of Mozambique recently succeeded, via direct dialogue with Renamo, in establishing peace corridors until a definitive ceasefire was reached. A general peace treaty was signed by both parties in October 1992 in Rome as a result of these dialogues. The Rome Accord (between the government and Renamo) includes a mechanism to guarantee assistance to the civilian population living in the war zones through the good graces of the International Committee of the Red Cross. These important actions must be safeguarded and expanded because they are fundamental to the defence of the interests of the Mozambican child.

Economic restructuring: social impact of the Economic Rehabilitation Programme

The Economic Rehabilitation Programme (ERP), introduced in 1987 to advance economic recovery, has instead worsened the economic situation of thousands of families in the urban centres. Subsidies were withdrawn from the great majority of food products and social services and most notably, in the health sector the cost of consultations, hospital rates and medicines rose substantially. To counteract these effects, it was established that minors below 18 years of age, the chronically ill, the elderly, the unemployed, blood donors, household employees and all the most vulnerable groups will continue to have free assistance. In addition, businesses, whether sole proprietorships or companies, must contribute to the health-care expenses of their employees.

Supplemental wages were introduced to support family members who were economically more vulnerable (Decree 6/90 of April 27).[9] State employees earning the minimum wage (under 52,200 mts, equal to two minimum salaries), with more than five persons in their family, receive 3000 mts, per month for each family member above five, the total not to exceed 15,000 mts. Such sums are readjustable in accordance with the inflation rate and budget possibilities.

The state, through the Ministry of Finance, also introduced a food subsidy. This subsidy, unlike the wage supplement, is available not only to state employees, but also to any family unit in a precarious economic situation, including individuals or urban families with incomes below one-half the national minimum salary. Families with children or pregnant women with nutritional problems also benefit from the food subsidy. This subsidy ranges from 7500 to 15,000 mts per month according to the number of family members. These totals are readjustable as changes occur in the minimum national salary. The state has provided special credit to support this subsidy but, in the future, the subsidies may be included in the general budget.

These measures are quite recent and have not yet had the desired impact upon the target groups. Their continued application as well as their expansion will demand a huge effort by the state which, on its own, can hardly support it. The donor community and the international financial institutions must not neglect the social component when prescribing economic readjustment programmes for Mozambique.

The National Commission for the Convention on the Rights of the Child

This Commission was created by the government in 1988 to coordinate Mozambique's involvement in the preparatory work of the Convention for the Rights of the Child. Commission members analysed the national reality, discussed the Mozambican child's interests, became involved in the preparatory drafting work and presented the Mozambican perspective at several international meetings.

Even before the UN General Assembly's approval of the Convention, the Commission took an active role in the dissemination of information about the Convention. It began the process of coordinating a Portuguese version, which has been agreed upon by the seven Lusophone countries, among which the Commission has been promoting the process that will lead to an official Portuguese version of the Convention's text. Once the Convention had been adopted by the UN, the Commission made the government aware of the importance of ratification. It then developed a programme for the national dissemination of the Convention with the involvement and participation of children, artists and humanitarian, non-governmental and popular organizations.

THE ROLE OF THE LOCAL, STATE AND INTERNATIONAL COMMUNITIES IN THE IMPLEMENTATION OF CHILDREN'S RIGHTS

The role of the local community

As we have repeatedly noted, the community is a crucial player in all projects related to the survival, protection and development of the child in Mozambique. Communities have both complemented state programmes or taken their own initiatives when the state has lacked capacity. With regard to the implementation of the right to family and the right to special protection in the event of abandonment and armed conflict, communities are instrumental in tracing and reunifying families and in socially integrating the orphaned, abandoned, traumatized and instrumentalized child. Rural communities welcome, love and care for thousands of homeless or orphaned children on a day-to-day basis. When reunification is not possible, communities seek substitute families, and the state provides a minimum support through SAS either in material goods or by helping to place children in new families. When necessary, communities attend to the needs of institutionalized (orphaned or abandoned) children. They help to create care institutions or to build infrastructures to house them, in collaboration with state agencies and humanitarian, religious and non-governmental organizations.

Communities play an important role in health instruction and education. They have contributed to the physical rebuilding of health and school infrastructures and, in some cases, have built units using local materials and traditional techniques. Communities have actively supported the vaccination campaigns and participated in the mother–child programmes, cooperating with the health institutions in the planning activities and in directing women and children to the care centre.

In the area of instruction and education, communities have organized to create schools for children who, owing to lack of space, could not attend the official schools. They have even developed their own literacy activities. Because the complete and harmonious development of the child involves more than institutionalized instruction, communities operate kindergartens for preschool age children. These centres offer recreational and formative activities and, in some cases, even include the participation of well known artists, such as Malagatana Valent Ngwenha.

Much concern has been generated among communities with regard to older children's use of their free time; it is difficult to offer productive recreational activities for adolescents. Nonetheless, since football is the most popular sport in the country, a few years ago, children's competitions were set-up. Initially, these competitions involved only children from the city of Maputo. However, by 1993, children from all the provincial capitals were involved, making it a true children's football championship. Teams made up of street children have also participated in the championship.

There is a growing awareness of the need for a complete solution to the problem of street children. Humanitarian, religious and non-governmental organizations have recently begun to offer street children some minimal care and protection through instruction, training and reaction in open centres.[10] However, we recommend that community and NGO involvement be encouraged beyond the construction of buildings and centres, since such actions reach only a small number of these children (25 per cent in Maputo). One concrete example is the formation of an organization called Association of Friends of the Child, currently being formed to defend the rights of the child, in particular street children. As a model, there already exists the Association for the Development of the Family, an NGO with a national scope which, among other objectives, aims for family stability through family planning with a view towards responsible paternity and maternity. However, this organization focuses more on healthy pregnancy and the child's right to health from birth through participation in family planning.

Mozambique's first national NGO, the Mozambican Association of Disabled Persons, addresses the special right to protection for the physically or mentally disabled child. This NGO intends to carry out national programmes to facilitate the active participation of disabled persons in society. Although its activities are not exclusively directed toward children, their work easily embraces children, an example being the work carried out in the Centre for the Visually Deficient in the city of Beira.

This overview of the Mozambican experience reveals not only the importance of the community in the protection and survival of the child, but also the community's capacity to collaborate with governmental and private bodies in a range of activities and to evolve their own actions in support of the child.

The role of the state

The government has long believed that poverty in Mozambique must be addressed via an integrated development policy, with special emphasis on economic and the social factors. To this end, the state created the National Institute for Rural Development (INDER). INDER coordinates programmes, projects and existing support in different state and society sectors as well as for other national and international agents, involving the community in the development process as the agents of its own development. INDER aims to increase productivity and output in the countryside to meet more of the population's basic necessities, while combating unemployment and encouraging people to repopulate rural zones. The integrated rural development policy will improve general living conditions and particularly those of the child.

Because the state views the child as the guarantee of society's continuity and development, despite the country's critical situation, it has not limited its pursuit of ways to improve child welfare. However, because child welfare has been the responsibility of only one department, the Ministry of Health, it has not been addressed in a holistic or systematic manner. Child-care programmes have thus been conceived and executed in a compartmentalized and fragmented fashion. To rectify this situation, the state recently created the State Secretariat for Social Action.[11] The Secretariat's mandate covers children up to 17 years of age and its obligations are:

1   to organize, direct and oversee the execution of support programmes for the child;
2   to direct, plan and promote the creation of social protection and support units for children, as well as elaborate norms for the pedagogical and administrative organization of these establishments, according to the requirement of the Ministry of Education;
3   to provide support for orphans, abandoned children and others lacking family support;
4   to support economically weak pregnant women and newborns;
5   to develop and initiate educational activities within the community about alternative child-care methods and the role of adults in the integral development and formation of the child;
6   to promote the realization of legal measures for adoption and guardianship, in collaboration with other agencies;
7   to organize, promote and oversee a system which guarantees protection, support, education and recuperation of the physically and mentally disabled child;

8   to promote the prevention of, and combat, drug addiction as well as the social reintegration of drug addicts in collaboration with other bodies.

Because a child may remain under the State Secretariat's protection until the age of 17, the harmonious development of the child is not disrupted. Previously, children were handed over to institutions directed by the SAS and, upon reaching school age, the child was transferred from institution to institution under the guardianship of the Ministry of Education, without continuity of care.

At the same time, the state has tried to offer incentives for initiatives that contribute to the child's improved development. In response to this opening, several religious, humanitarian and non-governmental organizations in close collaboration with the local community have been implementing activities specifically aimed at sheltering street, orphaned or homeless children. By means of the economic and social readjustment policy, the state intends, to the extent possible, to continue and to expand such measures as the supplementary wage, the food subsidy, the social security measures and the savings plan for school social activities. The state will try to maintain subsidized prices on basic foods such as corn, and will continue to support small agricultural projects.

Funds from international financial institutions, such as the World Bank, are important, though insufficient, to rehabilitate social structures such as schools and hospitals. Therefore, the state has taken several steps. The Economic Rehabilitation Programme includes a budget for the construction of new units and the repair of existing ones, mainly in large urban centres. Meanwhile, to make the recuperation of the units situated in rural zones possible, the state included a budget for this in the emergency programme. The state has also offered incentives to humanitarian, religious and non-governmental groups to participate in the recuperation and rehabilitation of social infrastructures in rural areas.

In an earlier paper entitled 'Penal law and the rights of the child: prevention of delinquency',[12] we recommend the creation of a centralized, governmental institute to coordinate the relevant state agencies, humanitarian, religious, non-governmental organizations and communities working on behalf of children. We propose that such a body would coordinate the implementation of holistic programmes and assist in obtaining resources for the total resolution of the problems of Mozambican children. With the creation of the Secretariat for Social Action by Presidential Decree 28/90, it would seem that such a body now exists. The Secretariat is responsible for providing protection and aid to children, either by defining and organizing multifaceted programmes, or by coordinating and directing programmes in direct collaboration with other state agencies and private institutions. Ideally, the Secretariat would prevent the promulgation of fragmented policies and disorganized programmes that have, until now, been the result of the decentralization of child-care policy within the government. Unfortunately, however, it will start off with a resource deficit. Thus, it is important that priorities in the realization of actions be defined and the phases for the implementation of each programme be determined following the methodology and the principles established in the Action Programme and agreed upon at the recent World Summit for Children. Although there is no shortage of political will, Mozambique needs to prepare and establish new frameworks, and raise funds, to support these programmes over the long term.

Nor does the creation of the Secretariat for Social Action diminish the need for a Commission on the Rights of the Child, which would be responsible for addressing implementation problems concerning children's rights and establishing a link between Mozambique and the United Nations. The Commission that was already established must now advance, under the rubric of the State Secretariat for Social Action, and must include the participation of governmental social sectors and citizens with recognized professional expertise and a clear interest in safeguarding the rights of the child. Finally, the creation of the State Secretariat in no way obviates the need for new civic associations which propose to carry out activities towards the defence of the rights of the child, as allowed for in the new Constitution.

The role of the international community

The Convention on the Rights of the Child permits the international community to take a supervisory role in the implementation of the enumerated rights. The international community may assist via bilateral or multilateral cooperation, but only at the request of the state in need. The principle of mutual advantage still governs intrastate cooperation. Thus, developing countries see few results from the signing of accords intending to improve the status of the child, since these countries can offer little or nothing in return. We anticipate that the international community of states might thus ignore the serious problems of children in developing countries.

However, the Mozambican experience yields a different perspective of the normative role of the international community in the implementation of children's rights. In Mozambique, the international community has developed a range of child welfare-oriented activities. Initially this intervention was spontaneous and individualized, but, recently, a higher level of international participation and organization – for example, involvement in plans with a national multisectoral scope, such as the emergency plan, or international activity in programmes and projects defined in partnership with the state and with the participation of the local community – has become evident. Often, the participation of the international community assures the realization of state plans and programmes, since the state does not have the capacity to carry them out. The international community has thus been an indispensable complement to state action, particularly with regard to the survival, protection and development of children affected by the war, enabling thousands of children to survive thanks to food, clothing and medical aid which provides for the basic needs of a considerable number of orphaned, abandoned and street children. We therefore believe that the international community has both an important role and a responsibility in the direct implementation of the Convention on the Rights of the Child, without lessening the state's responsibility. However, the responsibility of the international community extends beyond such participation. It should also act decisively to influence financial institutions to humanize their policies of economic structural readjustment by emphasizing the social component. Additionally, the international community must act together with donor agencies so that grants cease to resemble charity and begin to assume a dynamic role in community development. Only thus will it be possible to guarantee the implementation of the Convention of the Rights of the Child in many countries and, most specifically, in Mozambique.

NOTES

1   Art. 1877.
2   Civil Code, arts 1827 *et seq.*; 1845 *et seq.*; 1857 *et seq.*
3   Civil Code, arts 1921, 1973.
4   Arts 157 and 158 of Labour Law 8/85.
5   Art. 92, Constitution.
6   Art. 92(2), Constitution.
7   Arts 56 and 70, Constitution.
8   Law 8/85 of 14 December 1985.
9   Decree 6/90 of 27 April.
10 See A.M. Loforte (1994), 'Street children in Mozambique', *International Journal of Children's Rights*, **2**, p. 149.
11 Presidential Decree 28/90 of 10 September.
12 L.P. Sacramento and A.M. Pessoa (1991), 'Penal Law and the rights of the child: Prevention of delinquency' (unpublished).

9 New Zealand and The United Nations Convention on the Rights of the Child: A Lack of Balance

*Mark Henaghan**

THE SIGNIFICANCE OF CHILDREN'S RIGHTS AND THE CONVENTION: ESTABLISHING A BALANCE

Analysis of children's rights and their implementation requires keeping three potentially conflicting concepts in mind at the same time. First, there is the concept of the child's autonomy to express views and make decisions; second there is the concept of the family's responsibility to nurture and bring up children, and, finally, there is the concept of the state's responsibility to provide services which protect and enhance the lives of children. Each one of these concepts raises value choices of its own. When is a child old enough to make decisions? What weight should be given to children's decisions? When should children be consulted? Who is the 'family' that is responsible for the child? What is the basis for imposing responsibility on members of a family? Where does family responsibility end and state responsibility begin? What are the 'necessary' or 'appropriate' services the state should provide? Overriding these value choices, is the decision as to whom determines them. Who will determine the allocation of power and responsibility for children?[1]

The UN Convention on the Rights of the Child recognizes the three concepts about children's rights. Articles 12 and 13 recognize the autonomy of a child to express views freely, and receive information freely. Articles 3(2), 5,

*Senior Lecturer in Law, University of Otago.

165

14(2), 18, 27(2) recognize the 'primary' responsibility of parents and others, such as extended family, in bringing up, caring for, instructing and providing financial support for the child. Many other Articles[2] in the Convention place responsibility on the state to provide services which protect, educate and enhance the development of children. The Convention adds a fourth dimension – international cooperation in the implementation of rights – which is expressly referred to in Articles about education, health, culture, adoption, child support, child abduction, refugees and traffic in children. A major criticism of the Convention is that it has not practised what it has preached. There is no indication that children have been consulted as to the contents of the document. It is assumed that this is what they want.

The Convention reflects the political reality that there are different perspectives on how best to secure children's rights. Some push for more individual freedom of choice for the child,[3] others believe families need more recognition and empowerment,[4] and others still see the solution in increased state intervention and protection of children.[5] The Convention adds its own perspective of international cooperation to improve the living conditions of children globally. All have their place and are capable of being effective depending on the nature of the situation, the capacity of the child and the family, and the capacity of the state concerned. As Michael Freeman has clearly pointed out, 'the distinction between protecting children and protecting their rights has thus been drawn too broadly'.[6]

The significance of the Convention is not in providing concrete answers to complex issues of child policy.[7] The answer to most child policy dilemmas has been to say that we will act in the 'best interests' of the child, or that the 'child's welfare' is the crucial consideration. While these are laudable aspirations, they are frequently used as justifications in themselves – for example, 'the child must be placed in a foster home because it is in the child's best interests'. An award-winning British drama produced in the 1970s called *The Spongers*[8] which concerns a mother on social security trying to cope with a number of children, one of whom has Down's syndrome, provides an illustrative example. When the mother asks why that child is to be placed in an old people's home, she is told it is in the 'child's best interests'. Of course, the real reason is one of cost. The Convention provides a much more detailed framework for the accountability of such decisions.[9]

The temptation for interest groups to capture one segment of the Convention is always present. Frances Olsen[10] gives the example of Article 13, free access to information, which could be argued to make pornography widely available to children. That argument would need to be balanced against Article 19 (protection from exploitation) and Article 12 (children's own views on the matter).

THE THEME: A LACK OF BALANCE

New Zealand, which has been traditionally strong in state responsibility for the care and protection of children,[11] is weakening in that area. More and more responsibility is being placed on individual family members to care and provide for children.[12] Children's views are virtually non-existent in decision-making and the development of policy.[13] Consequently it depends on the capacities and capabilities of the family into which the child is born as to what chances and opportunities that child will have in life.[14]

WHY THE LACK OF BALANCE?

The social context

Legal policy in New Zealand is based largely on the married two-parent family:[15] the reality is quite different. Figures from the last census show that the number of single-parent families has increased, and the numbers of the traditional model of married couple plus children have decreased.[16]

Also, while New Zealand may seem to be a homogenous society, it is, in reality, made up of many cultures. Since the mid-1980s the concept of the Maori as the indigenous people of New Zealand has grown in strength. The Maori have been saying for 150 years, since the signing of a Treaty called the Treaty of Waitangi with the first settlers, that they have a special place as the *tangata whenua* (people of the land) in New Zealand, and that the state guaranteed as a condition of signing the Treaty that Maori *tikanga* (special ways) would be preserved. Donna Tai Tokerau Durie-Hall, of Ngati Rangiteaorere descent and legal adviser to the National Maori Congress, and Joan Metge, an anthropologist who has done a considerable amount of work with Maori people over a long period of time, have shown that the Maori recognize two kinds of family, the nuclear family and the *whanau*.[17] Whanau is defined as a group of relatives defined by reference to a recent ancestor (*tupuna*) comprising several generations, several nuclear families and several households, and having a degree of ongoing corporate life focused on group symbols such as a name, a land base (*turangawaewae*) and precious things (*taonga*). The experience of *whanau* affects the experience of family since, for Maori, children are not exclusive to their parents, they are also part of the *whanau*, and care of them flows between parents and *whanau* members. Grandparents (*tupuna*) are perceived to have a significant role in a child's life, helping with self-esteem, language development and emotional issues. Similar ideas exist in Pacific Island families, with the *aiga* (extended family) as the most crucial group. Since much of family law in New Zealand does not recognize the legal status of *whanau*, *aiga* or grandparents, it does not recognize the reality of those children's lives. One part of the balance, 'family' responsibility, is distorted. The legislation which does recognize the *whanau*, and wider family – the Children Young Persons and Their Families Act 1989 – was heralded as bringing a balance back into the reality of some families. Sadly, this has caused another part of the balance to be lost: legal recognition of wider family responsibility has had the effect of diminishing state support for the exercise of that responsibility.[18]

The political context

New Zealand signed and ratified the 1989 UN Convention on the Rights of the Child on 13 March 1993, three years after it was adopted by the United Nations. It was the one hundred and thirty-first country to ratify the Convention. A national programme of action for reaching the goals specified for the year 2000 has not yet been drawn up.

The New Zealand government attached three formal reservations to the signing. They relate to Articles 28, 32 and 37 on illegal immigrants, employment law and criminal custody rules.

Mr Don McKinnon, acting prime minister at the time of signing, explained the reasons for the reservations:

> Children who are not lawfully in New Zealand are not entitled to education and welfare benefits. We will reserve our right to continue to determine the entitlements of children in these areas according to their immigration status. Second, New Zealand's employment laws have traditionally not distinguished between children and adults, and we maintain that approach. Finally we have reserved our right to continue to mix juveniles and adults held in custody when circumstances require that.

The most outstanding feature of these reservations is their economic significance. They reflect a time of emphasis on the free market and the curbing of state support in New Zealand politics. The government would no doubt argue Article 4 of the Convention to justify their reservations: economic rights are to be undertaken to the maximum extent of 'available resources'.

There was little publicity for the ratification: 1993 was an election year in New Zealand and, as children are not eligible voters, little was done or said by government or opposition parties about the rights of children in New Zealand society. Most press coverage was given to a UNICEF report[19] which criticized 'monetarist'. 'free market' policies. Although New Zealand has long been cited as one of the world's 'most enlightened social democracies' since the mid-1980s it has begun to cut back on the former 'cradle-to-grave' social welfare system, the main political reason being given for this being the country that can no longer afford such a system. The report argued that the emphasis on the free market has produced a widening gap between rich and poor, and a deterioration in living standards in families with children. It linked these events with the facts that 'New Zealand now has the highest youth suicide rate among industrialised countries, and reported cases of child abuse have doubled since 1985'.[20] Nonetheless, however the statistics may be interpreted, there is undoubtedly more unemployment and more people struggling for a reasonable existence in New Zealand than there was 20 years ago.[21] It is acknowledged by all political parties[22] from all sides of the spectrum that times have become economically tougher in New Zealand. The crucial issue is how should interests be prioritized given that there is no longer sufficient funds to do all the things that have been done in the past. Article 18 of the UN Convention places the primary responsibility for children on parents and legal guardians, with the state having an obligation to render 'appropriate assistance'. The balance between parental responsibility and 'appropriate' state assistance can only be measured by the actual living conditions of children, not by political slogans.

After the 1979 International Year of the Child, a New Zealand Committee for Children was set up, with government funding, to monitor legislation and to ensure that the children's viewpoint was considered. Government funding ceased in 1987. New Zealand has had a Ministry of Youth Affairs, concerned with young people between 12 and 25 years old, since 1 July 1989. This branch of government, which has had a low public profile, carrying out advisory and liaison roles, changed its emphasis in 1994 to the provision of policy advice.[23] The Ministry is currently focusing on the areas of health, crime prevention, skills training, income and employment. Its main task is to promote 'equitable opportunities' for the youth of New Zealand. It also has the responsibility of preparing the report required under the 1989 UN Convention within two years of ratification; this report was submitted on 5 May 1995 but will not be completed until December 1995. Since the Ministry is concerned with children over 12, it has sought the assistance of the Commissioner for Children who deals with children from birth to 17. A briefing paper[24] to the incoming Minister of Youth Affairs states that the UN Convention on the Rights of the Child, 'provides an excellent standard against which policies, programmes and legislation can be measured for their impact on children and young people to age 18'. The strength of the Ministry is that, as part of government, it is in a strong position to influence policy; its weakness is that the government may not want to acknowledge its own deficiencies.

There are three more independent watchdogs on policy towards children in New Zealand – the Commissioner for Children, the Youth Law Project, and the Plunket Society. The New Zealand Commissioner for Children was set up under the Children, Young Persons and Their Families Act 1989,[25] primarily to monitor Department of Social Welfare practices under that Act. The Commissioner also has a brief to promote research and public awareness about the welfare of children up to the age of 17.[26] Given limited resources and powers, the Commissioner has done an excellent job through newsletters[27] and press releases to raise public awareness about the 1989 UN Convention and its significance for New Zealand society. Another group which has worked hard to raise awareness about the Convention is the Youth Law Project – a community law centre for children and young people.[28] This group has been clear and detailed in its criticism of where New Zealand falls short of the Convention.[29] The Plunket Society is primarily concerned with the health of the very young[30] and has been instrumental in child health and safety measures in New Zealand. Until children have political clout, it is likely to be the heroic efforts of such independent groups who make the small gains on their behalf.

The legal context: a glimpse of hope

The traditional view that international treaties are not an enforceable part of domestic law unless written into that law, has been undermined by judicial practice in New Zealand in recent times. The Treaty of Waitangi 1840 is an international document signed between the British Crown (the settlers) and some Maori chiefs (the indigenous people). The so-called 'principles of the Treaty' have been written into some domestic legislation.[31] Some New Zealand judges, including the President of the New Zealand Court of Appeal, Sir Robin Cooke, have made it clear that the 'principles of the Treaty' can be taken into account as an aid in statutory interpretation in statutes which do not mention the Treaty at all.[32] The assumption is that the wording of an Act should not be read inconsistently with the 'principles of the Treaty'.

Added to this judicial extension of the use of international treaties as aids to interpretation is the fact the New Zealand judges and lawyers are becoming more familiar with the use of 'rights' as a basis for arguing and deciding cases.

New Zealand enacted a New Zealand Bill of Rights Act in 1990. This Act is not overriding legislation as is the US Bill of Rights: it cannot be used to strike down legislation which is inconsistent with its principles. However, the Act can be used in interpreting other Acts, and can be used to fill gaps in the law. The major effect of the New Zealand Bill of Rights Act 1990 to date has been to apply a strong check on how police deal with suspects. The listing of 'rights' in legislation, even when many of them already existed in case law by virtue of the common law, appears to have given the 'rights' more legal bite.

In family law, Judge Inglis QC has begun to use the language of children's rights to justify decisions about the placement of children.[33] In New Zealand law, the parent–child relationship is expressed in terms of parents having a 'right' to control the upbringing of their children. This 'right' is seen as placing a duty on parents to nurture children to the stage where they become independent of their parents. Analytically, this gives children the right to adequate and appropriate care, the right to a stable and secure home, a right to be insulated from dissension and argument, the right to clear and consistent, but reasonable, guidelines and limits on the child's behaviour. This is an important check on the predominant focus on adult agendas, which has the positive effect of encouraging adult parties and their advisers to rethink how their behaviour impacts on the children rather than on each other.

The Convention has also been used in argument in the New Zealand Court of Appeal.[34] The context was a judicial review of the New Zealand Immigration Service to execute a removal warrant against a Western Samoan citizen who had come to New Zealand on a visitor's permit. While in New Zealand this person had married an applicant for permanent residence in New Zealand with whom he had a child who automatically became a New Zealand citizen. The applicant for review argued that he would not be able to support his family in Western Samoa, and that they would not come with him. He was the primary caregiver for the child, while his wife worked during the day. A paediatrician gave evidence that if the applicant had to leave his family behind, the separation would have a major psychological effect on the child. Articles 23 and 24 of the International Covenant on Civil and Political Rights (and the optional Protocol thereto), and Article 9, subsections (1) and (4) of the 1989 UN Convention on the Rights of the Child, which emphasize a child's right not to be separated from his or her parents against their will except by competent authorities, were cited by the father's lawyer.

The decision to deport the applicant was made before the child was born, so that there was no need to take into account the principles in the international treaties. The New Zealand Court of Appeal adjourned the appeal allowing the Minister of Immigration to reconsider the decision to deport, in the light of the changed circumstances of the child's birth.

The Court of Appeal commented on the relevance of international human rights conventions. Counsel for the father referred to the Balliol Statement of 1992, with its reference to the duty of the judiciary to interpret and apply national constitutions, ordinary legislation, and the common law, in the light of the universality of human rights. The Court acknowledged that the bearing on domestic law of international human rights and instruments was 'undergoing evolution' and, furthermore, that in a previous decision of its own, there had been recognition that some international obligations are so important that no reasonable minister could fail to take them into account.

The President of the Court of Appeal, Sir Robin Cooke, left open the argument for future cases that, since New Zealand's accession to the optional Protocol, the UN Human Rights Committee is 'in a sense' part of New Zealand's judicial structure, because individuals subject to New Zealand jurisdiction have direct rights of recourse to it. He concluded that:

> ... a failure to give practical effect to international instruments to which New Zealand is a party may attract criticism. Legitimate criticism could extend to the New Zealand courts if they were to accept the argument that, because a domestic statute giving discretionary powers in general terms does not mention human rights, norms or obligations, the executive is necessarily free to ignore them.[35]

Sadly, a New Zealand television documentary[36] has shown that points of high principle take time to filter down to the realities of people's lives. A Western Samoan woman mistakenly signed a removal warrant, thinking it was an application for residence. She has now been removed back to Western Samoa, leaving her two children behind with relations in New Zealand. She and her family were unaware of their legal rights and unaware of Article 9 of the Convention and how it could be argued. However, there is a potentially happy ending to this story now that the Minister of Immigration has undertaken to reassess the case.[37] The Minister, having become aware of the Court of Appeal decision, has put a freeze on the deportation of all those on temporary visas who have New Zealand children. The combination of the Convention and the courts are a powerful instrument to secure children's rights.

The other New Zealand case in which the Convention was given prominence was one which involved a contest for custody over three children who for three years had been in the custody of Exclusive Brethren grandparents.[38] The natural parents had left the Exclusive Brethren, and had 'withdrawn' from them. They had tried for some time to persuade the grandparents to let them see the children without success. The natural parents were given custody in the Family Court. In the High Court appeal, the UN Convention was used as a measure of the practices of the Exclusive Brethren. Fraser J commented that the Brethren were in breach of Article 13 (the free expression of ideas), Article 15 (freedom of association), Article 28 (opportunities for higher education – the Exclusive Brethren oppose university education), and Article 29 (to encourage children to treat all people with tolerance). Fraser J observed that the UN Convention on the Rights of the Child reflects 'the generally accepted standards of society in this country.' Ultimately, however, the case turned on the fact that, by law, the parents were the children's guardians and therefore had the right to decide their religion (Article 14(2)). The only way this could be done was to place the children in the parents' care. It is noteworthy that Article 12 of the Convention is not mentioned in the judgment. All three children, aged between 8 and 11 years old, wanted to stay with their grandparents. The judge accepted their views as genuine but did not give them weight. There is no analysis of why the children lacked sufficient age and maturity. There is also, no analysis of Article 30, the right to practise a religion of choice.

In terms of the three concepts behind children's rights, the child's autonomy was considered but not given weight, and the state's responsibility to ensure that certain lifestyles meet the standards of basic human rights for children was considered but not given explicit weight; instead, parental responsibility was prioritized.

EVIDENCE OF LACK OF BALANCE

The *child's* viewpoint

The child's viewpoint is underdeveloped and often non-existent in New Zealand. Article 12 of the Convention does not simply hand decision-making over to children, it recognizes that a child does have a viewpoint, which is to be given weight in accordance with the age and maturity of the child. Article 12 emphasizes that the child's views are to be put 'freely' by the child. A child is likely to value and perceive things in quite different ways than adults. Article 12 has the powerful effect of requiring decision-makers to listen to, and understand, a particular child's world. This gives respect and dignity to the child and is also likely to lead to better decisions. Bruno Bettleheim in his classic work, *A Good Enough Parent*, emphasizes this key principle:

> I feel that a parent's most important task is to get a feeling for what things may mean to his [or her] child and on this basis handle himself [herself] in ways that are most helpful to both; if he [she] does, this will improve the parent's and child's relations to each other. The best way to get this feeling is to remember what a parallel issue meant to us when we were children, and why, and how we would have liked our parents to handle it, us and themselves.[39]

It is widely accepted in child development literature[40] that children learn by how they are treated. When children's viewpoints are given respect and dignity, children learn from that experience to treat the views of others with similar respect.

Placement of children and financial decisions

In adoption, custody, access, guardianship and care and protection proceedings, there is provision in current New Zealand family law for the child's view to be taken into account. The provisions vary as to the mandatory nature of acquiring such views, the factors which may affect the weight to be given such views and the timing in proceedings when such views will be sought.

The Guardianship Act 1968, which deals with the placement and upbringing of children, makes it mandatory for the Family Court to ascertain the wishes of the child if the child is able to express them, and mandatory to take account of them to such an extent as the court thinks fit, having regard to the age and maturity of the child.[41] There are two principal limitations on the effectiveness of this provision. The vast majority of custody, access and guardianship disputes are resolved by conciliation processes, such as through counselling and mediation. There being no legal requirement that the children's views be heard or taken into account in these processes,[42] the degree to which children are involved is dependent on those who facilitate them.[43] If the matter does go to court, it is mandatory to appoint counsel to 'represent' the child, unless no useful purpose would be served.[44] There has been much debate in New Zealand on what this role signifies. Does counsel represent the child's wishes which would be consistent with Article 12, or does counsel represent what counsel thinks is best for the child?[45] It is possible to find reported cases where counsel appointed to represent the child have made submissions and recommendations quite contrary to the express wishes of the child they represent.[46] Research surveys of the role show that some counsel do not even talk with their child clients in order to ascertain their views.[47] The New Zealand Court of Appeal has not led by example on this issue. In an appeal in late 1993,[48] the Court insisted that submissions from counsel appointed to represent the child were crucial, and that such submissions had not been given sufficient weight in the High Court. Yet, two months earlier, in two major appeals[49] involving access to children where there had been allegations of sexual abuse, the same Court said that it did not want to hear from counsel appointed to represent the children in those cases. If children's rights are to be taken seriously, they cannot be switched on and off at the convenience of decision-makers. It is also possible to find cases where the views of the children concerned are not discussed at all in the judgment. The concept of the child's 'views', the child's 'wishes', is underdeveloped.[50] In the context of judicial proceedings between parents over a child, the child's 'views' are often seen as synonymous with the child's preference of parent. This is both an inappropriate and unfair burden to place on any child,[51] and requires the child to become part of the adult agenda. Children commonly do not want to choose, but that does not mean they do not have views. Their views, if they are allowed to be given freely, are likely to revolve around the important matters for the children, such as their everyday activities or the importance of keeping their friends. For children to be treated with respect and dignity, their views must mean their views, not merely their responses to adult questions based on the needs of an adult dispute resolution process. Article 12 will only be met when effort is made to understand how children see the situation. This requires a major shift of perspective.

The Adoption Act 1955[52] does not mandatorily require the views of the child to be ascertained, but does allow for 'due consideration' to be given to the wishes of the child, having regard to the age and understanding of that child. When the Adoption Act was passed, the most common type of adoption involved that of a very young child immediately after birth, so, understandably, there is no mandatory requirement for seeking the child's view. It is now more common for older children to be adopted into a reconstituted family, or to be adopted into a foster family.[53] In these situations the child, if old enough to express views, should have the right to do so.

Care and protection proceedings (which deal with abuse and neglect cases) do not mandatorily require the child's view to be obtained. The Children, Young Persons and Their Families Act 1989, states that 'due consideration should be given to the views of the child'.[54] The weight to be given the child's views is not to be determined solely by age and maturity, but his or her 'culture'. If a child comes from a culture which gives children less say in decision-making, then that child's views will hold less weight than if the child was from a culture which gives children more say in decision-making. This sliding scale according to culture is inconsistent with the Convention, since the document was written to apply to *all* children. Article 2 states that parties

> ... shall respect and ensure the rights set forth ... irrespective of the child's or his or her parents', or legal guardian's race, colour, sex, language, national, ethnic or social origins, property, disability, birth or other status.

The reason for the New Zealand caveat of culture is that strong concern about the nature of individual rights was expressed by the Maori and Pacific Island people.[55] The thrust of the concerns was that the interests of an individual cannot be determined in isolation, but must be determined as part of the interests of the wider family group. However, recognizing a child's right to give views does not necessarily undermine the wider family group. Article 12 does not say the child's views are determinative; it requires them to be heard and given weight based on the age and maturity of the child. Otherwise the child has no individual dignity or respect, the decision-making process becomes unbalanced in favour of the group over the individual.

The Youth Law Project has argued that parents should be required to consult children about major decisions affecting them such as a decision to go to live overseas, a proposed change of schools, a move to another town or city or a move to the household of a new partner.[56] The Project argues that, in Finland, parents have a legal duty to consult their children in such situations, and that a similar proposal has been made by the Scottish Law Commission.

With two exceptions, family law legislation in New Zealand does not specifically provide for children to initiate proceedings about their placement. There is provision in family legislation for 'any other person'[57] to apply with the permission of the court, and children could argue they come within this category. The exceptions are, first, for children aged over 16 to apply to the Family Court for a review of any decision by a parent or guardian on any important matter.[58] Second, there is provision,[59] put in by a 1991 amendment to the Guardianship Act 1968, for a child of any age to apply to be placed under the guardianship of the Family Court in custody and access proceedings because of the difficulties created by these proceedings, or their duration. Under these circumstances, the Family Court has authority to appoint an agent to care for the child. The New Zealand Family Court has used the provision creatively, allowing an 18 year-old to apply to free herself from the domination of her mother.[60]

The structure of the Guardianship Act 1968 does not allow children to apply for access to an absent parent. Even when a custodial parent applies on the children's behalf for the other parent to visit the children who were missing that parent, the structure of the Act is such that the Family Court has held there is no jurisdiction to make the order.[61] This makes it difficult for children to exercise their right, expressed in Article 9(3), to maintain direct contact with a parent. So, while unwilling children can be required by court order to visit a parent, unwilling parents cannot be required to see a child who may be missing them very much.

There is no mandatory requirement that children's views be ascertained or heard in property and financial disputes, although the interests of children are a relevant consideration in property disputes between married couples.[62] Research of the provision shows that it is rarely used in decision-making, mainly because children do not have independent party status in the proceedings. Property disputes between unmarried couples are determined by the principles of equity.[63] These look at the partners' contribution to the property, and have not developed to the point of consideration of children's interests. In decisions about child maintenance, there is no legislative mention of the interests of children or their views. The 1991 Child Support Act which deals with maintenance for children is a classic example of how adult priorities override those of children. The Act lists a number of objects,[64] but nowhere to be found are the interests or views of children. This is not only inconsistent with Article 12, it also infringes Article 3 of the Convention which requires that the best interests of children be a primary consideration in all actions concerning children. The Child Support Act was passed at a time when the amount owing on government support for children was high. Part of the push for the legislation was to transfer the collection of money owed from the Social Welfare department to the Department of Inland Revenue. The legislation was also passed to shift the burden of establishing liability. It is now an administrative matter for the primary caregiver to apply for child support from the liable parent. The Act sets out formulae for the amount to be paid. The formulae focus solely on the liable parent's income and circumstances and takes no account of the primary caregiver's circumstances. The burden is on the liable parent to initiate court action and to object if the assessment of amount is improper or unfair. The Act is based on the assumption that income support for children is an issue between caregivers and the state. Bill Atkin has summarized the Child Support Act 1991 as follows: 'Its focus is monetary ... and the interests of children are assumed to be bound up totally in the formula's assessment.'[65]

Children have more rights to express views on financial and property issues on the death of a parent. The Family Protection Act 1955[66] allows a child to contest a parent's will on the basis that adequate provision has not been made.

Education decisions

The Education Act 1989[67] provided that every secondary school Board of Trustees (the governing body of the school) should have one member appointed by the students to represent their interests. The Act was then amended[68] to allow Boards of Trustees to dispense with any student representation. The Youth Law Project[69] has pointed out that students do not even have the statutory right to be present or represented when a Board of Trustees is considering a student for suspension or expulsion from a school. While some schools may allow students to participate in educational decisions which affect them, there is no clear statutory right.

National and local elections

The present age of majority in New Zealand is 18. In 1986, a Royal Commission Electoral Reform considered arguments for lowering the voting age to 16. After a thorough review of available research, the Commission were not able to find any evidence that young persons of 16 lacked the capacity to make considered political and social judgements. In fact, as the Youth Law Project has pointed out, the Commission believed that from about the age of ten, children were likely to be sufficiently knowledgeable about political and social issues to participate in the democratic process.[70]

Environmental and planning decisions

The Commissioner for Children and the Youth Law Project have both argued persuasively that little consideration is given to the views of children when decisions are made about resource allocation, environment, open space, play and recreation, housing, transport, public facilities, health and safety. The Youth Law Project cites[71] the following examples: the lack of cycle tracks for safe transit of cyclists, the failure to provide for the special needs of children in designing public toilets and dressing sheds, the failure to protect children from poisoning by the mandatory use of childproof caps and containers, poor design and lack of imagination in children's play areas. While it is possible to find individual examples of child-oriented facilities, normally due to the efforts of a tireless individual on a council, or the push from a major organisation such as Plunket which has done a great deal for child safety in New Zealand, there is no right built into the decision-making processes for children to be involved. The Youth Law Project has recommended that the Office of the Commissioner for Children, should be expanded to include a consultative and advocacy rule in relation to environment, planning resource allocation and health and safety issues.

Criminal courts

New Zealand has made major efforts on behalf of child witnesses in cases of a sexual nature. Since 1 January 1990 there has been provision for children to give evidence via video, closed-circuit television, and behind screens.[72] This is to ensure the child will not be intimidated in giving their evidence and in being heard by the court processes and the presence of the accused. Juries are no longer to be told that children tend to fantasize and distort, a ploy which, in the past, has tended to undermine their evidence. Expert assistance is provided to help judges and juries understand the developmental level of the child giving evidence. These legislative changes have had the positive effect of judges and prosecution lawyers being made more aware of the needs of child witnesses. Specialist interview units are set up and staffed by police and social workers attuned to the needs of children who go through the criminal justice system. These changes have given children a better opportunity to be heard in the criminal courts. While they statutorily apply only to crimes of a sexual nature, New Zealand judges have an inherent jurisdiction to extend the use of the procedures to other crimes.[73]

A sign of hope

In their Statement of Intent for 1993–94, the Ministry of Youth Affairs lists as one of its outcomes, youth 'input' into the development of government policy and services, and 'participation' of young people in cultural, social and economic policies and services. These must become priorities if Article 12 of the Convention is to play its role in New Zealand society.[74]

Family responsibility for children

In the language of children's rights, a child has a right to be nurtured and provided for by that child's family. Children's need for nurture, identity, care and love is best met by those who most closely identify with the child – the child's family. Not all families are the same; not all families are capable of providing for and nurturing their children. Family responsibility must always be balanced by state responsibility and the child's views.

John Eekelaar[75] has pointed out two kinds of family responsibility: the practical exercise of it; and the status of biological and adoptive parenthood. Article 5 of the Convention recognizes that responsibility for providing 'appropriate direction and guidance' about the Convention may extend more widely than just to parents and may also include members of the extended family or community. The Convention places responsibility for the upbring-ing of a child primarily on parents or legal guardians;[76] responsibility for financial provision is placed primarily on parents or 'others responsible'.[77] The Convention recognizes that family responsibility is potentially wider than parental status, and that while it is 'primary', it is not absolute – it is not an end in itself.

The 1989 Children, Young Persons and Their Families Act which deals with children who are in need of care and protection and with young offenders under 17, legally recognized for the first time in New Zealand, the wider family of a child (the *whanau, hapu* and *iwi*).[78] This was a positive step in that it recognized the practical reality of Maori and Pacific Island family structures.[79] The Act set up the 'family group conference' as the primary means of dispute resolution. This conference involves the family network, with the support of a social worker and other relevant expertise, in the attempt to resolve the problem. The theory is that the family should have the first opportunity to protect and provide for the child. Written into the legislation are principles that the child's rights are to be upheld, and the child is to be protected.[80]

Independent evaluation of the Act, however, shows that the individual child becomes lost in the process.[81] The assumption of family responsibility becomes an end in itself. This is not surprising when a prime influence in passing the legislation was 'to save the public purse by reducing the cost of the care of the abused and neglected children by placing responsibility on the wider family'.[82] This has been borne out by lack of resources for operation of the Act. The New Zealand Commissioner for Children, Ian Hassall, graphically highlights the hollowness of 'family responsibility':

> The reliance on community resources required by the Act has not been matched by the provision of new programmes and services. Problems of finding suitable service providers, obtaining approval of the new programmes, funding the programmes and ensuring accountability have delayed developments. The intended reliance on iwi (tribal) authorities for services for Maori people has been handicapped by delays in creating and resourcing those authorities.
> ... the reality of family empowerment depends on resources and support services. Many families are living in very poor circumstances: without adequate incomes, in poor quality housing and without the support of others in caring for their children and acquiring skills in managing their families. The rhetoric of family responsibility can readily lead to the reduction of the support of the state sector which is essential to the wellbeing of many families.[83]

The sad reality of a philosophy of family responsibility as an end in itself without the child's safety as a priority, and without appropriate government assistance, is the fact that children die needlessly at the hands of their parents. In 1987 a 2-year-old child, supposedly under social welfare departmental supervision at the time, was killed by her mother. The result of a large-scale inquiry[84] into the handling of the case was to put the immediate safety of the child as the highest priority – the paramount rule is that 'the child must be made safe, now'. In 1993 11 year-old Craig Manukau was killed by his father – by a beating as a result of attending a school dance. The family was known to Social Welfare, because reports had been made by the school about his well-being. The Commissioner for Children who carried out an independent inquiry[85] into the handling of the case, emphasized the traps into which social workers can fall when family responsibility becomes an end in itself. Emphasis on, and deference to, the family and to the many problems experienced by the adult members meant that Craig's need for immediate safety and protection was not given the highest priority. The Commissioner for Children recommended that family group conference decisions, plans or recommendations be evaluated by one person taking a child protection focus and asking 'Is the child safe now?'

The Youth Justice part of the Children, Young Persons and Their Families Act emphasizes 'restorative justice'.[86] The idea is to heal the break in social harmony and the goal is for the victim and offender to come together in a process of reconciliation. The hope is that there will be a real change of heart by the offender and an effective repairing of damage to the victim. Evaluation of Youth Justice family group conferences carried out by the Office of the Commissioner for Children,[87] found that a third of young offenders felt involved, 11 per cent felt partly involved, and 45 per cent felt they had not been involved at all. In many cases, adults dominated the process, leaving the young offenders confused and unable to understand. For the family group conference to reach balanced decisions, the young person must listen and be listened to.

Foster parents often feel the impact of family responsibility. There is more pressure for them to take sole responsibility for a child, rather than to take the traditional role of acting in partnership with the state. The underlying reasons for this are financial: the more responsibility taken by the foster parent, the more there is justification to lessen financial support.

Overemphasis on family responsibility is evident in the distribution of property and income within families. Children's interests are merged with those of their carer(s). Article 27 of the Convention recognizes the right of every child to a standard of living 'adequate for the child's physical, mental, spiritual, moral and social development'. The Child Support Act 1991 does not separately address the interests of children; its emphasis is on collection from the liable parent.

Matrimonial property legislation recognizes the separate interests of children,[88] but this provision is very rarely argued because children are not parties to the proceedings and are not normally represented in them.

Focus on the economic interests of children as a distinct group in the community exposes the wide gaps between groups of children. Current government policy is to 'target' those most in need of economic assistance. While this may keep children in such families just above the poverty line, it in no way ensures that children from disadvantaged backgrounds have the same opportunities and range of services as others. Even when children try to make it on their own, the unemployment benefit, independent youth benefit, unsupported child benefit and domestic purposes benefit[89] all have age limitations or restrictive conditions as to eligibility which throws the young person back on to family responsibility. This is inconsistent with Article 26 which recognizes the right of every child to benefit from social security.

State responsibility for children

The dominant ideology of the free market in New Zealand puts children very much at risk. They are thrown back on the 'luck of the draw', of their own particular family. In a provocative and stinging analysis of children in New Zealand society, entitled *Children, Endangered Species?*[90] Lesley Max begins:

> In New Zealand, regrettably there is a diminishing number of people who appear to regard children as precious and deserving of particular planning, care and attention, not as appendages of their parents, not as impediments to work, but in their own right by virtue of their vulnerability and their potential.[91]

Health and disability

Measured against the 1993 *Progress of Nations*[92] published by UNICEF, New Zealand still looks a relatively attractive place for children. Only ten children per thousand die before the age of five, whereas based on per capita GNP, the country could be expected to have an under-five mortality rate of 13 per thousand. This ranks New Zealand equal 14th amongst industrialized countries. New Zealand has been set a target of eight per thousand for the year 2000, but is currently behind schedule on meeting that target. The country is ranked 25th amongst industrialized nations for maternal mortality rates. Maternal mortality rates are an indicator of the strength of health services generally.

These statistics must be evaluated in their historical context. In 1930 New Zealand was one of the first countries in the world to reach international mortality targets. Now it has slipped behind. While it is easy to blame the slippage on economic decline, that has been a global phenomenon. The more plausible explanation is one of priorities. Until child health is a top priority, the rhetoric of 'economic restructuring' will have no impact on the children and their parents who wait for a number of years for the child's life-saving heart operation.[93] Article 24 of the Convention guarantees every child the right to 'enjoyment of the highest attainable standard of health'.

Statistics hide the marked differences between socioeconomic groups and cultures in New Zealand. For example, the average Maori family has a per capita income half that of the non-Maori family. A New Zealand Planning Council Report,[94] after a comprehensive analysis of New Zealand society, concludes that 'Maori people are over-represented in almost every type of institution studied'. The reasons for this were attributed to:

... their generally disadvantaged social and economic position, a position which is associated with low rates of immunisation, poor infant health, greater risk of physical injury, diminished access to primary and preventative health services, high rates of alcohol intake, high rates of cigarette smoking, and a greater chance of apprehension for criminal behaviour.[95]

Similar problems apply to children of parents from lower socioeconomic groups. Current government policy is to target the most needy groups and to exempt payments for health services. Consequently, those who do not fit into the government-defined category of 'needy' will have to contribute to their health costs. This is likely to be a disincentive to obtain optimum health for their children. New Zealand is currently moving from a system of universal free health care, paid from taxes, to a system of 'user pays' in health, with the targeting of the most needy. As a result, those who can afford it take out health insurance to ensure they can obtain the optimum care. Others are thrown back on a state health system which does not appear to have the resources to meet all the demands. Such a situation does not guarantee every child in New Zealand the 'highest standard of health'.

Article 23 of the Convention recognizes the special needs of the 'disabled child' to achieve a 'full and decent life in conditions which ensure dignity, promote self-reliance and facilitate the child's active participation in the community'. According to the Youth Law Project, 'a series of restructurings and policy changes' over the last five years has left 'children with a disability and those seeking to provide help and support for them confused and disillusioned'.[96] Unlike Australia,[97] which requires court approval, the decision to sterilize a disabled child has been ruled in New Zealand to be a private one between parents and doctor.[98]

New Zealand has abortion laws.[99] A woman's right to choose and the child's need for protection before birth are balanced by the medical profession interpreting and applying specific statutory grounds for abortion.

Education

According to the *Progress of Nations*[100] New Zealand has 100 per cent of their children reaching grade five of primary education. This ranks New Zealand equal first among industrialized nations. However, the statistics do not tell the whole story. A major problem in New Zealand is truancy. An investigation carried out by a national newspaper[101] found that 2500 children aged between 11 and 16 were not enrolled at any school. In one South Auckland suburb, made up mainly of families in the lower socioeconomic groups, 389 children, aged 5 to 15, had left school and had not enrolled at another. Part of the explanation for this phenomenon is that the state resources to deal with truancy are not available.[102] Due to limited resources the Department of Social Welfare, which is legally responsible for truancy, has had to prioritize the more immediate problems of child abuse. Higher education in New Zealand was once heavily supported by the state. Now it is becoming more dependent on the individual and family means of the student, only the most needy being targeted for government assistance. Although the number of university students in New Zealand has increased over the last ten years, it is neither clear, nor has been carefully evaluated, whether all those with the capacity to attend, as required by Article 28 of the Convention, are actually finding their way to university.

Protection from abuse and neglect

New Zealand has made major efforts on the issue of sexual abuse: specialist sexual abuse teams have been set up; and government funding has been provided for ongoing counselling for the victims of sexual abuse. Up until 30 September 1992, lump sum payments of $10,000 were also available. There has, however, been a backlash of public opinion, with sexual abuse being perceived as a 'gravy train' and an 'industry' for the helping professions.[103]

This has had the unfortunate effect of child victims becoming penalized. Article 39 of the Convention requires the state to take 'all appropriate measures' to promote physical and psychological recovery and social reintegration of a child victim. The Victims Task Force recommended in 1993 that a properly founded scheme for providing information and support for child victims and child witnesses in abuse cases should be set up. This has not been done yet, but the Office of the Commissioner for Children has produced an excellent educational package for children who have to appear in court. Withdrawal of lump sum compensation has put child victims in a weak position. There is no clear right to sue for damages,[104] nor is there a criminal injuries compensation scheme in New Zealand.

There is less societal agreement on where the line of physical abuse should be drawn. While it is against the law corporally to chastise children at school, it is still lawful in New Zealand for parents to use 'reasonable' physical discipline to 'correct' their children.[105] Ian Hassall and Laurie O'Reilly, the Commissioners for Children have led a thorough and impressive campaign to educate parents on the alternatives to hitting children. In 1993, the office of the Commissioner for Children, commissioned a poll to assess how New Zealand parents disciplined their children, and determine the attitudes of New Zealanders towards physical punishment in the home.[106] One thousand New Zealanders aged 15 years or over and living in centres of population of 2500 or more, were surveyed. A very high percentage of those surveyed (87 per cent) considered it acceptable for a parent to smack a child. A much smaller percentage (3 per cent) considered it acceptable for a parent to thrash a child. This is a significant change in attitude. A 1981 survey found that 11 per cent thought it was permissible to thrash a child. A worrying sign is that twice as many men as women endorsed the thrashing of a child. Younger children under 10 are more likely to be smacked, and 36 per cent of those surveyed reported smacking young children by hand. A worrying statistic is that 13 per cent of those surveyed admitted thrashing their children of two years or over at some stage. A 1982 survey of children aged 13–14 found that 80 per cent reported having been smacked and 48 per cent having been belted (a more severe form of hitting).

While the figures show some change in attitude about severe thrashing, they still highlight a predominant attitude that it is acceptable to hit children. It is considered acceptable to hit the most vulnerable, defenceless members of our society. This attitude, combined with the finding that legislation designed to protect children puts their interests as secondary to those of their family, puts New Zealand children at risk.[107] A major review[108] of child protection legislation in New Zealand found that:

> ... the real danger is that with the emphasis on family group decision-making in the Act, there will be no, perceived conflict with the interests of the child provided all family members agree.

Government have agreed[109] to consider amending the legislation to make it clear that, in child protection issues, the welfare of the child is the first and paramount consideration. There is also an undertaking to improve the level of training for social workers who deal with abuse. Government has conceded that the number of social workers with formal social work qualifications has fallen to a worrying level.

Psychological abuse of children may well be the most significant problem for children in New Zealand society. Article 18 places responsibility on states to protect children from 'mental violence'. There is very little indication that psychological abuse is being dealt with, or even acknowledged, in New Zealand.

Child neglect is not always responded to swiftly. The Department of Social Welfare was publicly[110] criticized for its slow reaction to a family of children who had been living in neglected conditions in a shed beside their house. The children were all suffering chilblains and other serious health problems. It took the Department six weeks to respond to the first report about these children.[111]

Protection of family identity

Articles 7, 9 and 20 of the Convention recognize the right of a child to maintain identity with his or her natural parents and their culture. The Children, Young Persons and Their Families Act 1989 makes it very clear that, if a child is to be removed from his or her natural parents, the child should be placed either with relatives or, at the very least, with adults of the same culture.[112] New Zealand has traditionally had a system of closed adoption where secrecy prevailed, and the 1955 legislation which governs adoption reflects this approach. In 1986,[113] legislation was passed which enabled adopted children over 18 to make efforts to find out about and contact their natural parents. Natural parents of children born before the passing of the Act have a right to place a veto on their identity.

Simultaneously with this recognition of a child's right to know his or her basic identity, legislation was passed[114] which changed the legal status of children born as a result of new birth technology. The legislation deemed the donors (the natural parents) not to be the legal parents, and deemed the recipient parents to be the legal parents. There is no requirement in the legislation that identifying information be kept for the child's sake. Children born as a result of such procedures will most certainly not be able to exercise their right to know who their genetic parents are. The legislation was passed with adult concerns as the sole focus; there was no one represented the children's interests.

Discrimination and economic exploitation

Article 2 of the Convention makes it clear that all the rights in the Convention should be applied without 'discrimination of any kind'. The Human Rights Act 1993, which legislated for discrimination on the basis of age for the first time in New Zealand, specifically excludes children under 15. As the Youth Law Project has pointed out 'New Zealand law not only allows "youthism" [discrimination on the basis of age] but gives it statutory blessing'.[115]

Article 32 of the Convention recognizes the right of children to be protected from 'economic exploitation'. In New Zealand the Minimum Wage Act 1983 provides a minimum wage for all New Zealanders but does not apply to workers under 20 years of age. Also section 15A(3) of the Human Rights Commission Act 1977 expressly authorizes youth rates for young workers. Consequently, young workers receive less pay for equal work.

Criminal justice

New Zealand has youth justice legislation[116] which emphasizes the rights of young persons in the criminal justice system. At present, before any questioning of a young person begins they must be told their rights.[117] The police have proposed an amendment which would involve the telling of rights only after there are reasonable grounds of suspecting an offence, or where the questioning is intended to obtain an admission. There is provision for an adult to attend in a supportive role to ensure that young persons understand their rights[118] and can be supported through any questioning process. There is provision for youth advocates to represent young persons in proceedings.[119] The New Zealand Bill of Rights Act 1990[120] recognizes the right of a child charged with an offence to be dealt with in a manner that takes account of the child's age.

Institutional care

New Zealand has traditionally had a wide range of institutionalized care. This has now been downscaled, institutional care now being perceived as the 'last resort'. As a result, there are insufficient places for young persons requiring secure care, and they are sometimes placed in prison cells with adult offenders. This is a matter that New Zealand has reserved at ratification of the Convention. An important report[121] on residential care for young persons in New Zealand found that services need to be 'developed, supported and resourced and funded'. A positive improvement is that the Department of Social Welfare has drawn up Residential Care Regulations and a Code of Practice. These have been seen as[122] making 'great progress' for young persons in care, and as being more humane, sensitive and culturally appropriate.

Drugs

New Zealand has wide-ranging anti-drug programmes which are taken through the schools. They involve role play and discussion on the issue of drugs. There are also a wide variety of services to deal with alcohol and drugs.[123]

The sad reality is that those who fall out of the system, those who have drifted from their families and schools, do not have access to educational programmes about drugs. These are the children who begin glue-sniffing at an early age and live by their own wits and resources. They are also the young people who, when they are arrested, receive no visitors in their cells.

Privacy

Family court and criminal proceedings which involve children either as victims or witnesses are kept private. The public may not be present nor the press able to publish identifying information. New Zealand's comprehensive privacy legislation,[124] which spells out principles of privacy and access to information, applies to all citizens, including children.

Child abduction

New Zealand is a signatory to the Hague Convention on Child Abduction,[125] and New Zealand courts have taken a firm line on the enforcement of the Convention. If anything, concerns arise as to whether the obligation to enforce the Convention has begun to override other significant children's rights issues, such as hearing the child's own views, the child's best interests and protection from harm. In the most recent abduction case in New Zealand,[126] it was acknowledged the children wanted to stay in New Zealand, and that the father had assaulted the mother and made her in fear of him. Yet the children were returned to France in the care of the father, because of the Convention.

Adoption and intercountry adoption

The Adoption Act 1955, which has as one of its objectives the promotion of the interests of the child,[127] does not meet the requirement of Article 21 that the best interests of the child shall be the 'paramount consideration'.[128] The Social Welfare Department, in consultation with the Immigration Department, takes a hard line an intercountry adoption which it views as an 'option of last resort' which promotes the best interests of a child 'only in very special circumstances'. Pressure to adopt Romanian orphans opened the policy a little. The Department of Social Welfare has no legal powers to prevent New Zealanders adopting overseas children in the children's own country: any such adoption will depend on the laws of that country. The Immigration Department has the sanction of preventing the child re-entering New Zealand if the adoption has not been lawfully obtained. To ensure entry of the child back into New Zealand, it is essential to organize an overseas adoption through the New Zealand Department of Social Welfare. The Department follows international codes of practice and only works with governmental and transnational agencies, such as International Social Services based in Geneva;[129] it will not work with private agencies or overseas adoption brokers.

ACHIEVING A BALANCE: SETTING PRIORITIES

The Preamble to the Convention emphasizes that childhood is entitled to 'special care and assistance'. On the 1994 International Day of the Family, the public relations officer of the Dunedin Citizens Advice Bureau said, '... the problems people are seeking help with relate to the fact that they are unable to feed, clothe, and house themselves and their families adequately'.[130] At present in New Zealand there is no identifiable political will to eliminate cyclical disadvantage. Apart from the significant efforts made by the Commissioner for Children, the Youth Law Project and the *New Zealand Law Society Newsletter* to schools, little has been done by government to educate the public about the Convention.

The Convention is a wide-ranging – even overwhelming – document and, because of this, there is a danger that states will merely emphasize the easy bits, such as indicating legislation and legislative changes. It is crucial to prioritize the values laid down in the Convention. The key value which permeates the whole Convention, and which is often forgotten by institutions, is that each child is entitled to equal concern and respect.[131] While social and economic rights are subject to 'available resources', until the basics of sound health, education and welfare are addressed, the rest may not mean much to a child.

I make the following recommendations:

1 That the social, economic, and welfare opportunities of all children in New Zealand become the major priority for government policy.

2 That a goal of government policies be to balance the inequities of children from different backgrounds so that they have equal opportunities in life.

3 That the resources of the Office of the Commissioner for Children be expanded to include a spokesperson giving the child's point of view on all policy and legislation proposals.

4 That it be made law that, in all political, legislative, judicial and administrative matters, children from a wide variety of backgrounds will be consulted and their viewpoints considered.

5 That there be regular evaluation and monitoring of all policies that affect the lives of children.

6 That it becomes a priority in New Zealand to foster an attitude of international care and concern for the children of the world.

7 That the Convention and its values be made much more readily accessible to all children and families in New Zealand.

ACKNOWLEDGEMENT

The author wishes to thank Valmai Bilsborough for typing the many drafts of this paper. Thanks also to Tracey Hawe for her invaluable research assistance.

NOTES

1   As Robert Mnookin has said, 'Whoever enjoys the power of decision will influence not only the means, but the very objectives of child rearing'. R. Mnookin (1985), *In the Interest of Children*, New York: W.H. Freeman and Company, p. 511.

2   For example, Article 19 (protection from harm), Article 20(2) (alternative care), Article 7 (knowledge of identity), Article 11 (illicit transfer), Article 22 (refugee status), Article 23 (rights of the disabled), Article 24 (health), Article 28 (education), Article 32 (economic exploitation), Article 12 (right to express views), Article 34 (Sexual exploitation), Articles 37 and 40 (rights in the criminal justice system), Article 4 (promotion of rights in the Convention), Article 42 (making the Convention known).

3   For example, R. Farson (1978), *Birthrights*, Harmondsworth: Penguin; J. Holt (1974), *Escape from Childhood*, Harmondsworth: Penguin.

4   For example, J. Goldstein, A. Freud and A. Solnit (1979), *Before the Best Interests of the Child*, New York: Free Press.

5   For example, L. Max (1990), *Children: Endangered Species?*, New Zealand: Penguin Books.

6   M.D.A. Freeman (1983), *The Rights and Wrongs of Children*, London: Frances Pinter; N.H.: Dover, p. 60.

7   As Philip Alston puts it, '... it is surely correct that an array of legislative and other formal measures of implementation will ultimately be less important and less effective than measures designed to inculcate the values enshrined in the Convention into the consciousness of the masses as well as the decision-making elites': P. Alston (1991), 'The legal framework of the Convention on the Rights of the Child', *Bulletin of Human Rights, The Rights of the Child*, **2**, p. 1.

8   A BBC presentation, written by J. Allen and produced by T. Garnett. The story is about a single-parent family's struggle to survive with the help of so-called social services, set against the background of the 1977 Silver Jubilee Celebrations.

9   As Philip Alston puts it: 'The Convention as a whole goes a long way towards providing the broad ethical or value framework that is often claimed to be the missing ingredient which would give a greater degree of certainty to the content of the best interests principle.' Alston, *op. cit.*, note 7, above, at p. 8.

10 F. Olsen (1992), 'Children's rights: some feminist approaches to the United Nations Convention on the Rights of the Child' in P. Alston, S. Parker, J. Seymour (eds), *Children, Rights and The Law*, Oxford: Clarendon Press, pp. 192, 213. Frances Olsen shows the potential conflicts any list of rights must grapple with. She concludes 'overall it may stand to improve the status and lives of children' at p. 217.

11 The welfare state, created in the 1930s because of the depression was a dominant policy in New Zealand until the 1980s when it began to weaken because of economic and ideological pressures.

12   U Dolgopol (1994), 'The Convention on the Rights of the Child as part of the international system for the protection of human rights' in J. Harvey (ed.), *Implementing the UN Convention on the Rights of the Child in Australia*, Adelaide: The Children's Interests Bureau: 'There are many issues of concern to children ... which cannot be addressed if we focus exclusively on the family.'

13   G. Melton (1994), 'Human dignity and the experience of children: the UN Convention as a framework for policy in developed countries' in *ibid.*: 'What would it take for children to feel they are being treated with dignity?'

14   We should all step behind Rawls' veil of ignorance and emerge as a child: J. Rawls (1971), *A Theory of Justice*, Cambridge, Mass.: Harvard University Press.

15   See M. Henaghan and P. Tapp (1992), 'Legally defining the family' in M. Henaghan and B. Atkin (eds), *Family Law Policy in New Zealand,* Auckland: Oxford University Press, pp. 1–53.

16   The figures are from the 29th census taken on 5 March 1991. The number of legally married New Zealanders has declined by 23,319 between 1986 and 1991. During the same period, 46,245 more people were living in a defacto relationship, an increase of 40.2 per cent since 1986. There are more divorced and separated New Zealanders than ever before. Divorced couples have increased by 27.7 per cent between 1986–91. Separated couples have increased by 19.7 per cent. Statistics on same sex relationships and other family forms have not yet been officially compiled.

17   D. Durie-Hall and J. Metge (1992), 'Kua Tutu Te Puehu, Kia Mau: Maori aspirations and family law' in Henaghan and Atkin, *op. cit.,* note 15 above, pp. 54–82.

18   This issue is discussed in detail under the heading 'Family Responsibility'.

19   S. Hewlett (1993), *Child Neglect in Rich Nations*, New York: United Nations Children's Fund.

20   *Ibid.*, at p. 53.

21   As the UNICEF report, says; 'Between 1985 and 1990, New Zealand's GNP fell by 0.7 percent, the worst record of any industrialised country, while unemployment more than doubled' (p. 53).

22   New Zealand moves to a more representative form of government in the next election, known as Mixed Member Proportional. A binding referendum at the last elections in 1993 decided in favour of this system over the incumbent first-past-the-post system. The system is similar to that in place in Germany. A wider variety of interests are expected to be represented.

23   Ministry of Youth Affairs, Te Tari Taiohi, *Statement of Intent*, 1993–1994.

24   *Briefing for the incoming Minister*, Ministry of Youth Affairs, Te Tari Taiohi, November 1993, p. 12.

25   Sections 410–22, Children, Young Persons and Their Families Act 1989, set out the functions and conditions of the Commissioner.

26   Sections 411(1)(d) and (g) Children, Young Persons and Their Families Act 1989.

27   A newsletter, *Children*, is regularly published by the Office of the Commissioner for Children. It contains a wide variety of articles on law changes that affect children, research findings on children. It also contains a wide variety of child perspectives. A strong theme in the newsletter is the child's voice and viewpoint. The address for copies of the newsletter is Commissioner for Children, PO Box 12537, Thorndon, Wellington, New Zealand.

28   The Youth Law Project is a community law centre for young people under the Legal Services Act 1991. The postal address is PO Box 105159, Auckland Central, Aotearoa, New Zealand. Fax (09) 307-5243. The Centre produces a quarterly *Youth Law Review*.

29   Robert Ludbrook the founder of the Project wrote detailed submissions in 1993 on

New Zealand's lack of comparability with the Convention. These submissions are available from the Project.

30   The Royal New Zealand Plunket Society was set up by Dr Truby King to improve the health of young babies in New Zealand. The major workforce of the Society are Plunket nurses who provide community health services throughout New Zealand. The Society is also involved in ongoing research on child health matters. At present the Society is embarking into a major study on lead poisoning in children. The Society is responsible for a major campaign and changes of law on child safety in cars. The address of the Society for further information is PO Box 6042, Dunedin North, New Zealand.

31   For example, the State Owned Enterprises Act 1986, The Conservation Act 1986, Resource Management Act 1991.

32   *New Zealand Maori Council* v. *Attorney-General* [1987] 1 NZLR 641. *Huakina Development Trust* v. *Waikato Valley Authority* (1987) 12 NZTPA 129.

33   *Neho* v. *Duncan* [1994] NZFLR 157. *Tozer* v. *Newcomb* [1992] NZFLR 51. *Stove* v. *Stove*, (Family Court, Hastings, 31 May 1990, FP 020/222/88).

34   *Tavita* v. *Minister of Immigration and Attorney-General*, Cooke, P. Richardson, J. Hardie Boys, J. 30 November 1993, CA 266/93. [1994] NZFLR 97.

35   *Ibid.*

36   *20/20*, New Zealand, Television 3, Monday 2 May 1994.

37   *20/20*, New Zealand, Television 3, Monday 16 May 1994.

38   *H* v. *F* (1993) FRNZ 486.

39   B. Bettleheim (1987), *A Good Enough Parent*, London: Pan Books, p. 50.

40   Judith Wallerstein and Joan Kelly (1980), *Surviving the Break-Up*, New York: Basic Books shows clearly how parental behaviour affects children's behaviour.

41   Section 23(2), Guardianship Act 1968.

42   Section 23(2) refers specifically to the court and proceedings in court.

43   For a critique of this gap, see M. Henaghan (1992), 'Legally Re-arranging families' in Henaghan and Atkin, *op. cit.*, note 15 above at pp. 98–104.

44   Section 30, Guardianship Act 1968.

45   For an overview of the debate see S Jefferson (1993), 'Counsel appointed to represent children: the continuing confusion', *Butterworths Family Law Journal*, pp. 40, 47.

46   For example, *S* v. *E* (1981) 1 NZFLR 73, where the wishes of a ten year-old boy to live with his mother and brother and sister were advocated against by counsel for the child, because counsel thought the boy was too influenced by the 'holiday atmosphere' with his mother.

47   A. Harland (1991), 'The views of parents on counsel for the child', Family Court Custody and Access Research Report 4, Wellington: Department of Justice, pp. 73-86.

48   *J* v. *A* [1994] NZFLR 206.

49   *S* v. *S* [1994] NZFLR 26, *M* v. *Y* (1994) NZFLR 1. For a critique of the approach in these cases see M. Henaghan (1994), 'Court of Appeal ruling an access', *Butterworths Family Law Journal*, **1**, p. 74.

50   For example, *Makiri* v. *Roxburgh* (1988) 4 NZFLR 673, where the views of an eight year-old boy about moving from the care of his mother, with whom he had spent all of his life, to his father in a different area of the country are not discussed at all.

51   In *Dixon* v. *Dixon* [1992] NZFLR 527 a social worker was told by the family court that it is inappropriate to ask a four year-old to choose between parents.

52   Section 11, Adoption Act 1955.

53   In 1988, of the 867 adoption cases handled by the Department of Social Welfare, 376

were step-parent adoptions. These figures are cited in Adoption Practices Review Committee Report to the Minister of Social Welfare, August 1990.

54 Section 5(d), Children, Young Persons and Their Families Act 1989.

55 These concerns were expressed in *Puao-Te-Ata-tu (Daybreak)*, The Report of the Ministerial Advisory Committee on a Maori perspective for the Department of Social Welfare, September 1988. They were also expressed in *The Report of the Working Party on the Children, Young Persons* (Green Paper), December 1987.

56 Youth Law Project submissions to Government on the implementation of the Convention in New Zealand, 1993.

57 For example, section 11, Guardianship Act 1968.

58 Section 14, Guardianship Act 1968.

59 Section 9A, Guardianship Act 1968.

60 *X* v. *X* and *X*, Family Court, Hastings, 20 August 1992, FP 020/232/92, Judge Inglis QC.

61 *Cunliffe* v. *Cunliffe* (1992) 9 FRNZ 537.

62 Section 26, Matrimonial Property Act 1976.

63 Contrary to popular belief, couples living together are not covered by the Matrimonial Property Act 1976.

64 Section 4, Child Support Act 1991. The Act is currently under review. The review has been completed but there has been no change to the legislation.

65 B. Atkin (1992), 'Financial support: the Bureaucratization of personal responsibility' in Henaghan and Atkin, *op. cit.*, note 15 above, p. 255.

66 Section 3(l)(b), Family Proceedings Act 1955. Under section 3(1)(c) grandchildren can also claim. Section 3(1)(d) allows stepchildren to claim.

67 Section 94, Education Act 1989.

68 Section 94B(g), Education Act 1989 allows a Board to decide not to have a student representative.

69 Youth Law Project submissions on New Zealand's comparability with the Convention, 1993.

70 *Ibid.*

71 *Ibid.*

72 For detailed analysis and evaluation of the procedures see M. Pipe and M. Henaghan (1996), 'Child witnesses in New Zealand' in *International Perspectives on Children's Testimony*, London: Sage.

73 For example, *R* v. *Accused* [19891 1 NZLR 660, *R* v. *L* (I 990) 6 CRNZ 383.

74 An example in the April 1993 *Ministry of Youth Affairs Policy Matters Newsletter* is the development of policy on the basis on which young people make decisions about post-school activity. To gain insight into the issues, the Ministry conducted a 'small consultation exercise with young people in Wellington (a major city) and Blenheim (a small town)'.

75 J. Eekelaar (1991), 'Parental responsibility: state of nature or nature of state?', *Journal of Social Welfare Law*, p. 37.

76 Article 18, Convention.

77 Article 27, Convention.

78 Sections 2, 4, 5 and 13 which set up the principles and object of the Act specifically recognise the extended family, *whanau*, *hapu* and *iwi*.

79 See Durie-Hall and Metge, *op. cit.*, note 17 above for detailed discussion of the significance of the Children, Young Persons and Their Families Act 1989 for Maori people.

80 Section 13(a), Children, Young Persons and Their Families Act 1989.

81   *Review of the Children, Young Persons and Their Families Act 1989*, Report of the Ministerial Review Team to the Minister of Social Welfare, February 1992 (the Mason Report).

82   P. Tapp, in 'Legally defining the Family' in Henaghan and Atkin, *op. cit.*, note 15 above, p. 31. For detailed analysis of how cost considerations played a major part in the development of the Children Young Persons and Their Families Act, see also pp. 26–30, 175–8 of *Family Law Policy in New Zealand.*

83   Commissioner for Children (1991), *A Briefing Paper – An Appraisal of the First Year of Operation of the Children, Young Persons and Their Families Act 1989*, Wellington: Office of the Commissioner for Children, p. 12.

84   *Dangerous Situations, The Report of the Independent Inquiry Team Reporting on the Circumstances of the Death of a Child*, Department of Social Welfare, March 1988.

85   Commissioner for Children (1993), *Report to the Minister of Social Welfare on the New Zealand Children and Young Persons Service's Review of Practice in Relation to Craig Manukau and his Family*, 7 October.

86   As opposed to 'punitive' justice.

87   G. Maxwell and L. Orsborn, 'Let's Get Our Act Together', Paper presented at NZ Youth Justice Conference, Auckland, February 1994. Paper available from Office of the Commissioner for Children, PO Box 12537, Thorndon, Wellington, New Zealand.

88   Section 26, Matrimonial Property Act 1976.

89   See sections 60F, 58, 29 and 27G, 27B of the Social Security Act 1964.

90   L. Max (1990), *Children: An Endangered Species*, New Zealand: Penguin Books, at p. 8.

91   Hewlett, *op. cit.*, note 19 above, at p 53: 'New Zealand has the highest youth suicide rate among industrial countries, and reported cases of child abuse have doubled since 1985'.

      In September 1992 a meeting of people with considerable expertise in the area of young people's mental health met for two days in Wellington to consider ways in which the high rate of youth suicide in New Zealand could be reduced. A report, by H. Barwick (1992), *Youth Suicide Prevention Project: Workshop Report and Literature Review* is available from the Department of Health, PO Box 5010, Wellington, New Zealand.

92   Published annually by the United Nations Children's Fund.

93   During the 1993 election campaign, a mother of a child with a defective heart made a plea to the politicians for her child to have a needed operation. That plea is still unanswered, although there are signs that political pressure has grown to the point where the Minister of Health has indicated initiative may be taken.

94   *Care and Control – The Role of Institutions in New Zealand*, Social Monitoring Group of New Zealand Planning Council, Report No 2, Wellington, 1987.

95   There is debate between the 'old' welfare state, and the 'new' right which emphasizes individual responsibility, on what the best solutions are.

      As a selling point for health reforms, the government point to some Maori initiatives to provide health services to Maori people in a way that best meets their needs.

96   Youth law submissions to government on New Zealand's comparability with the UN Convention on the Rights of the Child 1993.

97   *Secretary Department of Health and Community Services* v. *JWB and SMB* (Marion's Case) [1991–1992] 175 CLR 218.

98   *Re X* [1991] NZFLR 49. Decisions to sterilize adults require court approval under the Protection of Personal and Property Rights Act 1988.

99   Contraception, Sterilization and Abortion Act 1977.

100 UNICEF (1993), *The Progress of Nations*, Geneva.
101 *Sunday News*, 3 April, 10 April 1994.
102 This was revealed at a seminar held for professionals who deal with child abuse, Dunedin, May 1993. Details of the seminar are available from Dr John Clarkson, Paediatrics Department, Medical School, University of Otago, Dunedin, New Zealand. The government has given a $2 million grant to deal with truancy, but a recent media report (16 May 1994, *Television One News*) shows it is not filtering through and that reports of truancy are left unanswered. The grant has been used to finance family group conferences (*Sunday Star*, editorial, 22 May 1994).
103 'Sex Abuse', *Metro*, March 1993, p. 72.
104 The Accident Rehabilitation and Insurance Act 1992 removes the right to sue if the matters are covered by the Act. It is arguable whether or not emotional distress due to sexual abuse is covered by the Act.
105 Section 159, Crimes Act 1961.
106 The results are published in Office of the Commissioner for Children (1993), *Children* (10), September newsletter.
107 The Mason Report, *op. cit.*, note 81 above.
108 *Ibid.*, at p. 11.
109 Response of the Minister of Social Welfare to the Mason Report, March 1992.
110 The case received major media criticism through newsprint, radio and television. The name of the family has been suppressed to protect the children. The children were removed from their parents and placed in foster care. The parents want their children back.
111 In Henaghan and Atkin, *op. cit.*, note 15 above, at p. 183, Geddis, Tapp and Taylor describe the outlook for the seriously abused child in New Zealand as 'bleak'.
112 Sections 5(b), sections 13(f), 13(g), 13(b), Children, Young Persons and Their Families Act 1989.
113 Adult Adoption Information Act 1986.
114 Status of Children Amendment Act 1987.
115 Youth Law Project submissions on New Zealand's comparability with the UN Convention 1993.
116 Children, Young Persons and Their Families Act 1989.
117 Section 215, Children, Young Persons and Their Families Act 1989.
118 Sections 215, 221 and 222, Children, Young Persons and Their Families Act 1989.
119 Section 323, Children, Young Persons and Their Families Act 1989.
120 Section 25(1), New Zealand Bill of Rights Act 1990.
121 The Mason Report, *op. cit.*, note 81 above.
122 By the Youth Law Project in its 1993 submissions on New Zealand's comparability with the Convention.
123 The Ministry of Youth Affairs produces a detailed booklet on adolescent Family Support Services and Programmes that deal with alcohol, drugs and other young people's issues.
124 Privacy Act 1993.
125 The Convention is implemented in the Guardianship Amendment Act 1991.
126 *B* v. *B*, High Court, Wellington, AP 49/94, 28 April 1994, Doogue, J.
127 Section 11 Adoption Act 1955.
128 The New Zealand Court of Appeal have held that even though the wording of the statute does not require the child's welfare to be paramount, because the effect of adoption is to change guardianship then the same principle as in the Guardianship Act

1968 should apply – the child's welfare is paramount. *Director General of Social Welfare* v. *L* [1990] NZFLR 125.

129   R. Ludbrook (1990), *Adoption: Guide to Law and Practice*, Wellington: GP Books, pp. 41–6.

130   *Dunedin Star Weekender*, Sunday, 13 May 1994, p. 2.

131   R. Dworkin (1985), 'Why liberals should care about equality', in his *A Matter of Principle*, Harvard University Press, p. 207 provides an excellent case for why values of individual respect and concern should prevail over utilitarian market values.

10 Children's Rights in Poland Three Years after the Convention

Wanda Stojanowska and Elżbieta Holewińska-Łapińska

INTRODUCTION

The preliminary draft of the UN Convention on Children's Rights, passed by the General Assembly of the United Nations on 20 November 1989, was submitted to the UN Human Rights Committee by Poland in 1978. Poland also submitted the amended draft of 1980 and the Polish delegation maintained the leading role throughout the 11-year gestation period of the Convention.[1]

The drafts mentioned above were prepared with the goal of trying to fulfil the principle of children's well-being, taking into account the Polish experience and Polish law. A large majority of children's rights included in the Convention were equivalent to the rights incorporated into Polish law many years before the Convention came into force – that is, on 7 July 1991.

Due to ratification procedures set by the Polish Constitution, the Convention signed on 26 January 1990 was ratified by the Republic of Poland on 7 June 1991, only after the Polish parliament passed a bill permitting the President to ratify the document.[2]

On 7 July 1994 three years had passed since the Convention came into force. In this short chapter we will discuss:

1 the outline of regulations in the Polish law concerning responsibility for children conveyed to parents, social organizations and the state;
2 regulations of the law on family relations, which do not correspond with the Convention;

3   important changes in the law made after the Convention came into force;
4   some examples of the Convention applied in practice.

We should stress that the problem of the Polish law's conformability to the Convention, and the practical application of the Convention, has been discussed at a number of academic conferences organized in Poland. The problem has also been discussed in many joint works and monographs.[3] This chapter is necessarily selective.

LIABILITY FOR CHILDREN OWED BY PARENTS, SOCIAL ORGANIZATIONS AND THE STATE

In accordance with the Convention, parents bear the primary responsibility for their children. Liability of other persons is subsidiary. The subsidiary responsibility of the state is applied in two aspects. The first concerns legislative and administrative activities in that the state should ensure health care, school education, social security, assistance in carrying out rights conveyed solely to the parents and the control of execution of parental duties. The second concerns the substitution of parents when, due to death or other circumstances, they cannot personally perform their parental duties. The state's responsibility in these situations includes: establishment of legal guardianship for the child; placement of the child with a substitute family or an educational guardianship institution (Article 20 of the Convention).

Responsibility for education and development of the child lies mainly with the parents (Article 18). The state respects their rights and duties (Article 14, para. 2) and makes sure that the process of education includes inculcation of respect for parents (Article 29, para. 1 (c)).

Except in situations where the children's welfare needs to be protected, children should not be separated from their parents against their will (Article 9). This provision principally takes into account the child's interest, likewise protecting him from the parents. The state's responsibility for the child is regulated in many other provisions of the Convention, such as Article 27, among others.

The Polish Constitution of 22 July 1952 is the main source of Polish law which constructs the concept of responsibility for the child and of the rights conveyed to him or her. Art. 79 of the Constitution is the most significant provision, stating that marriage, motherhood and the family remain under the protection and care of the state, and that the state especially values large families. This provision imposes a special duty on parents to bring up children as rightful and responsible citizens of the Republic.

Art. 80 of the Constitution imposes an obligation on the state to protect young people with care, provide for their education and assure the widest possible scope of development.

The provisions mentioned above reflect the concept of parental liability for the child's upbringing and the state's liability concerning the protection and care of families, described in the Convention. These provisions have been in force in Poland for the last 40 years.

The resolutions, included in the Convention and included in the Polish constitutional norms mentioned above, were specified in the Family and Guardianship Code which has been in force since 1 January 1965. The rights and duties concerning the child are regulated mainly within the institution of 'parental authority'. Art. 96 of the Code states that parents are to raise their child who remains under their parental authority, that they are to guide him or her, and care for his or her physical and spiritual development. They have the responsibility to prepare the child for work, for the good of society according to his or her talents.

The state may interfere with the exercise of parental authority by limiting authority (art. 109), suspension (art. 110) or deprivation (art. 111): Parental authority may be suspended if temporary obstacles to its performance occur. The court will deprive the parents of their parental authority if the obstacle is permanent, if the parents abuse their authority or in the event that they treat the child with crass ignorance.

Danger to the child's well-being is a prerequisite for the limitation of parental authority. Art. 109 of the Family and Guardianship Code provides for several forms of limitation, including placement of the minor in a foster family or in an educational guardianship institution. Both of these forms are provided for in the Convention. One method of limiting parental authority is to place the minor in an organization or institution created for vocational education or to another form of establishment which assures a limited form of child care. Those establishments or social organizations to which the child is sent are then given the responsibility for the child.[4]

Art. 100 of the Family and Guardianship Code imposes an obligation on the Guardianship Court and other state institutions to help parents to exercise parental authority properly. This can be done by putting parents in contact with the Family Diagnosis Advisory Centre, an auxiliary agency of the Guardianship Court.[5] The provision also allows parents to turn to the Guardianship Court for help in taking the child away from an unauthorized person.

Art. 572 of the Civil Proceedings Code imposes an obligation on the births, marriages and deaths registration office, the courts, the prosecutor's office, the public notary, local government agencies, the police, educational institutions, social guardians and auxiliary agencies of the Guardianship

Court to inform the latter where there is a need to institute proceedings. In this way, organizations and social bodies, among others, bear responsibility for children. This provision also facilitates the execution of the obligation to control the correctness of the exercise of parental authority.[6]

The state's duty to oblige parents to support their children, provided for by the Convention, is also set within four Polish norm-setting acts. The duty to pay maintenance is set by art. 132 of the Family and Guardianship Code. The creation of the Alimony Fund in January 1975 is an example of the state's care. Where money due under a maintenance award is not paid, persons domiciled in Poland are eligible to receive payments from the Fund. The Civil Proceedings Code provides procedures for the enforcement of alimony by the courts, but where there is persistent evasion of maintenance payments, criminal sanctions are provided for in art. 186 of the Criminal Code.[7]

A further example of the responsibility of social organizations for children is their authority to institute a maintenance action on behalf of citizens (art. 61 of the Civil Proceedings Code). The important role of organizations and social bodies and their responsibility for the child originates from the bill on proceedings for matters concerning minors dated 26 October 1982.[8]

Poland also has local educational systems which integrate the actions of different institutions and social bodies relating to the same child and youth population within a given area.[9]

The Polish legislator has tried to achieve safe conditions for the child's development within the family environment, as provided for by the Convention, by means of a wide network of norms of both substantive and procedural law in the area of divorce. Procedural norms establishing conciliation procedures and providing for a stay of proceedings where there is a chance of marital reconciliation (art. 440 of the Civil Proceedings Code) play an important role. Parental reconciliation is thought to be the best solution for the child because it guarantees contacts with both parents.[10] In theory, divorce is not allowed if the welfare of minors is jeopardized as a result of it but, in practice this law fails to stop divorce in families with children.[11] Family courts which have existed in Poland since 1 January 1978[12] and their auxiliary agencies, Family Diagnosis Advisory Centres,[13] play an important part in the fulfilment of the Convention's resolutions.

DIFFERENCES BETWEEN POLISH FAMILY LAW AND THE CONVENTION

The great majority of provisions in Polish family law conform fully with the Convention. It may be said that the children's rights included in the UN

Convention were put into effect by Polish family law when the Family Code came into force on 27 June 1950. Polish family legislation preceded similar solutions in Western European legal systems by approximately 20 years. Amongst its innovations were child welfare laws which applied irrespective of whether the parents were married, and which conferred equal rights on married couples and parents in the exercise of parental authority.

The main difference between the Polish law and the Convention is the reservation to Article 7 enforced by the Polish government during ratification: the Republic of Poland entered a reservation to the effect that the adopted child's right to meet his biological parents remains limited because of laws which allow adoptive parents to keep the child's origins secret. The decision to inform the adopted child about the fact of his adoption lies with the adoptive parents: it is an internal family matter. Norms regulating the court proceedings concerning adoption and the Law on Registry of Birth, Marriage and Death Certificates guarantee that third parties will not be able to access information about adoption.[14] Adoption is concealed from the child by means of art. 48 of the above-mentioned law which provides for the drawing up of a new birth certificate and the annulment of the old one, in cases where the child's natural parent(s) have expressed blanket consent – that is, they have not provided their own candidates for the future adoption of their child.[15]

This form of adoption was introduced into the Polish legal system on 1 March 1976. Adoption, for which the parents give such consent 'cannot be dissolved'[16] nor is it possible for a child's true biological identity to be established in a court.[17] In practice, this form of adoption concerns very young children, most frequently babies from extramarital relationships, where the fathers are not known. Usually, the mothers of these children, who have agreed to the adoption, have never personally taken care of the child or have done so for a very short period of time, and due to their living conditions and lack of emotional bonding with the child, they treat their consent for adoption as a form of deletion of the child from their life and memory. As was shown during the parliamentary discussion of the draft bill for ratification of the UN Convention, a great majority of the Polish public feels that keeping the secret of adoption is in the best interests of both the adoptive parents and the biological parents of the child.

Article 7 of the Convention also relates to problems concerning information about the genetic origins of a child in the event that the child was conceived artificially, where the semen donor is not the husband or partner of the mother, or where another woman's ovum has been implanted into the mother's body. Polish law does not regulate these matters and it is unlikely to do so soon, due to the negative approach of the Catholic Church to these matters. Nor can this be ignored, given the preponderance of Catholics in

Polish society. Thus, in the current legal system there is no basis for the establishment of paternity of the semen donor and, where a woman bears a child, she is regarded as the mother. Under these circumstances any child who has been born as a result of ovum or semen donation will be unable to discover his or her true genetic origins.[18]

There are no specific norms regulating international adoption in Polish law. Not all courts apply Article 21 (b) of the Convention; they wait instead, until a similar norm is introduced into the internal legal system. The dissolution of parliament in May 1993 interrupted the government draft of the appropriate bill, and the new Parliament elected on 19 September 1993 will probably resume the work.

The Supreme Court's stand, included in a resolution III CZP dated 12 June 1992,[19] should be taken into account; in this, the Supreme Court declared that the UN Convention on Children's Rights, ratified with the consent of parliament in the form of an Act, should be treated with legal consequences equal to parliamentary Acts, due to the fact that the Convention was published in the *Official Journal of Laws*. The Supreme Court explained that adoption mediation should be run in Poland by competent, specialized bodies cooperating with appropriate foreign organizations, based on applicable agreements and contracts. The Court advised courts to inquire first whether the child, who is to be adopted by persons with permanent domicile abroad, can be placed instead with a Polish family. The inquiry should always include a search for a Polish family through the mediation of the Central Bank of Information on Children Qualified for Adoption Families which is run by the National Adoption Guardianship Centre at the Friends of Children Society, a non-governmental, non-profit organization founded in 1919. The Friends of Children Society has organized adoptions for the last 30 years.

It is anticipated that the Minister of National Education will soon issue provisions describing the guiding principles for the activities of the adoption guardianship centres. Currently there are approximately 40 centres run by the Friends of Children Society; a few are run by the schools superintendents and one is run by the Archdiocesan Court in Łódź. New church centres are also being organized.

ACTS OF MAJOR IMPORTANCE REGULATING ISSUES OF THE CONVENTION ADOPTED AFTER 7 JULY 1991

Acts of major importance, regulating obligations set out in the Convention, adopted after 7 July 1991, are the following:

- the Act on the 'Educational System' dated 7 September 1991;[20]
- the Act on 'Family Planning, Protection of the Human Foetus and the Conditions for Admissibility of Abortion', dated 7 January 1993.[21]

These Acts, among other things, tackle important aspects of the Convention.

First, we will consider the controversial abortion legislation passed in 1993. Article 1 of the Convention does not set a point in time when the protection of the child's rights begins. According to legal status in Poland on 7 July 1991, in compliance with art. 8 of the Civil Code, every person has a legal capacity from the moment of birth.

Art. 1 (1)(a) of the Act on 'the conditions for admissibility of abortion', dated 27 April 1956, permitted doctors to perform a medical intervention when the woman in pregnancy has 'difficult living conditions' as well as in other circumstances. The practical application of this provision was very liberal. Interventions were made not only in medical establishments but also in private gynaecological consulting rooms. The pregnant woman's decision concerning the advisability of performing the intervention in the light of the provisions was not subject to verification.

The Act dated 7 January 1993 introduced a conditional legal capacity of a human being from the moment of conception and a severely limited admissibility of abortion. Doctors now frequently refuse to carry out an intervention, when it is permitted in the Act, referring to their beliefs and the ethics of the profession. Therefore, the scope of child protection has widened (cf. Articles 1 and 6 of the Convention). Even so, we cannot unequivocally state that children's rights are completely protected from the moment of conception.[22]

The Act on the 'Educational System' refers to the UN Convention on Children's Rights as early as the Preface Art. 13 of the Act, which carries into effect Articles 2 and 30 of the Convention, is especially important. It states that a public school should give students the opportunity of maintaining their national, ethnic, linguistic and religious identity, and especially the opportunity to study their own language, history and culture. The bases for organizing studies for children belonging to ethnic minorities are set forth in an Executive Ordinance of the Minister of National Education dated 4 March 1992.

Article 14 of the Convention was reconfirmed in art. 12 of the Act on the 'Educational System' and in an Executive Ordinance of the Minister of National Education dated 4 April 1992 concerning conditions and ways of organizing religious studies in public schools. A directive of the Minister of National Education, preceding this executive ordinance, reintroduced studies of religion into public schools. This caused much controversy and was referred for review by the Constitutional Tribunal by the Spokesman of the

Citizens' Rights. The Constitutional Tribunal dismissed the charge that the directive was made contrary to the Constitution and several Acts of Parliament,[23] and upheld it.

The freedom to form associations (Article 15 of the Convention) is dealt with by art. 56 of the Act on the 'Educational System', which states that associations and organizations aiming to enrich the forms of didactic, educational and guardianship activities may function in schools and education establishments, but that political parties and organizations may not do so.

Articles 11 and 35 of the Convention are being achieved by the ratification in Poland of The Hague Convention concerning civil aspects of child abduction abroad concluded on 25 October 1980. The above Convention has been in force in Poland since 2 November 1992.

REALIZATION OF THE CONVENTION ON CHILDREN'S RIGHTS IN PRACTICE

Within the scope of this chapter we can only draw attention to a few of the practical problems of implementing the Convention in Poland. What these show is that, in practice, there are areas where the content of the Convention is not complied with, and that much effort is required to further children's rights.

The matter which most shocks Polish public opinion is the limited enforcement of the Convention on the important matter of the organization and adjournment of international adoption. The number of such cases of adoption constantly rises. In 1989 they amounted to 11.4 per cent of all adoption cases adjourned in Poland and in 1991 15.5 per cent. For instance, within the district of the *Voivodship* Court in Warsaw, international adoption cases amounted to 15.8 per cent of all adjourned cases in 1990, while in 1991 it amounted to 44.1 per cent. There are, at a conservative estimate, about 5000 ordinary Polish families who have been accepted as suitable adopters and are waiting to adopt. The figure quoted is frequently three times as great. Since only a small proportion of children adopted abroad have special needs, or comprise a large family of brothers and sisters, a majority would be able to find an adoptive family in Poland.[24] Currently preparatory proceedings are taking place in Poland and in Italy against persons suspected of 'trading' Polish children destined for adoption by foreigners.[25]

A further problem which causes concern is the low detection rate of crimes against children, especially where the perpetrators are parents or other persons on whom the children depend. Polish research shows that 94 per cent of children who are victims of sexual crimes do not disclose their experiences.[26] Only a small number of perpetrators in 1000 disclosed cases involving child trauma each year will have either civil or criminal penalties imposed upon them for their acts.[27]

Family courts, which are invested with wide-ranging powers, are being notified about dangers to the child's well-being relatively late by the persons who are obliged to do so.[28] Out of misplaced respect for the privacy of family life third persons rarely react to harm done to children and do so unwillingly and too late. Guardianship educational establishments, where children are placed in cases of parental neglect, usually do not inform the guardianship court about the fact of neglect until six months after the parental infringement occurs. In this way, they want to give parents 'a chance to improve'.

During the period that the UN Convention has been in force, the economic situation in Poland has deteriorated. The Main Statistical Office data show that GNP per capita amounted to $2200 in 1992 and is sinking to the levels of 1982. Retail prices have risen seventeenfold during the period that the Convention has been in force, while service prices rose thirty-fourfold. The number of unemployed in 1993 reached 3 million, and, gradually, more unemployed are denied the right to benefit. This has a direct effect on children's living standards: 75 per cent of large families have extremely bad living conditions; 40 per cent of children from such families do not have a bed solely to themselves.

Also, during this period the number of nurseries, preschool groups, day centres, clubs and artistic schools has decreased. The quality of medical services has also decreased, due to lack of equipment and means for the modernization of medical centres.[29]

Ten per cent of the Polish territory, inhabited by 35 per cent of the population, is in a polluted environment designated as an environmental catastrophe. This has a direct effect on the course of foetal development and infant mortality.

SOME SOCIAL MEASURES

Despite considerable financial problems, steps have been taken in order to enforce the provisions of the Convention in practice. As examples we may cite the following:

1   The Ministry of Health, together with the Mother's and Child's Institute, has developed a programme to reduce infant mortality by improving care for pregnant women. Attempts have been made to popularize breast-feeding, and there have been improvements in intensive medical care for infants.

2   Different activities have been initiated for children with special needs. In the academic year 1992–3 free education at home was secured for 10,000 children and 500 education establishments were organized for 38,000 children, where the stay was only partially payable. The Friends of Children Society runs 20 education rehabilitation centres for children with child meningitis, dyslexia and dysgraphia and runs 20 help centres for physically handicapped children, children with brittle bones, cleft palate and lips, diabetic children and children on gluten-free diets. Monastic orders run 41 educational establishments and special primary schools as well as four special preschools.

3   All children and students over 18 qualify for free state health care; 95–100 per cent of children have access to free preventive vaccinations. In 1991 5,372,000 working families received family benefits and 391,000 educational benefits for preschool education for children up to the age of four years old.

4   Education in public schools is free. Compulsory education within the eight-grade primary school has been achieved. Only 0.05 per cent of children do not comply with the obligation. In March 1993 the government issued a set of general principles for the education policy. Reform of the educational system began on 1 September 1994.[30]

5   The Act on the 'Educational System' introduced the principle of a free right to establish schools and educational establishments by nationals and legal entities and provides subsidies for private schools up to 50 per cent of education costs in public schools. Private schools may obtain the rights of public schools in regard to issuing certificates and state diplomas. In the academic year 1992–93, 2571 primary schools (including 12 religious schools), 235 private high schools and 179 vocational schools functioned outside the government administration.

6   Despite the poor financial situation, Poland has helped children of refugees. In 1992 590 persons (together with children) sought refugee status. Children of refugees who have the right to permanent residence received the same protection as children of Polish citizens. On 14 August, 1992 the Polish government admitted 926 children evacuated from Croatia together with their guardians and teachers ensuring them an apartment, board, medical aid and education in their mother tongue.

CONCLUSIONS

In order to evaluate the application of the Convention in Poland, the following should be stated:

1 Polish law and its practical application achieve the principle of the child's superior well-being. The vast majority of regulations in Polish law comply with the Convention. Regulation of international adoption within the internal legal system is expected in the near future.

2 Despite objective financial problems hindering the achievement of the child's right to optimal health (Article 24), social security (Article 26), adequate living standards (Article 27), the right to rest (Article 31), within its existing means, the state treats children's (both of Polish nationality, ethnic minorities and refugees) needs preferentially, assisting in activities for children initiated by social and religious organizations.

NOTES

1 A. Łopatka (1990), 'Konwencja Praw Dziecka', *Panstwo i Prawo*, (3), hereafter referred to as *Pip*.

2 Bill dated 21 September 1990.

3 *Cf.* 'Konwencja Praw Człowieka', a joint work led by M. Balcereka, Warsaw 1990; *Konwencja o prawach dziecka a prawo polskie. Materiały z konferencji naukowej w gmachu Sejmu 19–20 marca 1991* (hereinafter referred to as *Materiały 91*); *Prawa Dziecka, Deklaracje i rzeczywistość*, Warsaw 1993 (hereinafter referred to as *Prawa.*); Papers from a conference held in Rembertów on 19–21 June, Wyższa Szkoła Pedagogiki Specialnej w Warszawie.

4 W. Stojanowska (1991), Odpowiedzialność za dziecko: rodziców, organizacji i ciał społecznych, państwa', *Materiały 91*, pp. 30–1.

5 *Ibid.*, p. 31 and J. Ignatowicz (1990) in *Kodeks rodzinny i opiekuńczy z komentarzemz*, Warsaw, p. 430.

6 Stojanowska, *op. cit.*, note 4 above, pp. 31–2.

7 *Ibid.*, p. 32.

8 *Ibid.*, p. 35.

9 M. Śnieżyński (1981), *Działalność opiekuńczo-wychowawcza w osiedlu*, Warsaw: Wydawnictwa Szkolne i Pedagogiczne.

10 W. Stojanowska (1979), *Rozwó a dobro dziecka*, Warsaw: Wydawnictwo Prawnicze, p. 38 *et seq.* following.

11 *Ibid.*

12 F. Zedler (1984), *Sądy rodzinne. Wybrane zagadnienia organizacyjne i procesowe*, Warsaw: Wydawnictwo Prawnicze.

13 W. Kubiak (1986), *Funkcjonowanie rodzinnego ośrodka diagnostyczno-konsultacyjnego w systemie wychowania prewencyjno-resocjalizacyjnego dzieci i młodzieży*, Szczecin.

14 Bill dated 29 September 1986.

15 E. Płonka (1986), *Przysposobienie całkowite w prawie polskim*, Wrocław; J. Ignatowicz (1984), 'Tajemnica przysposobienia w ujęciu prawa o aktach stanu cywilnego z dnia 29 września, 1986', *Ruch Prawniczy, Ekonomiczny i Socjologiczny*, (2).

16 Article 125(1), Family Guardianship Code.

17 Article 124(1), Family Guardianship Code.

18 *Cf.*, for example, Dyoniak (1989), 'Pozycja prawna dziecka urodzonego w następstwie

inplantacji embrionu', *Nowe Prawo*, (1); M. Działyńska (1993), 'Macierzyństwo zastępcze', *Studia Prawnicze*, (1), p. 97 *et seq.*; M. Safjan (1990), *Prawo wobec ingerencji w sferę ludzkiej prokreacji*, Warsaw, p. 415.

19   OSN 10/1992, p. 179.
20   *Official Journal of Law*, (95), p. 425.
21   *Ibid.*, (17), p. 78.
22   T. Smyczyński (1993), 'Nasciturus w świetle ustawodawstwa o przerywaniu ciąży', *Studia Prawnicze*, (1) pp. 74–85.
23   In a decision K11/90 dated 30 January 1991. Cf. gloss by M. Pietrzak in *Pip* (5), 1991; Hanna Gronkiewicz-Waltz and K. Pawłowicz in *Pip* (7), 1991; T. Rabska in *Pip*, (7), 1991; Z. Strus in *Pip*, (11), 1991.
24   E. Holewińska-Łapińska (1991), '"Adopcja zagraniczna" w świetle Konwencji Praw Dziecka', *Palestra*, (3–4).
25   *Cf.* 'Rodziły na sprzedaż', *Ekspres Wieczorny*, 26 May 1993.
26   J. Gromska (1993), 'Raport o przestępczości wobec dzieci, w tym seksualnej', *Prawa Dziecka*, Warsaw: Deklaracje i Rzeczywistość, (…), p. 183 *et seq.*
27   B. Mossakowska, 'Zespół Maltretowanego Dziecka w…': *Prawa* (…), p. 178.
28   Cf. Article 570, Civil Proceedings Code.
29   D. Słowicka (1993), 'Raport misji UNICEF', *Przyjaciel dziecka* (7–8), pp. 10–11.
30   Minister Edukacji Narodowej (1993), 'Profesor Z. Flisowski o działaniach MEN wobec zagrożeń w realizacji praw i potrzeb dzieci', *Przyjaciel Dziecka*, (7–8), pp. 1–3.

11 The UN Convention on the Rights of the Child and Russian Family Law

Olga Khazova

CHILDREN'S RIGHTS IN RUSSIAN LAW

The UN Convention on the Rights of the Child entered into force in the territory of the Russian Federation on 15 September 1990. As a result Russia undertook to review its national legislation and bring it into line with the Convention, and to ensure that every new legislative act, no matter what sphere of human relations it concerns, should be considered from the point of view of its conformity with the Convention.

Without giving a comprehensive description of recent Russian legislation, I must note the main statutes that, in one way or another, covered (or should have covered) matters connected with children. First of all came the Human Rights and Freedoms Declaration adopted in November of 1991.[1] The principal task of this document was to bring Russian legislation into line with universally recognized international standards of human rights and freedoms. The declaration proclaimed the principal and inalienable rights of citizens belonging to them from birth: the right to life, the right of freedom including that of movement, thought, conscience and religion, the right to personal privacy, privacy of home and private life, the right of property, the right of inheritance, the right to education and so on. These fundamental rights and freedoms were later incorporated into the new Russian Constitution of 1993.

The Law on Citizenship of 1991 assures every child in Russia the right to acquire citizenship.[2] Where the parents hold different citizenships and one of them is a citizen of Russia at the moment of the child's birth, the question of the child's citizenship is decided by his or her parents' mutual agreement.

If there is no such agreement, a child acquires Russian citizenship provided he or she was born on the Russian territory or if he or she would otherwise become stateless (s. 15). The citizenship of children aged between 14 and 18 years may be changed only with their consent. Similarly, under the Law on Entry and Exit,[3] a 14 year-old minor may leave the country only with his or her consent (s. 10). Legislation on Refugees and Forced Migrants of 1993[4] provides that state bodies are bound to render a refugee and a forced migrant all possible assistance, particularly with placing their children in school or kindergarten (ss. 7 and 6 respectively).

For the first time the law now stipulates the possibility of children participating in public associations. Under the Law of 1990,[5] the notion of public association also includes children and youth associations and permits membership in youth associations set up by the political parties from the age of 14 years (ss. 1, 9).

Child's rights are paid more or less adequate attention in the Fundamentals of Russian Legislation on Protection of Citizens' Health, adopted in 1993.[6] Several sections of this law are devoted to protection of minors' rights and interests. In particular, the age when minors are considered entitled to give 'voluntary informed consent to medical intervention or to refuse it' is lowered to 15 years. As to minors under 15, such consent is given by their parents (or their legal substitute). If parents refuse medical assistance that is necessary to save a child's life, the management of the hospital has acquired the right to institute court proceedings to protect the child's interests (s. 33). With the purpose of protection of minor's life and health, the Fundamentals also limit the possibility of use of new kinds of medical technology, treatment and medicines for children under 15 where this may directly endanger their lives (s. 43). An important innovation of the law is the provision that enables one of the parents, in the interests of the child's treatment, to stay with him or her in a hospital irrespective of the child's age. (This was an option previously much obstructed if ever possible.)

With the aim of preventing crimes against children, new sections of the Criminal Code introduce sanctions for the abduction of children (s. 125–1) and introduce criminal responsibility for swopping of a child in hospital committed from mercenary or base motives (s. 125).[7] However, this is definitely insufficient to prevent crimes against children. There are still no adequate measures against child abuse undertaken in Russian criminal law nor is there criminal responsibility for the sale of children.

In 1992 the Law on Education was enacted.[8] However, this, too, clearly seemed insufficient to protect children's right to education. The law is too declarative in character. Although it recognizes the right to education as one of the main constitutional rights, it fails to do enough to ensure that compulsory secondary education is universally applied in practice. It fails to provide a mechanism that could make it possible to check whether all children go to school or not. A great deal of evidence indicates that some children do not attend any school whatsoever. As one underlying reason for this situation, the shortcomings of the Law of Education undoubtedly cannot be ignored.

Among the recent legislative acts there are also those that should have had provisions on children, but do not in fact say anything on the matter. Of major concern are those statutes that concern the new realities of Russian life – pre-eminently the transition to a market economy. A specific example is the Law on Privatization of the Housing Fund,[9] which does not even mention the existence of children and their interests. This means that children's interests were entirely ignored in the process of privatization of dwelling houses, and children acquired no rights to the dwelling-place where they lived. Nor did subsequent transactions with the dwellings take their interests into account. Thus, it was not long before the chickens came home to roost, and a large number of children found themselves without a roof over their heads, because their flats or houses had been sold by their parents. Unfortunately, in the majority of cases it was too late to protect the rights of the children, because their dwellings had been sold and resold.[10] The number of abuses and disputes caused by this law led the Supreme Court to explain that minors have equal rights to their flats or houses and, together with adults, were entitled to participate in the process of house privatization.[11] There are no references in Russian law either to the child's interests on such a vital question for modern Russia as the right to dispose of a voucher. (Vouchers were given to all Russian citizens, children included, to be used in the process or privatization as their part in the national property.) Unfortunately, the list of such examples could be multiplied.

If we turn to the sphere of family relations, we will find no single special law on children's matters recently enacted in Russia. Moreover, there were no laws on matrimonial matters at all. The one legislative act adopted during this period was the USSR Law of 22 May 1990.[12] However, since it was the Law of the Soviet Union, there is a great uncertainty as to whether or not it continues to be in force on Russian territory. Russian lawyers and scholars differ on this matter, and the Supreme Court has given no clear explanations.

The above summary seems to be evidence enough that there is a lack of any general and consistent approach to problems connected with children. The protection of minors' rights and interests is fragmentary and unsystematic in character. It is perfectly obvious that, despite the enormous legislative activity taking place in Russia recently, the legal protection of children remains inadequate, and is paid insufficient attention. Therefore, on the whole, recent legislation, no matter what is its general significance, has failed to address the principal issue concerning children – it has not ensured a primary consideration of the children's best interests and has not treated them as individuals and as subjects of the law.

CHILDHOOD IN RUSSIA

There are several interconnected reasons explaining why this should be so – most being linked to the political and economic instability in the country. It has to be acknowledged, of course, that Russia, having entered into an obligation to raise the child's legal protection up to the level provided for by the UN Convention, then found itself in a difficult position given the social and political tensions and the economic and ecological situation in the country.[13] Negative, and sometimes even threatening, consequences of the latest reforms were not taken into account in a proper way.[14] Haste, with laws being adopted with insufficient attention given to their scientific basis, has no doubt played its negative part as well.

Recent years can be characterized by a slump in the material circumstances of the majority of Russian families. The ecological situation has also noticeably declined. The number of children with various disabilities, and children's sickness and death rate have increased. For the first time since the Second World War the death rate has exceeded the birth rate.[15] In 1992 the infant mortality rate 'reached' the level of 1920.[16] At the same time, the building of hospitals, maternity hospitals, schools and kindergartens is being seriously reduced. There are now more than one million homeless people in the country,[17] among whom there are many children.

The mechanisms for the protection of children who get into trouble do not work at all. Nobody today can estimate the true number of neglected children: almost 80 per cent of street children are believed to have parents.[18] The number of crimes committed by teenagers is constantly rising. If 10 years ago there were approximately 100,000 children involved in criminal activity, in 1994 this number appeared to have doubled. Every year 60,000 children, who have yet not reached the age of criminal responsibility, commit crimes.[19]

The problem of cruelty towards children and child abuse is stretched to breaking-point: 70 per cent of all child traumas are principally derived from family incidents. Every year nearly 50,000 children run away from their homes. Nearly 2000 children between the age of 7 and 17 commit suicide each year.[20] Indeed, suicide is the third most frequent reason for childhood death.[21]

In addition, because of the lack of an appropriate legislative base, Russia appeared to be absolutely unprepared to manage the control of international adoption or to prevent the sale of children abroad.

All of this is the stark reality of Russia today, and it becomes daily more and more threatening.

It is scarcely possible to resolve these difficult problems without a unified state programme on matters connected with children. However, such a complex programme is still absent. There is still no legal mechanism that could ensure the real fulfilment of state measures on childhood protection.[22]

Obviously, the absence of such a unified and complex programme to realize the Convention provisions could partly be explained – apart from the general chaos of Russian life – by the fact that neither Russian society as a whole nor the legislators are 'ideologically' prepared for the changes. Russia is just at the beginning of 'taking children's rights seriously'; this 'new ideology' has yet to be embraced in Russian consciousness.[23] For a long time the 'one-sided view' of childhood protection dominated in the law of the former USSR – the view of a child through the prism of his parents (or parent substitute). The child's interests used to be indirectly protected, primarily by means of protecting his or her mother's interests. The protection of children's rights was traditionally understood as a constituent part of the protection of motherhood and principally took the form of different social allowances and privileges granted to women with children. In such an exclusively paternalistic situation there was practically no place left for the child himself with his or her own rights and interests. This approach, unfortunately, still persists. The new Russian Constitution, in particular, not only says nothing on children's rights, but hardly separates children as subjects of law. 'Motherhood and childhood, family are under protection of the state' – that is all that the Constitution says about children. This is definitely not enough for a basic law adopted at the end of 1993 in a country which has ratified the UN Convention on the Rights of the Child.

This 'one-sided view' of the protection of child's interests in its turn may partly be explained by the absence of proper information. For a long time the 'Iron Curtain' obstructed new ideas from the West. Suffice it to say that Declaration of Human Rights adopted in 1948 became widely known to the general public (except to a close circle of dissidents and persons especially interested in problems of human rights) only 30 years later. As to the Declaration on the Rights of the Child of 1959, this document was practically not known at all in Russia until the end of the 1980s. For these purposes we can ignore the rare, brief paragraphs which occasionally appeared in the newspapers. Of course, in such conditions it was very difficult to think or speak about any rights at all.

To raise children's lives up to the standards of the Convention or even to approach this goal, it is necessary, as an initial minimum, to fulfil the requirement of Article 42 of the Convention and 'to make the principles and provisions of the Convention widely known ... to adults and children alike'.

Simultaneously, it is necessary to make widely known those obligations that were imposed on the Russian state by the fact of ratification of the Convention. The Convention on the Rights of the Child was published in Russia soon after its ratification, but only in small, or limited-readership, editions. For years there was practically no serious and widespread discussion of the Convention, and certainly lawyers, politicians, scholars and specialists in childhood protection, if such exist in Russia, did not participate. The majority of Russian children do not know, as before, about the existence of the Convention and about those rights and freedoms with which they are vested. And as far as adults are concerned they, it seems, are oblivious to the very concept of 'the rights of the child'.

PARENTAL RESPONSIBILITY

It is possible to speak about children's rights and their protection from different angles: from constitutional law, civil law, labour law, criminal law and, of course, family law. But without doubt, it is family law that plays the most significant part in the protection of the child's interests, since it is this which regulates the relationships within the family – 'the natural environment for the growth and well-being of all its members and particularly children'.[24] If we look at Russian legislation on marriage and the family through the prism of the Convention, it will become obvious that many family law provisions do not correspond to the Convention's requirements.

When we examine the Russian Code on Marriage and the Family the first thing we immediately notice is the absence of any clearly formulated general requirement that 'the best interests of the child shall be a primary consideration', as Article 3 of the Convention stipulates. There are many references in the Code to children's interests. For example, according to s. 1, one of the main tasks of the Code is to ensure 'every kind of protection is given to the interests of the mother and the children and that every child has a happy childhood'; s. 52 provides that 'parental rights cannot be exercised in contradiction with children's interests'; disputes on children's place of residence are decided in accordance with their interests (s. 55); adoption is permitted only in child's interests (s. 98) and so on. However, the mere mention of the necessity to take the child's interests into account, no matter how frequent, does not guarantee their actual protection. There is a long way to go to move the child's interests to the foreground and to give them a priority.

'For full and harmonious development' of the child's personality he or she should grow up in a family environment, surrounded by parents' care and protection – one of the essential conditions of a normal child's development being his proper family upbringing. Every child, 'as far as possible, has the right to know and be cared for by his or her parents' states Article 7 of the Convention. In Russian legislation, however strange it may seem, there is no reference to the child's right to a family upbringing or, in other words, his or her right to be brought up by his or her own parents. No doubt this must be considered as one of the main inconsistencies with the requirements of the Convention. The absence of a child's right to family upbringing stipulated by family law contrasts with the detailed regulation of the parents' rights and duties (in the Code the whole chapter is devoted to parents) At the same time, the right of the child to a proper family upbringing is, in reality, his or her most significant personal right.[25] How can we speak of protecting this right if it is not even mentioned in the law?

To perceive a child more as a subject than as an object of family relationships inevitably implies increasing parents' responsibility for their children. However, in Russian legislation the provisions providing for the responsibility of parents for children's family upbringing are often no more than declaratory, and in practice we sometimes find there is total irresponsibility.[26] Moreover, it is occasionally the legal rules themselves that encourage the growth of irresponsibility in parents. In this connection attention should focus on the following.

One obvious contradiction between the law and the child's rights and interests are the rules dealing with the (unfortunately rather widespread) situation when a child is born to an unmarried mother. In Russian law there is still in force a provision, introduced in 1944, that enables a woman who has a child outside wedlock to place her child in a children's institution to be supported and brought up at the expense of the state, irrespective of the reason why she has had the child.[27] The reasons behind the enactment of this provision in 1944 disappeared long ago,[28] and at present there is scarcely any reasonable ground for its preservation. But it is a law which, without any good cause, releases a woman from any responsibility for the life of her child and thereby grossly infringes the latter's rights and interests, depriving him or her of a mother and a home simultaneously.

ESTABLISHING PATERNITY

Legislation on the establishment of paternity is also open to serious criticism. In reality, it legalizes 'fatherlessness' when a father definitely exists.[29] Under the Code on Marriage and the Family (s. 48), a court considering a case on establishment of paternity[30] takes into consideration the following factors:

... residence in a common household of the mother and the respondent before the child's birth; or the mother and the respondent's common upbringing or maintenance of the child; or reliable evidence confirming the respondent's acceptance of his paternity.

Despite modern medical achievements and, in particular, genetic methods of determining paternity which makes it possible to establish paternity almost without doubt, the courts in Russia continue to be tied by the above-mentioned circumstances and do not consider themselves entitled to settle the cases on the ground of medical testing only. Statistics show that, in every fifth case, a court denies an application for the establishment of paternity. The majority of such rejections are based on the absence of the circumstances stipulated by law.[31] Furthermore, the latest genetic methods of proving paternity, such as DNA testing, are not in fact widely available in Russia because they are expensive. All such things make the process of paternity establishment extremely complicated and doomed to failure in a great number of cases. And if, in addition, to complete the picture, a woman decides to use her 'right as a lone mother' to place her child into state care, the child becomes an unwanted, 'an orphan', even though he or she has parents who may be young and healthy.

Sociological research, conducted in Moscow a few years ago, showed that nearly 52 per cent of children in children's homes were children of unmarried mothers, and that this phenomenon was increasing.[32] However, these women should not be blamed for the loss of moral values: there are objective reasons for this social phenomenon. Statistics show that births outside marriage usually take place among two age groups: those from 15 to 19 years of age and those from 35 to 40. A 35 year-old woman, as a rule, has the child intentionally and does not reject him or her child later. The case of the first age group is quite different. These young women usually do not have enough money to live on and often do not even have a place to live. These circumstances force them to leave their children, and they do so out of despair.

THE AGE OF MAJORITY

Under-age parents represent an especially vulnerable group. The legal regime regulating their rights is deficient in many ways. A distinction is drawn between under-age parents who are married to each other and those who are not. According to Russian family law, the statutory marriage age for both men and women is 18 (also the age of civil majority). Legislation provides that this may be lowered by dispensation, but not by more than two years.[33]

Although the law contains no grounds for dispensation, in reality it is usually sought where the prospective bride is pregnant or after the birth of a child.[34] A minor whose age of majority has been reduced by a competent body, after getting married, acquires full legal capacity as if he or she had already attained the age of civil majority.[35] Accordingly, he or she becomes fully independent from his parents or guardians.

But if this process has not been negotiated and a child is born to an unmarried minor between the ages of 16 and 18, then, although such young persons are entitled to register their child in the way prescribed by law (minors get identity cards at 16), the mere fact of the child's birth does not confer upon them full legal capacity. From the juridical point of view they continue to be of limited legal capacity and under the guardianship of their parents until they reach the age of majority. In particular, it means that they do not acquire full procedural capacity and their rights, as a general rule, are protected in court by their legal representatives.[36] Although there are some exceptions to this rule in the law, on the whole, the legal status of a 16 year-old minor parent is not defined very clearly. For example, in the law there is no clear answer to the question whether or not an under-age mother has the right to institute proceedings to establish paternity. There are different opinions expressed in regard to voluntary establishment of paternity by a 16 year-old father as well.

Such a 'discrimination' of unmarried minor parents seems to have no serious grounds and violates their rights, as well as those of their children. If the law permits lowering the marriage age with all the consequences ensuing therefrom, and recognizes thereby that minors of this age are psychologically and physiologically mature, it is logical to recognize them as equally mature if they happen to have a child. It is pertinent to note that, according to statistical data, 95.6 per cent of all conceptions in the relevant age group (of 16 and 17 year-olds) take place outside marriage.[37]

Much more serious is the question concerning minor parents aged under 16. Statistically they are a small group, but they create many big problems in practice. A girl who has not attained 16 years of age, who has a child, has no rights at all and cannot herself register her child. It may be done only by her parents (or their substitute). And if the parents, as is often the case, refuse to take and to register a child, what can the girl do then? In such a situation the position of a young mother is absolutely desperate. The only thing she can do is to use the right given to unmarried mothers and to place her child into the 'children's home'. According to the law, she places her child under state care temporarily and has the right to have the child returned at any time, but, in the event, when applying to the state body to take her child, it is 'suggested' to her that she gives consent to the child's future adoption. This implies that she has rejected her child, and it will be extremely difficult (if ever possible) to have him or her returned if the adoption has taken place. And since there is 'a great demand' for such children, they usually are adopted very quickly. That is why such applications are called 'refusals'.

Minor mothers who find themselves in such a situation are put under great pressure either from the maternity hospital administration and local authorities, or from their parents, or from all of them simultaneously. Poor living conditions, the inability of these minor mothers, because of their young age, to realize properly the consequences of their actions and their legal 'unprotection' render them merely toys in the hands of the adults. There have been cases where minor mothers have been greatly distressed by the loss of their children after their adoption by another family, but it has been too late to do anything about it. Thus, it is clear, that we have 'double breach' of minors' rights, both of the under-age mother and her child, and we can hardly speak about the 'child's best interests' in these cases.

In this connection it is impossible to ignore without comment the contradiction in the legislator's position. If a minor mother who has not attained the age of 16 is considered sufficiently adult to reject her child and give her consent to adoption, why is she not considered equally grown-up to 'accept' her own child and to act as his or her legal mother? While the question of legal capacity of minor children on the whole is a debatable one (though, we may mention that recognition of a minor as a person inevitably implies granting him or her certain rights), no one will doubt the necessity of protection of their rights. Therefore, as a minimum, the law must provide that the consent to adoption can be given only by a person of full age.[38]

CHILDREN WITH SPECIAL NEEDS

The right to family upbringing and to parental care must be equally granted to mentally or physically disabled children. For a time Soviet legislation was based on the contrary view; it pursued a policy of maximum separation of disabled children from the others. Unfortunately, the latest Russian legislation hardly constitutes progress. The Russian Law on Protection of Citizens' Health of 1993 provides that 'a minor with physical or mental defects may, at the request of their parents ... be kept in an establishment of the system of social protection ...' (s. 24). By a savage irony this provision is included into the section titled 'The Minors' Rights'! If such a child is not placed in a special children's home for mental defectives at birth and remains at home with his parents, he or she will encounter many problems when he or she attains school age. Since such a child creates a lot of additional problems for teachers, they will try 'to get rid of him or her' by all possible means.

The main thing that defines the future life of a child with special needs is the classification and diagnosis given him or her in the very beginning, since it is very difficult to change this later. If a disabled child is, in addition, an orphan, his or her position is absolutely hopeless, since there is no one to take an interest in him or her. Here, we can obviously refer to a form of 'psychiatric abuse' as, indeed, Freeman has pointed out.[39] Mistakes in the original diagnosis are common, and children with minor disabilities which could be further alleviated were they to develop within a normal upbringing, remain in institutions among severely disabled children. As is recognized in the report of one of the international commissions which examined children in the special children's homes, between 36 and 70 per cent of so-called disabled were perfectly normal.[40] That, with appropriate treatment, these children can be rehabilitated is demonstrated, particularly, by the work of the centre for the social and psychological rehabilitation of children with mental defects, opened in one of the districts of Moscow. This Centre is attended by 500 children, 350 of whom suffer from schizophrenia, feeblemindedness, epilepsy, mental retardation and communication disorders. As a result of studies in the centre 70 per cent of these children have been able to attend ordinary schools and kindergartens.[41] Unfortunately, such centres are still a rarity, and a child with correctable defects can easily be isolated with the mentally ill. The environment and treatment in such places are unbearable, and, of course, in such conditions a child is doomed to social degradation making the prospects of even partial rehabilitation totally out of the question. In such a situation, of course, we can speak neither about the best interests of the child nor the child's right to parental care; even less can we speak about the right 'to enjoy a full and decent life, in conditions which ensure dignity, promote self-reliance and facilitate the child's active participation in the community' (Articles 3, 7 and 23 of the Convention).[42]

REPRESENTING THE CHILD'S INTERESTS

The idea of strengthening parental responsibility for the upbringing of children is being constantly reiterated elsewhere. But there is little hope of this, since there is no clear and precise system of measures for ensuring children's proper upbringing in Russia. Under s. 52 of the Russian Code on Marriage and the Family, 'parents are obliged to bring up their children, and take care of their physical development and education ...'. Violation of this rule, for example by evasion of their duty of upbringing, abuse of parental rights, cruel treatment and harmful influence constitute offences entailing responsibility under different branches of law: family, civil, administrative and criminal. However, the 'abundance' of sanctions by no means indicates their effectiveness. There is no precise coordination between all these sanctions in Russian law, and it is not always clear why, in a specific situation, one set of rules applies rather than the other.

In this respect a few words must be said about the problem of representation of child's interests. Whenever a court considers a case connected with the upbringing of children, it must use a local authority representative from the agency on custody and guardianship. So-called 'disputes on children's upbringing' include that of child's place of residence when the parents are separated (ss. 34 and 55 of the Code); parents' claims to return children from persons not entitled to detain them (s. 58); cases on deprivation of parental rights and restoration of parental rights (ss. 59 and 63); taking a child away from parents (s. 64); annulment of adoption (ss. 111–118). The participation of custody and guardianship agencies consists of an investigation of living conditions and the mode of upbringing of a child. The agency is bound to take care of all neglected children and take measures, if necessary, to protect their rights.

However, the agencies of custody and guardianship are unable to fulfil all the tasks connected with children that are imposed on them by law. In each agency there is, at best, only one person who deals with children's matters – the inspector on childhood protection. And only 40 per cent of agencies have such inspectors;[42] in the remainder these functions are fulfilled by someone else, usually a 'school inspector' who has his own job to do and therefore considers these additional obligations as secondary. It goes without saying that it is very difficult to protect minors' rights properly in such circumstances.

The first and only attempt to widen the rights of children themselves in order to protect their own interests was made in the USSR Law of 22 May 1990. This law enabled a minor child to apply to the custody agency him or herself, if his or her parents were not properly fulfilling their duty towards their children or were abusing their rights. However, for reasons already stated, the future of this provision is quite uncertain and it is not working at present.

CONCLUSION

This is far from a complete survey of the failures of Russian law to address the rights of children as set out in the UN Convention on the Rights of the Child. There are many more gaps in Russian child and family law. However, I have selected a few problems which I believe show how laws and practices in areas crucial to the child's life and his future are inadequately addressed.

Russia needs to restructure radically the Code on Marriage and the Family and address the principles in the Convention. Such work has already begun. The Convention must be seen as a brilliant shining; it shows the country in what direction it must move. And Russia has a long way to go.

NOTES

1 'Deklaratzija prav i svobod cheloveka i grazhdanina', *Vedomosti S"ezda narodnykh deputatov Rossiiskoi Federatzii i Verkhovnogo Soveta Rossiiskoi Federatzii* (hereafter *Ved. RF*) (52), 1991, item 1865.
2 'Zakon o grazhdanstve', *Ved. RF* (6), 1992, item 243.
3 'Zakon o v"ezde i vyezde 1993', *Ved. RF* (32), 1993, item 1227.
4 *Ved. RF* (12), 1993, items 435, 427.
5 'Zakon SSSR ob obschestvennykh ob"edinenijakh', *Ved. USSR*, (42), 1990, item 839.
6 *Ved. RF*, (33), 1993, item 1318.
7 *Ved. RF*, (22), 1993, item 789.
8 *Ved. RF*, (30), 1992, item 1797.
9 *Ved. RF*, (28), 1991, item 959.
10 *Rossiiskaja gazeta*, 3 June 1994, p. 2.
11 *Bulletin Verkhovnogo Suda RF*, (2), 1994, p. 7.
12 *Ved. USSR*, (23), 1990, item 442.
13 See *Prava rebenka*, May 1992, pp. 63–4.
14 *Konventzia o pravakh rebenka i realnosti detstva v Rossii*, May 1993, p. 18.
15 *Vestnik Statistiki*, (8), 1993, p. 37.
16 *Vestnik Statistiki*, (9), 1993, p. 23.
17 *Rossiiskaia gazeta*, 3 June 1994, p. 2.
18 *Smena*, (124), 1 June 1991.
19 *Rossiiskaia gazeta*, 3 June 1994, p. 1.
20 *Rossiiskaia gazeta*, 1 June 1994, p. 1.
21 *Rossiiskie vesti*, 17 June 1992.
22 *Konventzia, op. cit.*, note 14 above, p. 15.
23 See M.D.A. Freeman (1992), 'The limits of children's rights' in M. Freeman and P. Veerman (eds), *The Ideologies of Children's Rights*, Dordrecht: Martinus Nijhoff.
24 Preamble, Convention.
25 A.M. Nechaeva (1991), *Pravonarushenia v sfere lichnykh semeinykh otnoshenii*, Moscow: Nauka, p. 48.
26 A.M. Nechaeva (1990), 'Konventzia o pravakh rebenka i deistvuiuschee zakonodatelstvo SSSR' in *Ja – rebenok, ja – chelobek*, p. 23.
27 *Ved. SSR*, (37), 1994, item 4.
28 In 1944 unmarried mothers were deprived of their right to sue in court for establishment of paternity. Actual (but not legal) fathers were denied of their right to establish paternity voluntarily. The child's father could be registered as the legal father only if he married the child's mother.
29 'Zakonodatelstvo o brake i semije i praktika jego primenenia', *Sverdlovsk*, 1989, p. 6.
30 Russian family law differentiates between judicial (compulsory) establishment of paternity and administrative (voluntary establishment of paternity).
31 A.I. Pergament and E.A. Pavlodskii (1988), 'Dinamika sudebnykh sporov, vytekaiuschikh iz brachno-semeinykh otnoshenii', *Pravovedenie*, (1), pp. 30–1.

32 Nechaeva, *Pravonarushenia* ... *op. cit.*, note 25 above, p. 206.
33 S. 15 of the Code on Marriage and the Family.
34 L.B. Maksimovich (1990), 'Pravovoe polozhenie nesovershennoletnikh roditelei', *Pravovedenie*, (2), p. 73 *et seq.*
35 S. 11 of the Civil Code.
36 S. 32 of the Code on Civil Procedure.
37 Pergament and Pavlodskii, *op. cit.*, note 30 above, p. 31.
38 Razvitie zakonodatelstva o brake i semie. M. 1978, p. 41.
39 M.D.A. Freeman (1992), 'Beyond conventions – towards empowerment' in M.D. Fortuyn and M. de Lange (eds), *Towards The Realization of Human Rights of Children*, Amsterdam: DCT, p. 19.
40 *Komsomolskaia pravda*, 1 February 1992.
41 *Extra*, 2 April 1994, p. 2.
42 Nechaeva, *op. cit.*, note 26 above, p. 37.

12 Swiss Law and the United Nations Convention on the Rights of the Child

Olivier Guillod*

INTRODUCTION

The UN Convention on the Rights of the Child (hereafter the Convention) was adopted by the UN General Assembly on 20 November 1989. Open to signature since 26 January 1990, it came into force on 2 September 1990, as the twentieth instrument of ratification was deposited with the Secretary-General of the United Nations (Article 49). By the end of 1993 some 150 states throughout the world had ratified the Convention. Switzerland is not among them.[1] This odd situation calls for a few words of explanation.

In 1924 Switzerland hosted the session of the League of Nations which adopted the Declaration of Geneva, usually considered the first step toward protecting children's rights.[2] Today, the Swiss reception of the Convention has so far been rather disappointing. It is due in part to the length and slowness of the political process leading to the ratification of an international convention.[3]

On 4 December 1989, two weeks after the United Nations had adopted the Convention, the Swiss government declared that it would sign the Convention as soon as possible, although some of its provisions could raise 'a number of problems'. It reiterated this stance in January 1991 in response to several questions from members of parliament. On that occasion, the Federal Council confessed that it was still undecided on whether to ask for various legislative amendments before ratifying the Convention or to make a few reservations (accepted by Article 51 of the Convention). It added that it

*Professor of Law, Neuchâtel University. I wish to thank Eva Leuenberger for her valuable research assistance.

would first seek to ratify the two UN Covenants of 1966[4] as well as the UN Convention against racial discrimination.[5]

On 10 April 1991 the Federal Council signed the Convention and declared that it was 'an act of international solidarity'.[6] In the following months many non-governmental organisations, several cantons and members of parliament invited the Federal Council to speed up the ratification process. The lower Chamber of Parliament wanted the Federal Council to prepare the legislative amendments needed in order to ratify the Convention without reservations. But the upper House asked for exactly the opposite – that is, ratification of the Convention with reservations because, so it said, ratification would come sooner.

In the second half of 1992 the Federal Council went through the usual process of consulting all interested parties (cantons, political parties, organizations defending children's rights, and so on). A summary of all their answers was made public in May 1993.[7] The answers are, overall, very positive: 24 (out of 26) cantons,[8] all political parties that took a stance[9] and 54 (out of 55) organizations[10] were in favour of ratifying the Convention. Comforted by these responses, the Federal Council prepared a report that was addressed to Parliament in June 1994.[11] It asked for Parliament to approve the Convention with a number of reservations having to do with Articles 7, 10, para. 1, 37 litt. c and 40.[12] A special Committee of the Upper Chamber of the federal Parliament (which took the matter first) held its first discussions on the Convention in spring 1995. Unexpectedly, diverging views entertained by members of the Committee seem to bury any hope for a swift approbation of the Convention. One cannot therefore expect the Convention to become part of Swiss law before 1997.

SWITZERLAND AS A FEDERAL STATE

Before trying to assess the compatibility of Swiss law with the Convention, one should keep in mind that Switzerland is a federal state. Since the legislative power is shared between the 'Confederation' and the cantons, one is compelled to examine 27 legal orders (federal law plus 26 cantonal laws) in order to discover possible incompatibilities of Swiss law with the Convention.

According to art. 3 of the Federal Constitution, the cantons are empowered to legislate on any matter that is not specifically attributed to the Confederation by a constitutional provision. Now, a number of fields in which the Convention recognizes various rights of the child lie within the legislative power of the cantons, especially education (Articles 28 and 29), public health (Articles 23, 24 and 25), welfare and family benefits (Articles

26 and 27) and almost all procedural matters (Articles 9 para 2, 12, 40, and so on).

In these fields, the laws of the cantons may differ on many points, although they usually do not diverge on fundamental principles. Actually, cantonal legal provisions must be consistent with constitutional freedoms as well as with the provisions of the European Convention on Human Rights which Switzerland ratified in 1974 and also with those of the UN Covenant on civil and political rights.[13] Several decisions of the European Court of Human Rights based on Articles 5 and 6 of the European Convention on Human Rights have brought about a number of reforms in the cantonal laws on civil, administrative and criminal procedures in recent times. The result is a better protection of the rights of individuals (adults and minors alike) involved in judicial and administrative proceedings.[14]

SWISS LAW AND THE CONVENTION ON THE RIGHTS OF THE CHILD

Preliminary remarks

The text of the Convention and its interpretation

As many critics have noted, the Convention provisions are not always of the highest clarity, rigour and precision. Vague expressions and non-imperative wording are common and therefore leave much scope for action or for interpretation by States Parties.[15] Use of an international terminology that does not systematically fit with the terminology used in national law sums into the difficulty of determining the exact meaning of several of the Convention's provisions.

There is absence of clarity, for instance, on the nature of various rights accorded to the child by the Convention. Following a classical distinction,[16] human rights are ranged in three broad categories:

1 *Individual rights* (so-called rights of the first generation, like the right to life, to freedom of movement, to a fair trial, and so on found in the UN Covenant on civil and political rights or in the European Convention on Human Rights). These rights are self-executing. Individuals may therefore sue before national courts for their vindication.
2 *Economic, social and cultural rights* (rights of the second generation, such as those found in the corresponding UN Covenant of 1966). These rights are mainly 'programmatic', in the sense that states must do their

best to implement them, but individuals cannot go to court to vindicate them.

3   *Collective rights* (rights of the third generation, such as the right of people to self-determination, development, peace and so on). They are outside the realm of the Convention on the Rights of the Child.

The Convention on the Rights of the Child contains an unspecified mix of rights from the first and second generations. Each of its provisions must therefore be construed according to its goals to determine the exact nature of the rights it grants to children. In its report to Parliament, the Federal Council expressed the view that some of the Convention's provisions were self-executing.[17] It also stressed that even the provisions which cannot be held self-executing are important in at least two ways: first of all, by becoming part of Swiss law, they compel authorities to put them into effect, even though they remain open to interpretation. Secondly, these provisions must be taken into account when construing internal legal provisions, either federal or cantonal and municipal.[18]

Not only is the nature of the rights recognized in the UN Convention unclear but their scope also often lacks clarity. Articles 13 para. 2 (restrictions to freedom of expression), 18, para. 1 (common responsibility of parents for the upbringing of the child) and Article 7, para. 1 (the right to know one's parents) are but a few examples of the lack of clarity surrounding the exact scope of the rights.

Under such circumstances, one may expect diverging interpretations of many Convention provisions by States Parties.[19] Unlike the European Convention on Human Rights, the Convention does not set up any jurisdiction to control how States Parties construe and apply the Convention. It merely relies on a system of periodical national reports (made public) to a Committee on the Rights of the Child (Article 42ff) which has no power outside that of addressing recommendations. Political pressure and pressure from public opinion should, it was hoped, prevent States Parties from disregarding the Convention once they have ratified it. This is, it is submitted, a rather optimistic view on the matter.

The options for Switzerland

Simply stated, Switzerland theoretically faces four options that may be combined:[20]

1   to ratify the Convention and at the same time amend national law wherever it seems to be inconsistent with the Convention provisions, interpreted in the most favourable way to children's rights (the 'maximalist option');

2   to ratify the Convention with reservations (the 'compromise option') – the most likely course of action, given the positions taken by most cantons and political parties during the 1992 consultation;[21]
3   to ratify the Convention and make an interpretative statement on some of its provisions in order to reconcile them with present Swiss law thereby presupposing a scarcely defensible restrictive interpretation of the Convention (the 'minimalist option');
4   not to ratify the Convention, which seems politically unthinkable.

General appraisal

Generally speaking, Swiss law is consistent with the provisions of the Convention.[22] This comes as no surprise because the substance of the Convention was largely influenced by the law and practice of Western nations and also because the Convention expresses a consensus (which, as we know very well in Switzerland, can be achieved only on those minimal rights that nobody really argues about) of all states (representing many cultural and legal traditions) and non-governmental organizations that took an active part in its elaboration.

The main purpose of the UN Convention on the Rights of the Child has been described in terms of prevention, provision, protection and participation.[23] It is built on a few fundamental ideas that are also basic tenets of Swiss law. Five of the most significant of these principles are:

1   The recognition of the *child as a legal subject* rather than an object of legal protection. Under Swiss law, children are considered persons – that is, subjects of rights and duties – from birth onwards. Unborn children are 'conditional persons' (art. 31, para. 2 of the Civil Code) entitled to patrimonial (inheritance and so forth) and personal rights that, however, may only be exercised after birth. This is consistent with Article 1 of the Convention which defines a child in a deliberately vague way[24] as 'every human being below the age of eighteen years'.[25] Children are legally incompetent and therefore are incapable of effecting a legal transaction as long as they do not have discretion[26] – that is, the capacity to act rationally (art. 16, Civil Code). Their rights are exercised on their behalf by their parents, provided the latter hold parental power, or by a legal guardian. As soon as a child has discretion,[27] he or she is capable of effecting some legal transactions, in the limits set forth in art. 19 of the Civil Code: he or she can, for instance, validly exercise purely personal rights such as applying to the judge for protection against injury to his or her person, asking for medical services or exercising most civil rights protected by the federal Constitution and the European Convention on

Human Rights,[28] several of which are also guaranteed in the Convention (especially in Article 13ff).

2   The *best interests of the child*, which must prevail in any decision concerning the child, at every level (state, family and so on). In Switzerland the legal status of the child is defined primarily by the Civil Code, in the titles dealing with natural persons (art. 11ff), the child–parent relationship (art. 252ff) and guardianship (art. 360ff). In these three areas, as in numerous others, the best interest of the child is of paramount importance.[29]

3   The *dignity of the child* that must be preserved by all third parties dealing with the child (the parents and the family, the school, the state and so on). Here again, the dignity of the child as well as, more generally, of the person is a basic principle of Swiss law. It is protected through the constitutional right to personal freedom, as the federal court has stated on numerous occasions.

4   *Non-discrimination*, as a fundamental tenet that must be observed in all matters touched upon by the Convention. Art. 4 of the federal Constitution (in public law) as well as art. 11, para. 2 of the Civil Code (in private law) express the same idea in Swiss law.[30]

5   *The primary role of the family* which requires the state to abstain from unduly interfering in family affairs and simultaneously to support the parents in their tasks and to protect family privacy. Swiss law has apportioned the responsibilities of family and state in the same way, but Switzerland still lacks a real and global family policy[31] despite art. 34 quinquies, para. 1 of the federal Constitution which mandates the Confederation, when legislating, to take into account the needs of the family.

Incompatibilities between Swiss law and the Convention

Overview

A comparative analysis of the Convention and Swiss law shows a number of real, apparent or potential contradictions between Swiss law and the Convention provisions.[32] If we choose the option of reading the Convention in a way most favourable to children's rights, obvious inconsistencies exist between Swiss law and Article 2 (non-discrimination), Article 7 (right to acquire a nationality), Articles 9 and 10 (family reunion), Article 9 (judicial review of decisions concerning the child-parent relationship), Articles 9 and 12 (right to be heard in judicial and administrative proceedings), Article 18 (common responsibility of parents for their child), Article 18 (right to benefit from child-care services), Article 21 (position of the child concerned by inter-country adoption), Article 22 (position of the child seeking refugee status), Articles 26 and 27 (right to benefit from social security and to a decent standard of living), Article 37 (right of the child deprived of liberty to be separated from adults) and Article 40 (procedural rights in criminal proceedings).

Substantive rights

Non-discrimination (Article 2)

Every state ratifying the Convention must ensure the rights set forth in the Convention to each child within its jurisdiction. Article 2 prohibits any discrimination among children, based for instance on 'race, colour, sex, language, religion, political or other opinion, national, ethnic or social origin, property, disability, birth or other status'. If we give a substantial and extensive meaning to the prohibition of discrimination, Swiss law does not fully meet the requirement found in Article 2 of the Convention. One may actually discover a number of discriminations, among which the following should be mentioned:

1 *Sex discrimination.* Despite a constitutional amendment (Art. 4, para. 2) adopted in 1981 that prohibits sex discrimination, the goal of equal rights has not yet been totally achieved. However, the problem is not so much in the legislation as it is in the practical implementation of apparently non-discriminatory legal provisions. For instance, girls and boys do not really benefit from equal opportunity in the education system of many cantons, contrary to Article 28, para. 1 of the Convention.
2 *Birth status discrimination.* The 1976 reform of the Civil Code provisions dealing with the child–parent relationship tried to put on an equal footing children born from married parents and children born out of wedlock. This objective has not been fully realized: the latter still suffer a number of minor disadvantages with respect to the former. The disadvantages especially concern the establishment of the child–parent relationship, the appointment of a guardian to the child,[33] the child's name and nationality, parental power over the child and the administration of the child property.
3 *Discrimination based on national, ethnic or social origin.* Here again, the problem is not so much one of changing laws but a more formidable one of changing mentalities.[34] In two specific situations, foreign children do not benefit from the same rights as Swiss children: when they are involved in intercountry adoption and when they seek refugee status.

According to Article 21(c), children affected by intercountry adoption shall enjoy the same protection as children involved in national adoption. Under Swiss law, one of adoption's prerequisites is that the prospective parents have given the child to be adopted care and education for at least two years. If the adoption is then finalized, no problem arises. By contrast, if, for any reason, the child is not adopted after the two-year period, the child concerned in an intercountry adoption does not enjoy the same protection as a child in a national adoption. He or she may be stateless, possibly without an identity and probably without adequate social protection because he or she will have no legal ties with the prospective parents and because those ties which he or she had with his biological parents were severed long ago.[35]

Article 22 para. 2 provides that a child who is seeking refugee status or who is considered a refugee shall enjoy the same protection as any other child temporarily or definitely deprived, for any reason, of his family environment. The fate of children seeking refugee status in Switzerland is governed by an administrative order issued in 1989 by the Federal Office for Refugees. The child having discretion may personally ask for refugee status, a fact that is frequently ignored or discarded by the Swiss authorities that rule on refugee status. Where the child does not have discretion, the competent cantonal authority shall decide whether the best interest of the child demands that he or she be sent back to his country of origin or be allowed to stay in Switzerland.[36] In general terms, the legal situation of these children, especially those who are unaccompanied, is adverse and not consistent with the relevant Article.

The right to acquire a nationality (Article 7)

The child's right to acquire a nationality at birth is not assured in all cases under Swiss law, which has adhered to the doctrine of *jus sanguinis*. A child born in Switzerland receives Swiss nationality if one of his married parents is Swiss or if his unmarried mother is Swiss.[37] By contrast, the doctrine of *jus soli* is not recognized: a child does not become Swiss solely because he was born in Switzerland. If neither parent holds Swiss nationality, the child may therefore be stateless,[38] depending on the national law of each of his parents.[39] In such a case, he or she may later ask for naturalization but does not have a right to it.

In light of that, the Federal Council could not but recognize the incompatibility between Swiss law and the Convention. It recommended therefore the adoption of a reservation in this respect, adding that this might be withdrawn in the future if the Federal Act on Swiss Nationality was amended.[40]

The right to family reunion (Articles 9 and 10)

Read together, Articles 9 and 10 of the Convention (and possibly Article 18 also) ensure the right of the child to live with his own parents or to maintain regular personal relations and direct contacts. Even though the wording of these two provisions leaves ample room for interpretation, it seems reasonable to say that they guarantee the child's right to family reunion.[41] Following this interpretation, Swiss law is not compatible with the Convention.

In fact, the Swiss regulation on the residence and establishment of foreigners denies the right of a few categories of foreigners living in Switzerland to bring in their family. This is especially the case for seasonal workers[42] (holding a so-called 'A' permit) who are allowed to come and work for one specific employer in Switzerland for nine months in a year (they must return to their country of origin every year for some time) but who are not allowed to bring in their spouse and children. Since these workers spend most of their time in Switzerland, they should enjoy the right to live with their family.

The legal situation is similar for people authorized to reside in Switzerland on a temporary basis. Several categories of foreigners are concerned: individuals who currently cannot be sent back to their country (for instance, people from Bosnia), foreigners who work in Switzerland only for a short time (up to six months), *au pairs* and health professionals completing their training (for a period up to 18 months), students and persons in Switzerland for medical reasons.[43] All these classes of people are presently denied the right to family reunion. However, even though their residence in Switzerland is legally assumed to be temporary (18 months is a fairly long time and higher education takes even longer), their children should benefit from Articles 9 and 10 of the Convention.

Finally, it is also doubtful that the restrictive conditions for family reunion established for foreigners holding an annual, renewable, residence permit (the so-called 'B' permit) are consistent with the Convention.[44]

It may be interesting to report briefly on the results of the 1992 consultation on this point.[45] One organization (of private employers) and two cantons deemed that the Convention was not sufficiently clear to conclude to a far-reaching right to family reunion and, consequently, asked for an interpretative reservation of the Convention by which Switzerland would say that its present law and policy towards family reunion are consistent with the Convention. A majority of those who took position on the issue considered that present Swiss law was not consistent with the Convention. But they split as to the consequences to be drawn: two cantons and two political parties (from the right) asked the Federal Council to make a reservation whereas several cantons, political parties of the left and all interested organizations called for amending the law to ensure the right to family reunion. The Federal Council opted for a reservation instead of amending Swiss law on the matter. But it declared that it would examine concrete measures allowing Switzerland to withdraw the reservation in the future.[46]

The right to be raised under the common responsibility of both parents (Article 18, para. 1)

The Convention merely asks States Parties to 'use their best efforts to ensure recognition of the principle that both parents have common responsibility for the upbringing and development of the child'. Under Swiss law, parents are denied common responsibility for the upbringing of the child when they are not, or are no longer, married: art. 297, para. 1 of the Civil Code restricts the joint exercise of parental power to spouses.

In divorce proceedings, the judge must therefore decide which parent shall continue to have parental power after the dissolution of marriage.[47] The first draft of a bill amending the Civil Code provisions on marriage and divorce[48] allows divorced parents to exercise jointly the parental power on their children.

The situation is presently similar for unmarried partners: the mother (alone or living with a partner) has exclusive parental power as regards her children, even when her partner has acknowledged paternity. This unsatisfactory situation for the father may well be improved in the future. The first draft of a bill amending the Civil Code provisions on marriage and divorce gives the cohabiting father a right to ask for sharing parental power with the mother.[49]

The right to benefit from child-care services (Article 18, para. 3)

This right is recognized by Article 18, para. 3 of the Convention to the children of working parents. Commenting on this provision, Hausammann wrote that 'in this respect, Switzerland is a developing country'.[50] The cantons currently do not formally recognize the right to benefit from child-care services. It would be their responsibility under the Convention to take drastic measures to improve the availability of facilities and services for the care of children. The Federal Council viewed Article 18, para. 3, as a mere 'programmatic' provision. It therefore stressed in its report that cantons kept a wide margin of action to try and fulfil the Convention's purpose in this respect.[51]

The right to benefit from social security (Article 26) and the right to an adequate standard of living (Article 27)

Both rights are generally recognized and satisfactorily implemented, at least for children who reside in Switzerland. A number of problems may, however, arise with certain categories of foreign and stateless children who stay only temporarily in the country (assuming that they, too, enjoy all the rights recognized in the Convention).

The lack of a maternity insurance is also deplored (and, I submit, deplorable), even more so because Article 34 quinquies, para. 4 of the federal Constitution, accepted by Swiss voters in 1945 provides that 'the Confederation shall set up legislatively a maternity insurance'.[52] That would indeed be an important, though indirect, step towards the goals expressed in Articles 26 and 27 of the Convention.

During the 1992 consultation,[53] several private organizations also called for a substantial raise in family benefits which presently far from cover even the basic cost of raising a child.[54]

The right to know one's parents (Article 7, para. 2)

I wish to end this incomplete review of substantial rights with a more positive assessment. A constitutional provision (Art. 24 novies (g)), adopted by the Swiss citizens and cantons on 17 May 1992, has recognized the right to know one's biological parents. Although this provision is part of an article dealing with genetics and medically assisted procreation, it is widely assumed that the constitutional right to know one's parents belongs not only to children born of artificial procreation with the gametes of donors but also to adoptive children.[55] A few legal writers had accepted this idea of the adoptive child's right to know his biological parents even before art. 24 of the federal Constitution was accepted.[56]

Swiss law goes beyond Article 7, para. 2 which recognizes the right of the child to know his parents only 'as far as possible'. Furthermore, this provision of the Convention does not, in my opinion, apply to artificial insemination,[57] especially because the sperm donor cannot be said to be a 'parent' within the meaning of the Convention.

Procedural rights

The general right to be heard (Article 12)

The right to be heard has been recognized for a long time by the federal court, as a fundamental procedural right based on art. 4 of the federal Constitution. Cantonal provisions on civil, criminal and administrative procedure also recognize this right. However, the right to be heard is enjoyed by people intervening as parties in the proceedings. It is therefore doubtful that the child's right to be heard is implemented 'in any judicial and administrative proceedings affecting the child' in accordance with Article 12, para. 2. Indeed, many proceedings between the child's parents may affect the child himself. It remains to be seen whether a general provision should be introduced in Swiss law or whether it may be enough to interpret existing Swiss law according to the Convention.

The special right to be heard in proceedings leading to the separation of the child from his or her parents (Article 9, para. 2)

Article 12 recognizes to the child who is capable of forming his own views the right to express them in all matters affecting him or her. In judicial and administrative proceedings the child shall be heard, either directly or through a representative. Article 9 provides for the same right in proceedings resulting in the separation of the child from at least one of his parents (as for instance in separation and divorce proceedings where the judge must rule on the child's place of residence).

Matters of procedure are left to individual cantons. Substantive law on divorce, separation and on the parent–child relationship is found in the Swiss Civil Code and this may only set out fundamental procedural rules necessary to implement uniformly federal law. At this time, the Civil Code does not compel cantonal courts to hear the child in divorce or separation proceedings. Cantonal laws on civil procedure do not provide for such a right either, although many judges have started acknowledging it in their day-to-day practice.[58]

The first draft of a bill revising the Civil Code provisions on marriage and divorce[59] improves the child's legal position in divorce and separation proceedings. Indeed, art. 144, para. 2 provides that the judge 'shall hear the [divorcing couple's] children personally and in an appropriate way, as long as their age or other important reasons do not exclude a personal hearing or require the child to be heard through a representative'. Knowing the usual pace of reforms in Switzerland, the new provisions on marriage and divorce will, however, not go into force before ratification of the Convention.

The right to a judicial review of decisions separating the child from his parents (Article 9, para. 1)

Article 9, para. 1 of the Convention provides that the decision to separate a child from his or her parents against their will must be taken by 'competent authorities subject to judicial review'. Not every decision of this kind is subject to judicial review under present Swiss law: a number of competent (cantonal) authorities are not judicial ones and arts. 314 and 314a of the Civil Code require judicial review only for cases of deprivation of parental power and deprivation of the child's liberty for personal assistance.

In other procedures leading to a separation of the child from his parents (for example, a child placed with foster parents according to art. 310 of the Civil Code), no judicial review is guaranteed, and there is actually none in a number of cantons. As the federal court indicated recently in a case involving a father's right of access, this situation is not compatible with Article 6 of the European Convention on Human Rights.[60] Cantons are therefore already under an obligation to modify their organic and procedural rules on the matter. These modifications will make Swiss law compatible with the Convention as well.

Procedural rights in criminal proceedings (Article 40)

A special status of the child in criminal matters results from the Swiss Penal Code. Up to the age of seven, a child cannot commit a crime or misdemeanour (art. 82 para. 1 of the Penal Code). Between the ages of 7 and 15, children may be tried for criminal conduct before special juvenile courts set up in each canton. The court may not impose criminal sanctions upon the child but shall take special measures like educative measures, treatment orders or disciplinary punishment (art. 84ff of the Penal Code). Between the ages of 15 and 18, children are treated, as a rule, much the same way as younger children but may also be punished with imprisonment for up to one year.

According to the relevant provisions of cantonal law, the proceedings before a juvenile court develop in a very informal way. But the proceedings must be consistent with Article 6 of the European Convention on Human Rights that recognizes the right to a fair trial. Despite this, there remains a number of procedural rights that Article 40 of the Convention seems to guarantee but that are not quite recognized in a number of Swiss cantons. This is especially so of the following:

1 *The right to have legal assistance* (Article 40, para. 2 (b)(ii)). Such a right is recognized only in part in several cantons (for instance, Zurich,

Basel and Bern) because it was thought that the presence of a lawyer would hinder, rather than enhance, the educative value of the proceedings before the juvenile court. But the federal court has already ruled that the constitutional right, based on Article 4 (as well as deriving from the European Convention on Human Rights) to have legal assistance also belongs to minors involved in criminal proceedings, at least in 'serious or difficult cases'.[61]

2   *The right to a competent, independent and impartial authority or judicial body* (Article 40, para. 2 (b)(iii)). This right is also recognized by Article 6 of the European Convention on Human Rights.[62] But problems are not yet solved because, in some cantons, the juvenile court comprises a judge who exercises the functions of examining magistrate and sitting judge and simultaneously plays the role of the child's protector. During the 1992 consultation, several cantons and the Swiss Association of Judges expressed the view that it would be regrettable to change the law in this respect because it would irretrievably alter the educative nature of the present proceedings.[63]

3   *The right not to be compelled to give testimony* (Article 40, para. 2 (b) (iv)). The laws on criminal procedure of many cantons do not exclude children from the general duty to give testimony.

4   *The right to have the free assistance of an interpreter* (Article 40, para. 2 (b)(vi)). According to legal provisions in a number of cantons, people (including children of course) involved in criminal proceedings may ask for an interpreter[64] but such assistance is, as a matter of principle, not free of charge.

To sum up, Swiss law is presently not in accordance with the Convention as to the right to have legal assistance, the right to a competent, independent and impartial authority and the right to have the free assistance of an interpreter. The Federal Council shared this view since it proposed to make a reservation as to Article 40 on these three counts.[65]

The right to be detained separately from adults (Article 37(c))

Once again, the wording of the Convention leaves room for interpretation: it recognizes the child's right to be detained separately from adults 'unless it is considered in the child's best interest not to do so' (Article 37(c)). But if we want this provision to be meaningful, it will be necessary to make a reservation or to amend Swiss law.[66] Indeed, cantonal provisions on the execution of criminal penalties, save in Geneva, do not require that children be separated from adults.[67] Both reforms might be difficult to push through politically because many cantons observed in the 1992 consultation that they lacked the necessary institutions and detention centres to implement thoroughly this right. This explains why the Federal Council proposed to make a reservation on this point.[68]

CONCLUDING REMARKS

Overall, the compatibility of Swiss law with the Convention on the Rights of the Child is quite good. But, on a number of points, Articles 7, 10, para. 1, 37 (c) and 40, Switzerland will have to make reservations (as proposed by the Federal Council in its report) or amend a number of its legal provisions. The first option, which should be a temporary solution until Swiss law is adapted, will probably be retained by Parliament

Whatever Parliament finally decides, the impact of the Convention should go beyond the technical task of adapting Swiss law. It ought to lead to federal and cantonal authorities alike adopting policies more respectful of the rights of the child and to a transcending of the old conventional view of the child as a mere object of legal protection, a view still harboured by a number of people who are charged with the job of implementing the law.

NOTES

1   Incidentally, Switzerland is not even a member of the United Nations! On 16 March 1986, the Swiss citizens and cantons alike refused in a national referendum to join the United Nations.

2   See Cynthia Price Cohen (1989), 'United Nations: Convention on the Rights of the Child. Introductory Note', *ILM* **28**, p. 1448; UNICEF (1992), *Les enfants ont des droits – chez nous aussi. La Convention relative aux droits de l'enfant et la Suisse,* Zurich, p. 7.

3   The procedure under the Swiss Constitution to ratify an international Convention is a three-step process: the government (Federal Council) first signs the Convention; then Parliament (Federal Assembly) approves it, with the possible addition of a national referendum; finally the government ratifies the Convention.

4   Both Pacts were approved by the Federal Assembly on 13 December 1991. The instruments of ratification were deposited on 18 June 1992 and the Pacts went into force on 18 September 1992.

5   The Convention was approved by the Federal Assembly on 18 June 1993 along with a modification of the Penal Code which was later accepted by Swiss voters in a national referendum held in September 1994.

6   Christina Hausammann (1991), *Die Konvention über die Rechte des Kindes und ihre Auswirkungen auf die schweizerische Rechtsordnung,* Bern: Studie im Auftrag des Schweizerischen Komitees für UNICEF (unpublished paper from the Seminar für öffentliches Recht der Universität Bern).

7   Federal Department of Foreign Affairs (1993), *Procédure de consultation relative à*

l'adhésion de la Suisse à la Convention des Nations Unies sur les droits de l'enfant, du 20 novembre 1989, Bern, 5 May.

8   The cantons of Appenzell Innerrhoden and Thurgau were against ratifying the Convention. Their position is based partly on a defence (for this author, outdated) of federalism, partly on the belief (for this author, erroneous) that present Swiss law is good enough and partly on the conviction (for this author, correct but unproductive) that one does not need additional international provisions protecting children but better implementation mechanisms of existing legal provisions. The canton of Zurich favoured a delayed ratification and called for many reservations.

9   Covering the whole spectrum of political opinions, from the left to the right.

10   The only exception was the organization of Edmond Kaiser, 'Sentinelles', which rejected the Convention as too vague and not going far enough in the recognition of children's rights.

11   Message sur l'adhésion de la Suisse à la Convention de 1989 relative aux droits de l'enfant, from 29 June 1994, *Feuille Fédérale* [F.F.] 1994, V pp. 1–102.

12   F.F. 1994 V 80.

13   See Claude Rouiller (1992), 'Le Pacte international relatif aux droits civils et politiques', *Revue de droit suisse*, p. 107ff.

14   See generally Mark Villiger (1993), *Handbuch der Europäischen Menschenrechtskonvention (EMRK) unter besonderer Berücksichtigung der schweizerischen Rechtslage*, Zurich: Schulthess.

15   For a critical view on the Convention, see for instance Irène Théry (1992), 'Nouveau droit de l'enfant, la potion magique?', *Esprit*, p. 5ff.

16   See for instance Karel Vasak (1977), 'A 30-year struggle – The sustained efforts to give force to law of the Universal Declaration of Human Rights', *UNESCO Courier*, November, p. 29.

17   F.F. 1994 V 22. This is a noteworthy divergence with the view expressed by Germany in its interpretative declaration (*Bundesgesetzblatt* 1992, II, no 34, p. 990) and by the highest court in France (Cass. civ., 10 March 1993, *Dalloz* [D.] 1993 Jurisprudence [J.] 361; 2 June 1993, D. 1993 J. 153; 15 July 1993, D. 1994 J. 191; Cass. soc. 13 July 1994, *Semaine Juridique*, Ed. G., no 2, 195, pp. 17f), the two countries most looked to when legislating in Switzerland.

18   F.F. 1994 V 21f.

19   In the following pages, I shall stick to the interpretation of the Convention most favourable to children's rights.

20   The reader should keep in mind the first three when going through the list of incompatibilities between Swiss law and the Convention.

21   This is the option recommended by the Federal Council in its report to parliament (F.F. 1994 V 80). It remains to be seen which course of action will be chosen by parliament.

22   Federal Dept. of Foreign Affairs, *op. cit.*, note 7 above, p. 2ff; Hausammann, *op. cit.*, note 6 above, p. 29.

23   See, for instance, Thomas Hammarberg (1990), 'The United Nations Convention on the Rights of the Child and how to make it work', *Human Rights Quarterly* **12**, pp. 97, 100; Nathalie Kocherhans (1991), *Droit, enfant et travail. Mise en perspective d'une Convention internationale*, Neuchâtel (unpublished paper from the University of Neuchâtel, School of Law).

24   Despite para. 9 of the Preamble, nothing can be drawn from Articles 1 and 6 of the Convention as to the status of the unborn child or, *a fortiori*, of the in-vitro embryo: see P. Alston (1990), 'The unborn child and abortion under the draft Convention on the Rights of the Child', *Human Rights Quarterly*, **12**, pp. 156, 168ff; Olivier Guillod and

Marina Mandofia Berney (1993), 'Liberté personnelle et procréation assistée', *Revue suisse de jurisprudence*, p. 207ff.

25   Starting from 1 January 1996, the age of majority is 18 in Switzerland (art. 14 Civil Code). It was formerly 20.

26   According to art. 16 of the Civil Code, discretion (*discernement*) is the capacity to act rationally. The notion is the same as the one used in Article 12, para. 1 of the Convention: 'capable of forming his or her own views' is actually translated in the French text of the Convention by *'capable de discernement'*.

27   The Civil Code does not determine an age for discretion. It depends especially on the maturity of the child, on his intellectual development and on the kind of legal transaction he effects. Discretion may be accepted for one decision and not for another even though both are taken the same day. But discretion is, as a matter of principle, assumed.

28   See Peter Saladin (1976), 'Rechtbeziehungen zwischen Eltern und Kinder' in *Familienrecht im Wandel, Festschrift Hinderling*, Bâle/Stuttgart: Helbing & Lichtenhahn, pp. 175ff; J.P. Müller, *Commentaire de la Constitution fédérale*, Zurich/Berne/Bâle: Schulthess/Stämpfli/Helbing & Lichtenhahn, Introduction before art. 4, no 103; F.F. 1994 V 24f.

29   F.F. 1994 V 27f.

30   See G. Müller in *Commentaire de la Constitution fédérale*, art. 4 no. 2; F.F. 1994 V 25f.

31   See G. Müller (1986), 'Zum Verhältnis von Verfassung, Familienpolitik und Familienrecht', *Festschrift Hegnauer*, Berne: Stämpfli, pp. 231ff.

32   A number of them were mentioned in the 1991 study of Hausammann, *op. cit.*, note 6. The 1992 consultation (*op. cit.*, note 7) revealed additional inconsistencies. For the position of the Federal Council, see F.F. 1994 V 22ff.

33   See O. Guillod (1992), 'Le curateur au ventre: une acception nouvelle?' in *Instants d'instance. Mélanges Jean Hoffman*, Neuchâtel, p. 113ff.

34   An obvious and dramatic example of such an assertion was given by the Swiss authorities many years ago, when they developed a vast programme in which they invoked the best interest of the child to rob gypsy families of their children, to place them under guardianship and often to commit them in educative, or even mental, institutions. A nomadic way of life was said to be inherently bad for the child.

35   Federal Dept. of Foreign Affairs, *op. cit.*, note 7 above, p. 13; F.F. 1994 V 49f. See also M.-F. Lücker-Babel (1991), *Adoption internationale et droits de l'enfant: qu'advient-il des laissés-pour-compte?*, Fribourg: Editions Universitaires.

36   One immediately sees what use can be made of the notion of 'best interest of the child'. F.F. 1994 V 51f.

37   Art. 1 of the Federal Act on the Swiss nationality. If the parent–child relationship is legally abolished later, the child keeps the nationality he acquired at birth only in the case where he would otherwise be stateless: see art. 8 of the same Act.

38   A problem may also arise with children involved in an intercountry adoption which is not finalized, as has already been mentioned.

39   But then, which country must implement the right to acquire a nationality? The state where the child was born or the state of origin of either parent?

40   F.F. 1994 V 29. Other countries (Kuwait, Monaco, Thailand and Tunisia) have made a reservation on the same point.

41   The Federal Council expressed a contrary view in its report to parliament: F.F. 1994 V 35, quoting S. Detrick (1992), *The United Nations Convention on the Right of the Child – A Guide to the 'Travaux Préparatoires'*, Dordrecht: Martinus Nijhoff, p. 181.

42   Art. 38, para. 2 of the federal Order limiting the number of foreigners (OLE).
43   See art. 14a of the federal Act on the residence and establishment of foreigners and arts 20 and 38, para. 2, OLE.
44   The requirements are: 'sufficient' financial means and 'adequate' lodging: see art. 39 and 40, OLE. The waiting period, which had usually been 12 months, was recently suppressed: see F.F. 1994 V 36.
45   Federal Dept. of Foreign Affairs, *op. cit.*, note 7 above, p. 7.
46   F.F. 1994 V 38. Other countries (for instance Germany and the UK) have made an interpretative statement as to Articles 9 and 10 saying that the Convention must be construed in accordance with their own immigration laws.
47   The federal court affirmed this narrow interpretation of the law in 1991: ATF 117 II 523. In about 90 per cent of cases, it is the mother who retains parental power.
48   *Message concernant la révision du code civil suisse* (to be published soon in Feuille Fédérale), pp. 125ff and proposed article 133 para. 3 CC.
49   *Idem*, pp. 161ff and proposed article 298a CC.
50   Hausammann, *op. cit.*, note 6 above, p. 30. As a father of two small children I can readily confirm her opinion.
51   F.F. 1994 V 47.
52   Federal authorities are not the only culprits: such an insurance, as part of a global package on health insurance, was voted down by Swiss citizens in 1987.
53   Federal Dept. of Foreign Affairs, *op. cit.*, note 7 above, p. 14.
54   A recent study from the Swiss National Research Fund, as reported by the press (see, for instance, *Le Nouveau Quotidien*, 23 August 1995), concluded that the cost of raising one child was about 1 450 Swiss francs a month and the total cost of raising two children approximately 2 200 Swiss francs. Monthly family benefits for a child are between 130 and 200 Swiss francs a month, depending on cantonal law.
55   Guillod and Mandofia Berney, *op. cit.*, note 24 above, p. 213. This position was adopted in a Report accompanying the first draft of a federal Act on medically-assisted procreation; Berne, June 1995, p. 66.
56   See, for instance, Cyril Hegnauer (1988), 'Kann das Adoptivkind Auszüge über den ursprünglichen Eintrag seiner Geburt verlangen (Art. 138 ZStV)?', *Revue de l'état civil*, p. 2ff.
57   The same view has been expressed by J. Rubellin-Devichi (1991), 'Droits de la mère et droits de l'enfant: réflexions sur les formes de l'abandon', *Revue trimestrielle de droit civil*, pp. 695, 701.
58   Federal Dept. of Foreign Affairs, *op. cit.*, note 7 above, p. 9; F.F. 1994 V 33.
59   See *op. cit.*, note 48 above.
60   ATF 118 Ia 473; see also O. Guillod (1991), 'Les garanties fondamentales de procédure en droit tutélaire,' *Revue du droit de tutelle* p. 41ff.
61   ATF 111 Ia 81; F.F. 1994 V 72.
62   The exact meaning of Art. 6 ECHR for minors is still (partly) disputed: see F.F. 1994 V 73. In any case, the reservation Switzerland had made about Article 6 ECHR was held invalid: see ATF 118 Ia 473.
63   Federal Dept. of Foreign Affairs, *op. cit.*, note 7 above, p. 18. They, accordingly, asked the Federal Council to make a reservation.
64   A limited right may also be inferred from art. 4 of the federal Constitution: see ATF 118 Ia 462.
65   F.F. 1994 V 80.
66   A similar provision can be found in the UN Covenant on civil and political rights.

Switzerland made a reservation on this point when ratifying the Covenant. F.F. 1994 V 67.

67 A problem might also arise with respect to the federal provisions on civil commitment (arts 397a to 397f of the Civil Code).

68 F.F. 1994 V 67. Other countries made a similar reservation, for instance Australia, Canada, Iceland and the UK.

Index

Index of Articles of the Convention

ARTICLE